OOPS!

I Forgot My Wife

OOPS!

I Forgot My Wife

A STORY OF COMMITMENT AS MARRIAGE
AND SELF-CENTEREDNESS COLLIDE

Doyle Roth

P. O. Box 64260, Colorado Springs, CO 80962

Oops! I Forgot My Wife
ISBN: 0-93608-318-2
Copyright © 2004 by Lewis & Roth Publishers. All rights reserved.

Cover Design: Resolution Design (www.resolutiondesign.com)
Cover & Interior Illustrations: Dan Pegoda (dannagin@aol.com)
Editorial Team: Stephen Sorenson, Shannon Wingrove, and Paula Graham
Typography: Tim Howard

Library of Congress Cataloging-in-Publication Data
Roth, Doyle, 1944-
    Oops! I forgot my wife : a story of commitment as marriage and self-centeredness collide / by Doyle Roth.
        p. cm.
    Includes index.
    ISBN 0-936083-18-2
    1. Marriage. 2. Communication in marriage. 3. Commitment (Psychology) I. Title.

HQ734.R773 2004
646.7'8--dc22

                                                                                                2004048933

Printed in the United States of America
First Printing / 2004

To receive a **free catalog** of books published by Lewis & Roth Publishers, call toll free: **800-477-3239**. If you are calling from outside the United States, please call 719-494-1800.

Lewis & Roth Publishers
P.O. Box 64260
Colorado Springs, CO 80962-4260
www.lewisandroth.com

CONTENTS

Have you ever tried to do two things at once? That's what I've just been doing. I've been busy sitting in my recliner while at the same time staring at my dusty computer keyboard. You see, I'm caught between Monday Night Football and writing this "acknowledgments" page. I'll get back to you after the football game.

OK, I'm back. What I was thinking about was how in the world this book ever came into existence. Frankly, I've never written anything longer than a hunting supply list. What in the world made me think I should write a book? (It would be laughable except that writing this book has probably reduced my life expectancy by ten years.) You see, I'm a rancher, not a writer. While I do some public speaking, my heart is really in working with people individually.

Before it ever dawned on me to write a book, my young friend Michael Murphy asked a very stirring question. "How is an old guy like you going to pass on to others your insights about mentoring and relationships?" That question resulted in this book. As the idea took shape, many of my friends and colleagues were very supportive of the idea. For instance, my lifetime friend, Alex Strauch, already a well-known author, gave me excellent counsel right from the start. "Are you *crazy?*" he counseled. I should have listened because my first two drafts landed in the trash alongside last month's magazines and newspapers.

Then it happened. I began to understand my communication style and how to transfer ideas to the printed page without forfeiting my identity in the process. (Two wonderful friends—Dr. Craig VanSchooneveld and Barney Visser—were determined to preserve this in my writing.) I wanted to write in a style consistent with how I relate to people in counseling—more personal than formal, yet very direct. A combination of relationship, story, and teaching. The email format was "just what the doctor ordered."

After forty years of marriage and thirty years of marriage counseling, determining the subject of the book was easy. What was tough was deciding which theme to emphasize: *men are terrific* or *people are self-centered.* Of course, my lovely wife Nancy disagreed with the first one and was partial to the second in hopes that my spending time thinking about it would be beneficial to our own marriage. We finally compromised by taking a little from both and emphasizing *the self-centeredness of men.* For some reason it hasn't been that hard to come up with illustrations of how male self-centeredness impacts marriage.

I must tell you something up front. Even though Nancy, our children, and their families make veiled appearances in some of my illustrations, I love them dearly. They have all been a tremendous source of encouragement during this project. We've laughed, cried, and disagreed through almost every email. It's embarrassing to say this, but they have all lived this "self-centeredness of men" story by living with the author of this book.

What's been amazing to me is how God has raised up the necessary people to finish this project when I was running out of gas. A miracle in itself was the way Paul Santhouse showed up and put the finishing touches to the text. He is a fantastic brother in Christ and I thank him for his perseverance. I'm also thankful for Eric Anderson's design skills, Dan Pegoda's wonderful art work, and the editorial genius of Stephen Sorenson and Shannon Wingrove. Thanks to all of you for your labor of love. You've all worked very hard! Why not take the next six months off?

There you have it. The message, the process, the people, and now the book in hand. *Enjoy!*

INTRODUCTION

This is a story. A work of fiction. A tale.

But it's also true. True to life and true to marriage. Not that you could actually email any of the characters, but that you will see many of their same attitudes and experiences reflected in the "normal" marriages of your city, neighborhood, and church. You will even recognize some of what you read from firsthand experience, because when we peak into the lives of others, we often see ourselves. Stories about human nature are always true.

This story goes beyond human nature, however. It also features perseverance, redemption, renewal, and the value of confrontation. When friends and mentors stay committed through ugly times and deep disappointment, hope is unleashed. And when troubled couples find hope, miracles are not far behind.

So get ready to read someone else's mail (email, actually). It reveals the story of how Gerry, Sue, and Carter stood with their friends through the midst of a storm. And beyond.

FROM: Gerry

TO: The Reader

SUBJECT: How it all got started

I remember the exact moment I realized my wife and I were headed for divorce. It came to me during one of our shouting matches. I had just thrown out an accusation guaranteed to cut her to the quick—a handy trick I'd used many times to move us from gridlock to resolution. Normally she'd stop dead in her tracks, get teary-eyed, and start back-pedaling. From there I could usually get us onto the same page and moving to the more important things of life (like, "What's for dinner?").

But this time it didn't work that way. When I hurled my accusation, she actually smiled at me (unpleasantly) and muttered, "Whatever." Though at one level I sensed the match was over, I still tried making my point from different angles, but none of them took. In fact, she didn't even let me finish. Right in the middle of my last attempt, she left the room—not in tears or in a rage, but disinterested. As if she couldn't be bothered to continue. That's when it struck me. She didn't care. Not about me, not about the argument, and not about our marriage. She was done.

My hunch turned out to be correct. She even had an escape plan in place, and if it weren't for the intervention of a close friend I'd be single right now.

Now, I say "a close friend," but it didn't start out that way. Up to that point, Carter was a bit of an enigma to me. A successful businessman, he was also a rancher with an enormous spread of land southwest of town. He could talk stocks and investments with the best of us, but then he'd always throw in some crazy comment about having to go spread manure and head for his truck. He had a way of dismissing us younger guys with colorful putdowns and questions about our manliness. Jokingly, he'd refer to us young bucks as sissies, slackers, slugs, or varmints of one kind or another, yet there's not a single one of us he didn't intentionally pursue with friendly intent. Over time I came to see how deeply he cared about us and wanted to see us grow into men. (He was also clear about what a man is supposed to be. "A man," he'd say, "stands for something. A man is more concerned about a stain on his character than a stain on his pants. A man cares more about keeping his integrity above reproach than about keeping his SUV spotless. A man opens the car door for his wife, and at all times treats her with honor and respect.") To be honest, he made being a man something I wanted very much for myself.

One weekend, when a bunch of us were hunting together, he abruptly turned to me and asked how my wife, Sue, was doing. Aside from being totally unprepared for such a question during a hunting trip, I was hesitant to let him know. "She's great," I said, then changed the subject. He didn't let it rest, however. The next morning at breakfast, he asked again. I told him things could be better, but we'd be OK. By the look on his leathery, unshaven face, I knew that he knew I was full of bull.

I'd always wondered how he got to be an elder at our church. His rough and gruff manner didn't strike me as typical of a churchman, yet behind his crusty appearance there was definite warmth. That morning over the campfire things began to make sense. Although he thoroughly understood the demands of business and never made me feel guilty about my "workaholic" tendencies, he was unapologetically straightforward about the self-serving way most men approach life. He shared stories from his life and marriage and didn't try to make things sound perfect and wonderful. At some point that weekend, I realized he was an authentic Christian, and I decided I trusted him.

The night Sue walked away from our argument, she also left the house "to go visit a friend." To be honest, it was pretty ugly. I told her not to hurry back, which I thought would finally trigger those tears of remorse I'd been looking for, but she only returned an emotionless, "Don't worry, I won't," and drove off. I slammed the door for effect, but something in my mind was going, *uh-oh*. This time seemed different. She is so disinterested. She doesn't love me anymore. The more

I considered it, the more convinced I became. After a couple hours of brooding, I admitted to myself that we'd crossed a serious line in our relationship. I'd always fought to win, and now winning wasn't the issue. I didn't have a clue what to do.

That's when I thought of Carter. Not that I wanted counseling. Sue and I had already tried that several times, and it only made things worse. We'd sit in somebody's office explaining what each other did that made us hurt or angry, then we'd go home and fight about what we said. I'm sure the counselors were moved by our situation and genuinely tried to help, but I was too stubborn to give any ground. Somehow I couldn't picture Carter letting Sue and me get away with that. After staring at his number in our church directory for several minutes, I picked up the phone.

True to form, Carter greeted me with, "Hello, Slacker," and told me to get my "sorry rear end" down to his office the next day, preferably together with Sue. Fortunately, Sue agreed to come (more out of respect for Carter than for my sake). Right away I knew this session would be different. From the moment we walked in the door, Carter's loving but no-nonsense approach hit us right between the eyes. He used the Bible to explain what was going on in our hearts, and he used ranch and animal analogies to help us see what we were doing to each other. Even now I can't help but view cows with a subtle kinship, not to mention horses, turkeys, pigs, goats, elk, deer, fence posts, barbed wire, manure spreaders, and a host of other things I'd never heard of before. (I now understand why Jesus used so many parables in His teaching.)

Initially Sue was taken aback by Carter's blunt statements and willingness to confront, and his illustrations were certainly not easy for my male ego to swallow. More than once I decided not to come back. (Imagine being compared to a pig, a posthole digger, or a pile of manure. One time he referred to me as a fence staple—sharp, crooked, and bent toward myself.) I can still see his boots on the desk and the mud on his jeans. It's one thing to resist the "opinions" of a professional, but who can resist the observations of a cowboy? When somebody is willing to put truth in your face, it has a way of defining reality. Gradually I came to see my behavior as unacceptable and my childish tantrums as outright sin. I was an abusive husband—not to mention proud, arrogant, insecure, and totally self-focused—and Carter didn't mince words. But he also didn't lord it over me. He'd had his share of failures and freely told us about them. His marriage had been on the rocks at one point, and the journey back from that experience left him with a humility I could not resist. Sometimes a spade has to be called a spade, and I'm grateful he had the courage and gentleness to do it well. His belief in Sue and me helped us rediscover our belief in ourselves, and the years since then have been better than I'd ever imagined they could be. Which brings me to the present.

For some time after our meetings with Carter, Sue and I made it a point to invite him and his wife, Minnie, over every now and then to meet our friends. Whether it was their age, experience, or earthy humor, they always fit in well and seemed to spark probing conversations. At one of those get-togethers, Sue's good friend from work, Stacy, started asking lots of questions about Jesus Christ. She and her fiancé, Mitch, became regular fixtures whenever Carter and Minnie came around, and they even had Carter do their premarital counseling.

About six months later, my job took me several hours north to Cheyenne, Wyoming, and a few months after that Mitch and Stacy also moved there. However, as things steadily improved for Sue and me, we began to feel concern for Mitch and Stacy. We saw them less frequently, and when we did get together with them, Sue and I always felt troubled afterward. Consequently, we weren't surprised when the doorbell rang late one Thursday night.

I've decided to share their story with you because it meant a lot to me, and to many of the guys at my church. Once again, Carter played a significant role, only this time he met us in our own homes—via email. In many ways I actually think email was exactly what Mitch needed. For one thing, it's much easier to get personal "impersonally" via the computer than sitting face-to-face in somebody's office with your spouse. It also gave Mitch time to reread each message after calming down from his initial reactions. (Carter is nothing if not "to the point.") All I know is that we saw miraculous things happen in all of our marriages, and Stacy gave me permission to share the whole story with you. So, here goes. . . .

FROM: Gerry

TO: Carter

SUBJECT: Meltdown at the "Not-So-OK Corral"

Hey Carter!

Remember me? How are you doing, my friend? It's been ages since we talked. I trust you and Minnie are more in love than ever. Sue and I will never forget your kindness to us, and you'll be happy to know we're still thriving together.

Better grab yourself a cold drink—this email's a doozy. I'll call you soon so we can catch up, but I wanted to send you a heads-up first.

Something we've long feared has finally happened. Last night about 12:30 AM our doorbell rang. Groggily, I climbed out of bed and stumbled to the front door. Looking through the peephole, I saw three distorted figures standing on my porch. As best I could tell, it was a woman with two little children, all holding hands. A certain anxiety crept into my chest, and when I opened the door my fears were realized. There stood my best friend's wife, Stacy, with their two kids, Tanya and Rusty.

I figured something terrible must have happened. The children had blankets tucked under their arms, and Rusty was hugging his bear and sucking his thumb. Tears were running down Stacy's cheeks. Mascara was smeared across both sides of her face, and her hair was a disaster. Frankly, they looked like refugees. So where was Mitch?

Disoriented, I just stood there looking at them. As Tanya began to sob, Sue appeared from behind me and had the common sense to invite them into the house. She took charge of the situation and put the little ones to bed in our guest bedroom. She seemed to know at once what was going on. As I watched the two women hug each other, it dawned on me. Mitch was up to something.

I'm sorry to break this news to you because I know how much you love Mitch and Stacy. You've been close to them and have prayed for them for years. We both knew Mitch needed a spiritual overhaul and figured God would do it in His time. Well, I think that time has arrived.

Carter, you know I'm no marriage counselor. It hasn't been that long since *we* were in your office getting counseling. Sue and I are certainly doing better, but I wasn't prepared for this morning's encounter. As we sat down at the kitchen table about 1:00 AM with warm cups of tea, Stacy began venting unbelievable anger, bitterness, hostility, and frustration toward Mitch. They apparently had a huge disagreement earlier last evening, which heated up again later on to the extent that Stacy went into another room. When she came back, Mitch was sound asleep. His I-don't-give-a-rip attitude pushed her over the edge. She couldn't stand another minute in the house with a snoring husband who didn't seem to care that his wife was dying inside. So she gathered up the children, put them and her broken heart into the car, and headed for our house. Listening to all this, I wondered if Mitch was having a good night's rest.

As Stacy cried, pounded her fist on the table, and expressed how deeply she was hurting, I remembered how badly I had hurt Sue during our marital trouble. Mitch's complete disregard for Stacy, combined with his careless treatment of her, was breaking her heart, and it made me more upset than I can tell you. (Why is it so much easier to see the pain in somebody else's wife than in your own?) Stacy was in a state of emotional and marital meltdown. Her family was breaking apart, her children were in our spare bedroom, and her husband was sound asleep as if he hadn't a care in the world. As I listened to Stacy cry, I wondered what Mitch was going to think when he woke up in his big empty house.

Carter, it was really helpful for me to have gone through our counseling sessions with you. I kept trying to think of what you would say, but finally realized you wouldn't say much of anything. This was the time to listen, not talk. I think Stacy just needed to get everything out. Sue seemed to understand this. She kept asking questions and encouraging Stacy to explain how she felt.

Let me tell you something, Carter. This is one angry woman we've got here. I jotted down some things she said about Mitch because they rang a bell with me, too. As you think about them, remember we're not talking about the same Mitch you knew several years ago. We're now dealing with Mr. Successful Businessman. He's still a tad shy of six feet tall, but he's probably up to 190 pounds (too much fast food). His hair has gone from brown to partly cloudy and his new goatee almost makes him look sophisticated. Sue says he has dropped from an eight to a six on the handsomeness scale, but that's still four points lower than he thinks of himself. He seems awfully concerned with how he looks. Designer duds, oxford shirts (heavy starch), and $200 loafers. No manure under his heels! Only the best ties and eyeglasses, and a spotless white hardhat for his job-site visits—not so much to protect his head as to keep his hair from getting messed in the endless Wyoming wind. (OK, I confess I'm not feeling too fond of Mitch at the moment.)

Anyway, here are some of the "high points" from Stacy's ocean of fury:

1. Mitch is nothing but an image manager. He's extremely concerned about what others think. Dress right, act right, fool everybody. Stacy is terrified that talking to us will set him off because of how it will tarnish his lovely image. According to Mitch, only weak people go for counseling.
2. He has also become a Jekyll and Hyde. Who he is at home is totally different from who he is everywhere else. At home he's unbearable to live with, but to everyone else he's Mr. Wonderful. Kind of like the guy who yells at his family all the way to church and then becomes Mr. Smiles when he steps out of the car.
3. Mitch is an even worse workaholic than I was. He enjoys what he does and makes a great salary, but he's so stingy with his

time and money that the family doesn't benefit from it. He comes home to refresh himself, be waited on hand and foot, pat the kids on the head, take on some calories, have sex, and continue with his self-centered life. Stacy says he would rather take a promotion with a divorce than decline the promotion and keep his family.

4. Speaking of which, he's totally disinterested in the needs of his family. He sees his home life as merely an intermission in what's most important to him—his work. In a sense, he leaves his energy, creativity, personality, humor, patience, and love at the office. His total lack of involvement in his family make him pretty irrelevant and boring.

5. He is disconnected from his children. He understands that they need discipline, but never takes the time or initiative to get involved with them or deal with them gently. All he does is yell and order them around. He can't seem to understand what it's doing to the kids.

6. Mitch needs to be the center of attention. Stacy says she and the kids have to focus on his needs at all times. She would like to invite friends over, but he gets frustrated when her attention is diverted from his needs. When he's home, it's all about him.

7. She says he's a "marital cripple." He is completely clueless about how to have a good family. As you know, his parents are divorced, so it's not like he has ever had a healthy model. Still, Stacy says he's not even trying.

8. He's abusive to Stacy. This was the real shocker for me. He apparently orders her around as if she's an animal and emotionally beats her down whenever she tries to communicate how she feels. He puts her down with sarcastic, insensitive, and hurtful jesting. Did I ever do this? What kind of man gets his jollies by hurting his wife, anyway? He even does it in public, which is humiliating to her. After listening to Stacy for so long, I now think my best friend is a total control freak. However, I think he's about to be put on notice that his controlling days are over. Believe me, Carter, this woman has had it!

I can't tell you how many times she used the word "self" to describe him. Over and over and over. According to Stacy, he's a self-centered, self-serving, self-absorbed, self-righteous, self-willed, self-defensive, self-justifying, self-sufficient, self-deceived, self-loving, self-exalting, self-satisfied, and self-consumed man. (Did you get all that? Would you like me to repeat it? Me neither!)

Granted, Stacy is really upset, but if even half of what she said is true I think we've got a menace on our hands.

It was 5:30 AM before Stacy started to wind down. All of a sudden she stopped talking and said she needed to rest. I could only think of how sad it was that this marriage was ending. There's no way this lady is going back into that situation unless something miraculous takes place. Her belly is plum full of a man who is soundly sleeping just three miles away in the comfort of his empty house. Little does he know that the biggest nightmare of his life will be starting as soon as he wakes up, like a bomb going off in his pajamas. All I can think to do is wait for his call when he opens his eyes to nobody. Do you think he'll shave and put on some cologne first?

Actually, that's why I'm emailing you. I know he'll be calling soon, and I think I'll direct him your way for some of that famous-recipe counseling you dish out. He knows what a huge difference you made in my marriage, so I'm guessing he'll take my advice and contact you. *If* he'll admit there's a problem, that is. Of course, the empty house should serve as a nagging reminder, don't you think?

Don't mince words with him, Carter. I think your two-by-four-between-the-eyes approach is the best thing for all of us guys. It sure knocked me back to reality. Your having the guts to tell me my behavior was unacceptable really got my attention. I needed to hear that from somebody I respected. None of us enjoys hearing stuff like that, but it paves the way to better things. I know you can't take him to lunch from a hundred miles away, but give him the best you've got via phone and email (preferably email). I think you can make a difference for those two. They sure need it right now.

By the way, I remember how you always loved that *Life at the Lazy-U* comic. Well, I've been meaning to send this one for weeks.

Have you seen it yet? Based on what's about to happen to Mitch, I think it's pretty timely.

Uh oh! The phone is ringing. I have to go, but I expect you'll be hearing from Mitch in a very short time. Brace yourself.

Love to you and Minnie,
Gerry

FROM: Mitch

TO: Carter

SUBJECT: What's new?

Hey you old rip, how the heck are ya? Every since I moved up here, I've missed seeing you. I assume Minnie is doing well. What a sweetheart she is. I still can't figure how such a beautiful woman ended up married to such a strange character. I sure miss our weekly racquetball game and steaks at your ranch. We always had such great parties. Let's do it again!

I know you don't understand why I moved to Wyoming, but I could make a lot more money up here. We bought a really nice house outside Cheyenne and even updated the old pickup. I wanted something a little nicer for the family so I bought a fancy Z28. It's a ragtop no less! We kept Stacy's old clunker, though, because it does much better with car seats and spilled milk shakes (which happens all the time). Rest assured the Z is spotless.

Well, it's 9:00 Thursday morning, and I finally decided to take a day off from work. It's about time I caught up on some household chores Stacy's been after me to do. She's a great woman, but she sure knows how to put the pressure on when something's not to her liking. I guess all marriages have little disagreements here and there. We had a small one last night. Frankly, it was no big deal, but Stacy must have decided she needed to visit with Sue (Gerry's wife) about it. Dealing with these emotional females must really frustrate you as a marriage counselor. The smallest disagreements make them go ballistic. You know what I mean, don't you? I just talked to her on the phone a little while ago, and she said she wasn't feeling the best. Apparently she has a bad headache from not sleeping well last night. That probably explains her lousy attitude. One thing for sure—she still sounded pretty angry. I hope Sue helps her work through whatever's rankling her. Anyway, she said she'd be home later this morning so I'll figure out what her problem is when she arrives. Hope she makes it by 10:00 so I can get down to the club for a good workout before lunch. I'll have lunch with Stacy and the kids, then see if they want a quick ride in the convertible. Without the milk shakes, that is!

Hey Carter, I've got some great jokes for the next time we talk. The guys I work with are hilarious—I don't know where they come up with this stuff. Sure breaks up the seriousness of office life.

Hang on a minute—the phone's ringing. Maybe it's Stacy.

Well, I'm back again. It was my mom. I told her about Stacy heading over to Sue's to discuss our argument, and she couldn't believe it. To be honest, I can't believe it either. She ought to be talking with me, not with everybody else in town. Hopefully she'll get all this complaining out of her system soon because I'm getting real tired of it.

Sounds like she's opening the garage door. I'll get back to this email as soon as I check in with her.

Sorry for all the interruptions, Carter. It's only 10:35 and Stacy has already come and gone. She was here for fifteen minutes, then she slammed the door and left! Said she had to run back to Sue's house. Apparently she only came home to pick up some clothes for the kids and didn't want to stick around for lunch. That's too bad. It would have been nice to have a couple hours without the kids—know what I mean?

Actually, now that I think about it, this whole thing is pretty weird. She didn't look a bit good and didn't want to talk about it. I tried to tell her I'd be done with my workout around 11:30 and that we could discuss last night over lunch, but she just kept gathering up clothes and toys for the kids. I even told her about some of the friends I've made at the gym, but she didn't show the slightest interest. Maybe this is her "time of the month." You know what that's like for us husbands, right? I told her to be back in time to fix supper, but I think that was a mistake because she immediately started crying and drove off. I hope Sue will encourage her to get more exercise because she sure needs to lighten up a little bit. Sheesh.

I guess since Stacy doesn't want to be here for lunch, I'll meet a couple guys from work and slam some fast food. Maybe I can talk them into eighteen holes this afternoon, provided I can get Stacy to bring the kids over at 5:00 instead of 4:00. (She said she wants them to see me. I don't get that. First she hauls them to Gerry's house and then arranges to bring them back "to see me." What's wrong with this picture? Women . . .)

Well Carter, it's now 4:00. I didn't have a chance to send this earlier because my buddy Stu called about our golf game. Since we couldn't get a tee time, I went over to the club instead. It's probably just as well because Stacy came by with the kids about fifteen minutes ago and she would have been mad as a hornet if I'd not been here. She said she couldn't wait until 5:00 because she had errands to run. Then she tells me she's not coming back until 6:30 so "could I please fix the kids some supper." Can you believe this? She swoops in and drops the kids without any consideration for my time, then orders me to fix supper for everybody. Good thing there are leftovers in the fridge I can nuke without too much trouble, no thanks to her. I can't believe this. How am I supposed to get her list of chores done? She sure is acting weird today.

OK, the kids are *finally* playing in the backyard. I've got the game going on the TV. It's actually pretty nice to have some peace and quiet for a change. Hey, have I told you about our backyard? It's huge. We got the biggest lot in the neighborhood and landscaped it to the hilt. I sure hope you and Minnie can come up for a visit before the snow flies. We'll have a killer barbecue! (By the way, the snow flies pretty early up here, so we'd better get something on the calendar.)

What a day. I know, this is gonna be the strangest email you've ever received. Kind of like a running documentary. Actually, I have to run now because a guy from the office just called and wants to meet me at the pub for an hour. Said he has to bring me up to speed on how the day went. Wait till he hears how *my* day went. Anyway, I think I'll send this now and get back to you after I "fix supper." Actually, the neighbor said she'd watch my kids while I'm out, so I'm going to see if she'll feed them supper, too. Hope so.

OK, gotta run. Please say hello to Minnie for me. I've got some things to ask you, but I'll wait till later and email you again. I'll also try to find those jokes. Sorry for this crazy email! Take care.

Mitch

P.S. I didn't have time to do the chores. Oh well, I'm sure Stacy will understand. After all, she's the one who's always telling me how hard it is to watch the kids all the time!

FROM: Gerry

TO: Carter

SUBJECT: Flying dishes

Hey Carter,

I left you a short voicemail message, but you and Minnie must be out for the evening. Have you heard anything from Mitch? Things are heating up, and I'm wondering if you should give him a call.

Stacy went over there after supper to pick up more clothes and things, and while she was there Mitch kept confronting her about what she was doing. At some point he must have grabbed her wrist or something because she screamed at him, jerked her wrist out of his hand, and in the process knocked over a lamp. I don't know exactly what she said, but according to Stacy he lost his temper, chased her into the kitchen, and started throwing dishes. He must have scared her pretty good because she ran to the phone and dialed 911, which prompted Mitch to shove her aside and rip the phone cord out of the wall.

When she finally got back to our house the kids were still crying hysterically. I waited for Mitch to show up (praying furiously I'd know what to do when he got here), but he never came. I feel sick that I let her go over there alone, but I had no idea he'd do that kind of stuff. Beside, he's my best friend. What am I supposed to do? Tell you what, Carter. Even in the worst days of our marriage troubles, I never got to the point of physical violence. This has me real nervous, Carter. Please pray for us.

OK, Sue just came in and read my email. Lest I get too high and mighty here, she reminded me of a few times I backed her against the wall when we used to argue, so I guess I was also pretty aggressive.

Amazing how easy it is to forget the bad old days. (At least for me! Sue apparently hasn't forgotten . . .)

Talk soon (I hope),
Gerry

FROM: Mitch

TO: Carter

SUBJECT: Not the best day of my life

Hi Carter,

I was hoping there'd be some of your cowboy wisdom waiting for me when I logged on tonight. I could sure use your advice right now. I think Stacy has gone off the deep end. You and Minnie must be off gallivanting or something.

You wouldn't believe what happened this evening. When I got back from meeting my buddy for dinner (the neighbor fed the kids), Stacy was here filling a suitcase with clothes and personal things. I couldn't believe it and asked her what she thought she was doing. I mean, what would you do if you came home from one of your meetings and found Minnie in the bedroom loading a suitcase? What was I supposed to do? Help her pack? She started crying and wouldn't say anything, which really ticks me off. Every woman in the country uses that trick to get out of having to defend whatever they feel like doing. I told her I wasn't buying that crying routine and I demanded an immediate explanation for what this whole stupid thing was all about.

Carter, I was blown away. She told me she wasn't happy in the marriage and was leaving. It didn't register with me at first until she said she'd be staying over at Gerry and Sue's until she could find an apartment. I guess hearing the word "apartment" brought me to my senses. I have to confess I got kind of angry. But who wouldn't be angry to find his wife skipping out? It must have scared her when I raised my voice a little because she went running into the kitchen. Unfortunately, when I followed her in there I knocked some of my lunch dishes off the counter and they made a huge crash. Before I knew it she was calling the police. Now, the last thing we need around here is the police making a big deal of everything, so I told her to hang up immediately. When she didn't, I unplugged the phone and went into the other room to cool down. Since the kids were both crying I figured I'd let her calm them down before we got to the bottom of this, but she snuck them out of the house and drove away without even apologizing or saying goodbye.

What's wrong with her, Carter? She has no right to treat me this way after all I've done for her. There's not a single one of my friends' wives who has it as good as Stacy. I can't believe what a spoiled brat she's turned into.

And get this. A few minutes after she left, the doorbell rang. I figured she took the kids for a little drive to get them quieted down and was now coming back to apologize. I mean, how could she even think of leaving me? I provide her with everything she wants! I bring home the bacon, put her in a better house than any of her friends have, and provide total security. And what about the kids? They need me. I'm their father, for crying out loud. So I go to the door prepared to set the record straight once and for all. I decided to tell her she was never, ever to do this again to our family. Enough is enough. Does that make sense? The only thing is, when I opened the door—it was the police! How frustrating. The only thing they said was, "Is there a problem here?" I told them the problem just left with my two kids.

Carter, my wife and kids are gone. What am I supposed to do? Drive over to Gerry's and tell them to come home? I tell you what, it'll be a cold day you know where before I go sniveling after Stacy in front of my friends. If that's what she expects of me, she's crazier than I thought.

Well Tex, I've been sitting here for the past several hours waiting for her to call and apologize. It feels like I'm sitting in a mortuary. How mean can a woman get to do something like this to her husband? Does she understand how this feels? I walk around the house and all I can see is the time I've sacrificed at work to make this place nice for her and the kids. She doesn't realize what it takes for me to put this rather large roof over her head. Carter, do you think you could talk some sense into her? Does she actually think she'll be satisfied living in an apartment with two little kids? It's so like her. She never gives an ounce of thought to what she's doing. Sorry, I need to answer the phone. Caller ID says it's Stacy. I'll keep you posted.

Hey, get a load of this. It's 11:00 at night and I've just finished a forty-five minute conversation with a woman I don't even know anymore who is supposed to be "my wife." She's telling me she wants a "controlled separation" for at least two months. What the heck is that? Have you ever heard of such a stupid thing? Here's the deal. She said she's willing to work on our marriage provided I get personal counseling at the same time. She said a bunch of stuff about anger management and called me a control freak. If you ask me, she's been watching too much daytime TV. She also wants us both to get marriage counseling together. She will "consider" getting back together after a "controlled separation" *if* she sees significant changes in my attitude and in our relationship. In the meantime, I'm not supposed to put any pressure on her to return home. (Can you believe this?) She says we can do things together as a family—like going out for dinner or taking the kids to the park—but she will call the shots and set the pace for how much we do. Hello? Hello? She seems to have forgotten that I'm not the problem here! She's the problem! Has she already forgotten that she's the one who left? As far as I'm concerned, she can just find an apartment and when she gets her life figured out she can ask to come back. Nuts with a "controlled separation." If she wants a divorce, she can go for it. In the meantime, I've got an early morning tee time, so I'm going to bed.

Please send me some of your sage advice, old buddy. Did you ever have this much trouble with Minnie? I'd bet not. You found yourself a classy one. Wish I could say the same.

Mitch

P.S. I'm thinking she's the one who needs some "personal counseling," wouldn't you say?

FROM: Mitch

TO: Carter

SUBJECT: I forgot to ask you this

I just finished watching TV. An unbelievable talk show was on, and you know what I saw? Some nut-case woman ranting and raving about her husband. She sounded exactly like Stacy. You know something, Carter? I think Stacy's been watching way too much TV lately.

Anyway, I can't sleep, so I decided to sit down at the computer. I watched my clock go all the way from 11:30 PM to 3:17 AM. Carter, I've never felt so pathetic. My whole life is swirling around in my mind like a herd of antelope. Frankly, I can't believe my marriage has come to this. What does Stacy expect of me? I thought everything was going along fine, and now I'm facing a "controlled separation." What about the kids? Has anyone stopped to think about them? And what am I supposed to do about the laundry, the meals, the yard, our sex life (yeah, right). All I know is that my marriage is in the tank. What am I supposed to do? I know this is going to damage our reputation in the community and at my company if people find out. I wonder what the neighbors think? How can she do this to me?

Maybe I should do some counseling to make her happy again, but with who? Actually, this is what I wanted to ask you earlier today (or yesterday, or whenever that was). I hate to impose upon you and our friendship, but somebody needs to help me make some sense of this. I'm not asking for counseling, really. (You know I think counseling is for sissies.) I'm sure I could figure out what to do with Stacy if she would cooperate, but I don't know how to get her to listen. Suddenly she won't let me say anything. If she were home, we could take our time working this out, but now that she's gone time seems to be on her side and working against me. To be honest, tonight it feels like there's no hope for putting this mess back together. I guess we'll have to see what happens.

It's now almost 6:00 in the morning. I think I'll call the starter at the golf course and cancel my tee time. I don't think I could even see the ball, let alone hit it. I'm completely worn out and the day is just beginning. Guess if I hurry I can still shower, grab some breakfast, and make it to the office on time. Before I go, I'd like to ask what your thoughts are about this whole confusing mess. Do you think we need counseling, or is that just an excuse for her to bail out of our marriage? Gerry told me yesterday I should talk to you about it all. Can you give me some reasons why I should come to you for counseling?

Talk about a couple of nutty emails—these are surely the weirdest I've ever sent. Maybe it'll give you some insight into what kind of help Stacy needs. It sure beats me.

Hope to hear from you soon,
Mitch

P.S. Get this—just as I was getting ready to send this email the phone rang. Stacy wanted to know where I left the checkbook. Isn't that just like a woman? They break your heart and then run off with all your hard-earned money. A long separation is sounding better all the time.

FROM: Carter

TO: Mitch

SUBJECT: What on earth is going on in Wyoming?

Well, my friend, there's no need for me to ask what's new by you. During the past thirty-seven hours, I've received two emails and two phone messages from Gerry, a long phone call from your lovely wife, and a series of rather informative emails from you. It took me quite a while just to process everything I heard and read. Please be assured of our constant prayers for you and Stacy as well as the children.

Let me start off by telling you I can certainly sympathize with you and Stacy, having once experienced the meltdown of my own marriage. I feel so sorry for your children who are caught in the tension of your fighting. And poor Gerry! I can sure understand the stress he's feeling as he tries to decide when to listen and when to talk. I know he and Sue care a great deal for both of you, and I'm thankful they're right there alongside you. I wish I could be there as well. But for now we'll have to make the best of these lousy emails. (I couldn't reach you at any of your phone numbers.)

Actually, I've discovered emails aren't so bad for this sort of thing. They give you time to process information, which is important for old geezers like me. With emails I can read them over and over, whereas phone calls are finished the second you hang up. I'm of the age now where I always forget nine-tenths of what is said as soon as it's said. (Don't laugh—it'll happen to you someday!) Besides, if you get angry at one of my emails and delete it, I can always send you another copy!

Before I continue, how do you like Wyoming? I couldn't believe you gave up pine trees for sagebrush, elk for jackrabbits, deer for antelope, and bears for badgers. I understand from Gerry that you live in a small residential area on the edge of Cheyenne. According to the cen-

sus report, your moving up there gave Wyoming its anticipated pop-
ulation increase for the year. How does it feel to live in the middle of
a cow town where all they talk about is the latest price of beef, whose
horse is the fastest, whose tractor has the best air conditioning, whose
hay is the tallest, and whose manure is the deepest? It feels like just yesterday you were still here in Colorado. Time flies while you're making
mistakes! Wyoming instead of Colorado? Mitch? (You know I'm just
razzing you. Minnie and I love you and just want it all to work out.)

The move must have been stressful. Anytime you move a family,
the stress piles up like unread magazines. Of course, as you know, stress
piles up whether you're moving or not. The informative email I
received from Gerry yesterday made it sound like everything is piling
up. So the marriage is pretty iffy, huh? I was glad to also get a phone
call from Stacy, who was reaching out for help instead of wringing
your neck and heading south with a guy twice the man you are at half
your belt size. That woman must love you, or she'd have left years ago.

Gerry, Sue, and even Stacy seem to think I might be able to break
through your thick skull with a series of emails. Frankly, nothing
makes me happier than to come alongside those I love and give them
a hand, but the question is, *are you really looking for help*? I wasn't so
sure from your emails. Sometimes other people care more about our
marriages than we do. For instance, my mom sure cares a lot about
mine. You know something, Mitch? I care about your marriage, but
I'm not going to force any "counseling" your way unless you're interested in it. We all believe in you and know you'll do everything you
can to straighten out this mess. Since Gerry and I have gone through
his marriage problems together, he thought we might as well all pitch
in and go through yours together. But it's your call. What about it, you
slacker? Everyone would love to help if you're interested. As for my
part, I'll shoot off emails every now and again between racquetball and
ranch work. Maybe some barnyard theology from an old "rip" might
just give you and Stacy something to think about.

By the way, Minnie says hello! She also says if you don't straighten
up she's going to head up there and give you the talking-to of your life.
Believe me, you'd better straighten up now while you're ahead.

Mitch, I don't know how such a lousy fisherman ended up with such a great catch as Stacy, but I think the time has come for you to decide whether you want to pull out the net, ask for help, and land the woman of your dreams, or whether you're going to play "catch and release" with your whole family. The ball is in your court!

Shoot me an email and let me know what you think. And meanwhile, try not to throw any more dishes. That could get expensive. If you have to throw something, use cow pies. No sharp edges.

Write back soon. I'm anxious about you and your family.

Carter

P.S. In case you're too busy to keep up with the really important things of life, I've attached one of my favorite comics, *Life at the Lazy-U*. Does it remind you of anybody? Nah, I didn't think so.

FROM: Carter

TO: Mitch

SUBJECT: Wedding bells

Mitch, my friend, I can't stop thinking about you and Stacy. Minnie and I were just reflecting on the day you got married. Do you remember?

Something special took place that day. Not only did you say goodbye to all your money and most of your free time, but you also gave up your singleness. It sounds to me like you still think you're a single guy with an opposite-sex roommate. Two people sharing the same carpet. Just as you forget to put your dishes in the dishwasher when you're done eating, have you also forgotten the marital covenant you entered into? Remember standing in front of that official-looking guy and promising you'd perform certain duties for a certain beautiful young lady? That meant more than just turning up the furnace, you know. A covenant was made, and vows were taken. Words like *love, cherish, faithfulness*, and *for better or for worse* were enthusiastically exchanged during that ceremony. Congratulations! You've now made it to the "for worse" part of your marital journey, and you've done it in style! Think of it this way. Most men don't get to the "for worse" part until they've been married many years, but you've succeeded in getting there with breakneck speed. Way to go! I'm sure you've set a record of some kind. Maybe I should send you a prize. How about a small trophy? What do you say?

You know something? Minnie and I went through similar struggles early in our marriage. To be honest, we were a total disaster. Yet our marital problems became the launching pad for changing our entire lives. The thing is, both Minnie and I needed to be willing to change. It wasn't enough to just sit through counseling. We needed to submit ourselves to it and change our nasty attitudes and selfish behaviors. Many people are eager to help, but the big question is, "Are you willing to receive the help and be changed?"

As you already know, Mitch, I'm not one to mince words. I'm going to tell you what I think. But isn't that what we men most want to hear? I sure do. Why waste time massaging our anemic egos, right? Let's get straight to business. You aren't going to be a sissy and try to get your ego stroked somewhere else, are you? Nah, I know you better than that. Now that we've gotten this disclaimer out of the way, how about we get to work on your marriage?

Let's reminisce a bit. Remember when the two of you thoroughly enjoyed being together? I can remember you guys constantly laughing together over absolutely nothing. You were "in the hunt" back then and could hardly wait to snuggle up to your sweetie. While you were dating, you treated her very special. I was so impressed!

Actually, I should say that *most* of the time you treated her special. Throughout the premarital counseling, some of our mutual friends tried to help you both make the right decision. We were all trying to help you see through the fog of courtship. However, at that star-spangled point in your relationship nobody was going to tell you anything. You wanted to get married, and that's all you both could see. We pointed out some weaknesses in the way you communicated with each other, but you both assumed things would improve over time and that it was no big deal. I even talked with you about your abusive tendencies and your need to be less controlling. Stacy defended you back then, remember? She hasn't forgotten. Yesterday, your wife was reflecting with regret on your premarital counseling and wishing she had listened more carefully.

There were also many positive things about your relationship. You worked well together, like a pair of draft horses. What's happened since then? I can feel the distance between you. I suspect you seldom do anything together except eat, sleep, and bark at each other. Well, my friend, that's unacceptable! Yes, I know you share the same hot water tank, but I'm thinking about personal things. For example, what about making time to talk together, plan together, go to the movies together, and all that? Hello? Hello? Are you still there? From what I'm hearing, whenever your wife brings up the subject of doing something together you tune her out. You have to go to the office, the club, the golf course, or the recliner for a quick nap. You may not like hearing this, but from Stacy's perspective it's the truth. However ruffled your feathers may feel, you know she's right. Plenty of distance has crept between you.

How many times have all of us guys encouraged one another to spend more personal time with our wives? We all know the more time we enjoy together the better our marriages will become. Hasn't that been true? Now look at your marriage. You two can hardly be civil to one another. Furthermore, you're not even living in the same house. Remember what it was like before you were married? It was spicy, exciting, inspiring, thrilling, open, honest, understanding, caring, comforting, assuring, and all that stuff. What happened to the romance? When did the fun and pleasure you enjoyed disappear? Can you remember? What happened to the person your wife married? Mitch, what happened to you?

Frankly, marriage isn't that hard when we follow the owner's manual. You have one, don't you? It's called the Bible. I know you have one because I gave it to you, remember? You know something? I got a similar owner's manual when I bought my new Ford F-250 4x4 pickup truck in 1968. It was a little book that told me how to take care of my new vehicle. I was so proud of that truck! Fact of the matter is, I still use it at the ranch.

Now relax, I'm not comparing our wives or marriages to pickups. I simply said the owner's manuals are similar. They both tell us how to take care of something important. In the manual for my truck, I'm told to use gasoline for fuel rather than sawdust. I'm told it'll work better if the tires are inflated. And, however good cold water tastes in hot weather, I'm told oil works better in a hot engine. It's all in there. Distilled water belongs in the battery, and brake fluid in the master cylinder, not vice versa. I'm even told not to slam the thing into reverse while barreling forward because the air bags will deploy. (Actually, my truck didn't come with air bags—that's what padded dashboards were for.) A lot of engineering goes into new vehicles these days, and if you don't want trouble, you'd better pay attention to the owner's manual!

You know something? The same is true with the owner's manual for marriage. It contains a wealth of information on how to keep a marriage running smoothly and efficiently. It tells you how to keep things moving forward in your relationship and how to avoid hitting reverse at high speeds. Can you think of anybody who needs advice like that right now? It tells you how to turn each other on and how to cool each other off. Seat belts of commitment are provided for the occupants of the marital relationship because there are many bumps and tussles along the way. The warning lights in a marriage are highly visible and signal serious problems. My friend, this is exactly where you are in your marriage. The warning lights are on, the doors are open, and you are sitting on the pavement all alone. At least you had plenty of warning before landing there. Stacy has been telling you for more than a year that she's been running out of gas. Did you listen? Or did you simply turn up the radio?

God's Word tells us how to take care of our marriages and how to keep them from breaking down. Have you ever consulted it? If not, there's likely to be even more trouble ahead!

Mitch, I know you've decided for whatever reason not to become a Christian. That's your business. But deciding not to pay attention to the owner's manual for marriages impacts more people than just yourself. It was written by the One who designed your marriage, and He knows what He's talking about. Do you want to enjoy your marriage? Do you want to squeeze as much out of it as you possibly can? It's all in the manual. The problem with guys like you and me is that we think we already know it all. We think we don't need any marriage manual telling us how to be happily married—we learned all there is to know about marriage when we were in high school. We think we can solve all our problems without outside assistance.

I got news for us, Mitch. That's a load of bad hay. When it comes to marriage and family matters, men are as sharp as marbles. We need the help of a marriage manual, the accountability of other men, and patient wives. Otherwise our marriages will be in the junkyard with a whole lot of other worn-out, battered, and abandoned old marriages. Look at it this way—your marriage has broken down. Want to see what the manual has to say and get your marriage back to its original, high-performance condition?

With your permission, I'm going to email you several things to think about during the coming weeks. Together, let's try not only to save your marriage, but let's get it running better than ever. What do you say?

While you think about it, put on some reading glasses and find that manual. The days of letting it gather dust under the front seat of your Z28 are definitely over.

Carter

P.S. If anybody can repair his marriage, you can. Trust me, you'll be fine. What do you say?

FROM: Carter

TO: Mitch

SUBJECT: Don't follow you; you're lost!

Calling Crazy Mitch! Hello? Where are you, my friend? During the past week, I've heard twice from Gerry, once from your lovely wife, and once from Sue. But still no Mitch. Have you decided to pack it in? Or are you suffering from that most common of all male diseases, the refusal to ask directions?

I know, what man needs directions? It's a contradiction in terms. Women ask for directions, but never men. We don't have time to ask for directions. Besides, we can figure it out. After all, we're *men*, and *men* don't need directions! Right?

Let me tell you something. Just this past week, I played a round of golf in a tournament with some business friends. It was at a course I've never been to, so I needed detailed directions to even find the place. What was even worse is that I needed more directions once I got there. I needed directions to the restroom, to the starter, to the golf carts, and to the first tee box. I even needed directions to my ball most of the time.

But the real problem occurred after the tournament. Once I returned my golf cart, took off my golf boots (I installed golf spikes on my cowboy boots), and tossed my bag into the truck, I realized I'd misplaced the paper with my directions for reaching the place and getting back home again. So what do you think I did next? What a dumb question. I started the truck, made my way to the entrance, waved at the attendant, knowingly glanced up and down the street and turned left. (Did I say left? I meant right. Or was it left? Where was I anyway?)

Things started to look pretty familiar for the first twenty minutes of driving around, until I recognized a woman I had seen ten minutes earlier still watering her lawn. That made me a little nervous, but not nervous enough to ask her how to get out of there. In fact, it wasn't until the fourth time I passed her, nearly thirty minutes later, that I actually considered stopping. Thankfully, I didn't have to, because just then I remembered where I'd left my directions. Within ten minutes, I was waving at the parking lot attendant (again) and threading my way back to the main drag. So it only took me an hour and ten minutes longer than necessary to find my way out of there, and the enormous homes with impeccable landscaping provided wonderful scenery along the way. Incidentally, when you're "learning a new neighborhood" (never say "lost"), it's better if you can justify your travels by enjoying the scenery. That way it's like you actually planned to go exploring.

When I was a young buck like you, it took me about six years of marital hell to realize I needed directions. I wandered around way too long trying to figure things out by myself. What a shame! It would have been so easy to ask someone for directions. But I was too self-directed and self-ruled to look to others for assistance. In the Bible, 1 Corinthians 10:12 says, "Therefore let him who thinks he stands take heed that he does not fall." Our self-confidence in believing we can fix our problems often brings us to ruin. The true essence of all biblical teaching is to give us directions about how to live skillfully and with discernment. Paul the apostle tells us the Scriptures are inspired for the purpose of instruction, correction, and training so we'll be equipped to live life properly. (You can find where he says this in 2 Timothy 3:16.) Those who try to put their marriages together without the Word of God are just as foolish as I was trying to find my way out of that neighborhood maze without directions.

Life was never meant to be lived without the use of directions. Don't be foolish. Not only are good directions available, people all over the neighborhood of your life are eager to help you if you'll only stop long enough to ask. Don't become one of those tourists who burn up all their vacation time driving in circles because they won't ask for help.

Mitch, are you tired of going around in circles yet? Are you dizzy enough? Frustrated enough over trying to put your marriage back together without the help of directions? Trust me, your marriage needs less "exploring" and more direction. I know how that feels because I've "been there and done that." Please stop whatever you're doing up there with all your new free time and start asking for directions. I'll wait to hear from you this time. Honest. (But please don't make me wait too long. I'm not getting any younger.)

The Grungy Old Cowboy

P.S. The Bible says, "There is a way which seems right to a man, but its end is the way of death." (That's in Proverbs, chapter 14, verse 12.) It seems to me that we'd both better be careful about being too self-directed. Marriage is a lot like that proverb. What "seems" right often ends in divorce. Look out, the sky might be falling!

FROM: Mitch

TO: Carter

SUBJECT: OK! OK! I can hear you, you grungy cowboy!

Oh Unrelenting One,

Boy, you don't beat around the bush, do you? I guess you haven't changed at all since those days at your house when you used to harass me about becoming a Christian. I still think about those conversations, but I suppose I shouldn't tell you that—it'll only encourage you. I have to confess, you made me mad with a few of the things you wrote, but I'm guessing you're on the money with some of it, too. Thanks for caring about Stacy and me.

You wouldn't believe what a lousy couple of days I've had. I feel like I'm trapped on a gigantic emotional roller coaster. One minute I'm so mad I can't sit still, and the next minute I'm so lonely I can't move. There are times I can actually feel my face turning red with frustration, and the next second I've got tears rolling off my cheeks and ruining my starched shirts. Carter, what is going on with me? I took a ride in my new car with the top down hoping to feel better, but I ended up driving over to Gerry's house to see Stacy—and she wasn't even there. What does it mean when you even feel depressed in the car of your dreams? It made me want to return the car.

Carter, what if Stacy gets an apartment and meets another guy? The thought of my children calling someone else "Daddy" just kills me, let alone picturing them playing in the courtyard of some apartment building. But you know something? She brought this on herself! She has a nice house to live in, but if she wants out, that's her doing! If she thinks she's had it tough in the past, just wait. She's really going to have it tough in the future. Of course, so am I. A divorce, thousands of dollars a month child support, visitation schedules, outrageous attorney fees, selling the house, dumping the car, no more eating out, doing my own laundry, and a lifetime of bitterness don't sound like a picnic either. These problems are too huge. I don't know where to begin. Maybe tomorrow I'll figure it out. Better yet, maybe my old cowboy friend will give me a hand.

Carter, I would like very much for you to throw in with us and help Stacy and me sort through our marriage problems. I realize I can be pretty bull-headed sometimes—about once a month Gerry tells me I'm as stubborn as a mule. But I'll try to consider your counsel. It won't be easy, and I guarantee you'll hear back from me when I think you're out of line, but please feel free to "knock some sense" into this hard head of mine. I believe you and Minnie love us as if we were your own kids, so that makes it easier to take your abuse . . . I mean advice.

I've always respected the way you look at life (except for your unfortunate narrow-mindedness about God) and wish we could get together like we used to. Remember all the fun times we had in Colorado? I hope you're still working on your racquetball game. We played a lot back then, and I really miss it. None of my friends are as easy to beat as you were. Hah! Hey, do you remember the game where we were going at it big time and I bumped into your arm while trying to avoid your left-handed kill shot? It was like one of those slow-motion replays watching you miss the ball and hit yourself right in the mouth with your racquet. I'll never forget all the excuses you gave for the loss. When are you going to suck it up and finally admit I smashed you?

While I'm ragging on you, I just thought of a time when we laughed out our guts. Remember when we were fishing on the Fryingpan River that cold day in March? I'll never forget it because I almost froze to death. Not only did you catch more fish than I did, you stayed a whole lot dryer than I did. About all I remember is losing my balance and heading downstream in five feet of rushing water. I vaguely remember passing by the hole you were fishing and hearing you laughing and telling me to try walking the shoreline next time because it's a lot dryer. You were even waving your cowboy hat at me, you merciless cob. When I finally climbed out of the water, you were already headed to the truck to start the heater. At that point I knew we were done fishing for the day. After all, how could I fish without a fly rod? I still can't figure out where that thing went.

Well, Carter, it looks like I'm in over my head again, and I'm about to drown. I'm scared and cold-hearted, and I need you to start up the heater and help me warm up to my wife. (How's that for Mission: Impossible?) Let's get going before I freeze to death.

What do you say, Rev?
Mitch

P.S. Before we begin, could you explain something? What's this "controlled separation" thing all about?

FROM: Carter

TO: Mitch

SUBJECT: Understanding counselors

Greetings, my dear friend. I was both glad to get your email and sorry to hear about your roller-coaster feelings. Still, that's better than feeling like you're on the Titanic. Always remember: things can get worse! Your marriage could actually sink.

I'm thankful that you acknowledge my love for you and Stacy. It's a relief to know you both understand I'm only trying to help. I might even assume the new name you tagged me with in that last email. Frankly, I like being called "The Rev" even though I'm not one. A business associate also calls me that. When you consider all the names men call each other (buddy, partner, slacker, weenie, turkey, looser, ugly, and bowlegs) what's one more?

It really made me chuckle when you referred to yourself as stubborn and bull-headed. I like your style! As I recall, you had a hard time agreeing with me before you were married, so why should I expect anything different now? I'll bet you've always been pretty independent and you've been right most of the time. You're very gifted, Mitch, but be careful! Your self-confidence can lead you astray. It must seem pretty humbling to be collecting opinions from Gerry, Sue, and the old Rev. But who knows? Some opinions out there could be the ticket to saving your marriage.

You raised a couple of good questions in your last email. One concerned the "controlled separation," and the other had to do (indirectly) with my qualifications as a counselor. This last one is just about the most important question every couple must ask before committing themselves to counseling. "Who does this guy think he is?" is a valid question, along with, "Can he be trusted with our most valuable possession?" Who wants just anybody messing around with his marriage? I'm guessing you're feeling some initial apprehension, which is understandable. After all, it's your marriage, and you're responsible for protecting it. Although I'm delighted you gave me the green light to move ahead, you still deserve an explanation as to my qualifications and what hope we might have for putting this thing (your marriage) back together.

If you're wondering about credentials, I'll need to offer an apology. In reality, I'm sort of an impostor. I've never formally studied psychology, nor have I gone to school to become a "licensed" or "professional" marriage counselor. I have however, broken horses to ride, taught bulls to lead, and trained dogs to growl. How can marriage problems be any more difficult than these? My only credentials are the hundreds of couples who have been referred to me during the past thirty years, not as a therapist, but as a friend. (A rather bold friend, I might add.)

My first counseling challenge was Minnie and myself. We had *extreme* marital problems at the front end of our marriage, and those problems served as the beginning of my education. You could say I was trained at The School of Hard Knocks. Like Moses, a guy in the Bible who learned God's ways by spending forty years in the wilderness cleaning up after sheep, I learned God's ways by spending years in the wilderness of an adversarial marriage cleaning up after myself. Look at it this way. Someone who has been bucked off a horse as many times as I have is bound to become a better rider. Not the kind of thing one can learn from a book, or even a library of books. Minnie and I have had to work real hard at our commitment through the years. Even after almost forty years, many attitudes and actions still need to be corrected. Trial and error, trial and more error! However, we're working on them together these days, and we wouldn't trade our relationship for anything in the world.

Of course, there are terrific marriage counselors out there. Many do an outstanding job of helping hurting families. If you and Stacy later decide to go that route, we'll support you all the way. But I'll warn you now, there's lots to learn about getting counseling these days. For one thing, the terminology has changed since I was young. Let me give you some examples:

1. Today they call counseling "therapy." When I was a kid, therapy was a trip behind the woodshed with Father.
2. You've no doubt heard of "group therapy." Well, years ago, group therapy was when the town fathers got the whole bunch of us kids together and thumped us all.
3. Today couples have "issues." When I was growing up, they called it sin.
4. I hear a lot of talk about "dysfunctional families." Fifty years ago, those same families were known as "normal."
5. Today, if someone is drunk, he's either "under the influence" or "alcohol dependent." What's wrong with drunk?

In fact, most of what we used to call "personal responsibility" is now hidden behind a host of unthreatening, nonjudgmental, warm and comfy terms that hold our ancestors or environments more responsible for our behavior than we are. Mitch, I guarantee you won't misunderstand any of my terms. You'll know the definition of every word I use without a doubt.

Here's one strong concern I have, though. Wouldn't it be better to work with a counselor who has a personal relationship with God? I know the difficulties you face with this God stuff, but the Bible provides tremendous instruction about marriage even for those who don't necessarily believe. I use the Bible in counseling because it tells me the "truth" rather than giving me just another "theory." The Bible's wisdom about anger, selfishness, and so forth applies to all people, believers or not. Shouldn't you decide about this? Stacy tells me that she turned to Christ last December. She even tells me you know a little about the Bible and have memorized a few verses. But she doesn't believe you are interested in following biblical teaching. Now, that's a problem only God can help you with! When He decides to build a fire under your backside, some of these things will begin to make more sense. I believe God is reaching out to you through your marital problems. He wants you to listen to the Bible, Mitch. It's made a huge difference in my life to know the One who wrote the owner's manual on marriage. I can help you understand how the Bible says you should live, but knowing its Author will make even more of a difference for you.

I told Minnie how glad I am that you are willing to "work" on your marriage. However, I need to know that you realize your marriage needs more than an "adjustment." Things are more serious than you think. Your marriage needs major corrective surgery, not just a few bandages. Denying or avoiding this issue isn't going to buy you anything but more trouble. Mitch, you must face the fact that your wife is at the end of her rope. It's time for you to go to work on your marriage every day just like you'd work on dieting or breaking a pack mule. Breaking a pack mule requires long-term commitment, and dieting means disciplining yourself every day to watch what you eat. (Incidentally, you might want to consider a diet because Stacy has lost sight of your belt buckle.)

Let me remind you of something I tell every couple. I'm not better than you, nor am I more qualified than you are to solve your marital problems. I've just had more experience dealing with these kinds of problems than you have. Frankly, I'll bet the farm you already know what you need to do. Deep down, you know it's going to take a huge sacrifice on your part to make your marriage work. But you are resisting it. I know how you feel because I've been there. You just don't want to make the necessary sacrifice, do you? Are you still thinking you can do your own thing, talk Stacy out of this separation, and have a great marriage? Sorry, sport. That's not the way it's going to work from here on out. In fact, it hasn't worked very well to this point either, has it?

I've been informed that you told Stacy, "Maybe I shouldn't have married the woman I did." Now, I've heard plenty of radio psychologists say, "The person you marry is the most important factor in determining whether your marriage will succeed or fail," but I've got news for you. Your wife is not the problem. Did you get that? A successful marriage doesn't depend on *finding* the right partner but on *being* the right partner.

As far as whether there's any hope for your marriage, I won't lie to you. Your marriage may not survive. But there is hope as long as you stop telling yourself there's no problem. You keep telling Stacy you'll try harder, but all three of us know that up to this point you've made little (if any) effort to change your life. In poker, they call this "bluffing." The success of your marriage is directly related to your personal commitment to becoming the man God wants you to be. The future of your marriage is in your hands, not mine (or any other counselor's). It's a problem only you can solve. Your wife wants you to love her, care for her, and treat her special. But unless you take some initiative starting right now, that's all going to be history.

Well my friend, I've tried to answer your questions. Although I'm not a professional counselor, I will come alongside as your friend and fellow learner. I will stand with you and pray for you. I will tell you what I think in no uncertain terms and listen carefully to what you say. I will share my experiences, both good and bad, and share your experiences as you go through them. We will cry together, laugh together, and learn how to become better husbands together. But the responsibility for how your marriage turns out remains on your puny shoulders.

That's where we are. Next, we have to talk about where we go from here. In the meantime, plop into your recliner, kick back with a soda, and take five. It wouldn't hurt to get a soda for your wife as well. Oh, I forgot. She isn't living with you anymore. Well then, how about cleaning up the house and finishing those chores she's been asking you to do for the past six months? What do you have to lose? Sorry, wrong question. What do you have to gain?

The Rev

P.S. Go dig your Bible out from wherever it's gathering dust and look at what God promises in 2 Chronicles chapter 7, verse 14: "If My people who are called by My name humble themselves and pray and seek My face and turn from their wicked ways, then I will hear from heaven, will forgive their sin and will heal their land."

That certainly smells like hope to me, wouldn't you agree? The question is, are you ready to humble yourself, pray, seek God's face, and turn from your wicked ways? Stacy is waiting. And speaking of working on your marriage, have you seen the attached *Life at the Lazy-U*? Take my advice, Mitch. There are better ways to work on your marriage.

FROM: Stacy

TO: Carter

SUBJECT: What's happening to Daddy and Mommy?

Hi Carter,

Thanks for your encouragement on the phone yesterday. Our conversations bring rare moments of hope to my world of despair. How did I come to this place? Just when I think I'm at the end of my tears, another pang of grief seizes me and I'm crying again.

This afternoon it was just awful. I was at the kitchen table calling about apartments when I noticed my daughter, Tanya, walk into Gerry's study. Now, I've told both children to leave "Uncle Gerry" alone when he's in there. (To be honest, I'm terribly anxious about becoming more of a burden to Gerry and Sue than we already are. Overnight houseguests send Mitch through the roof, so I'm trying my best to keep us out of Gerry's way.)

Anyway, as soon as I saw Tanya walk in there I ended my phone call and walked over to the study door to apologize. As I came to the door, however, I heard her ask, "Uncle Gerry, what's happening to Mommy and Daddy?" Curious what he would say, I waited just outside the door.

Gerry did a good job (he'll make a great father some day). He asked her what she meant, and she proceeded to ask question after question about what's going on between Mitch and me. At first he tried to answer her questions, then he suggested she ask all the questions she could think of while he wrote them down. I think she felt honored by this because she went on and on. I had no idea she was thinking so deeply about our situation. Kids sit in front of the television and you think they're off in another world, but they're not.

I listened as long as I could, but eventually ran into the bathroom for more tissues and to wash my face. I'm in agony over what this is doing to our children.

When they were through talking, Gerry came out and showed me the list of questions she asked him. I couldn't even read through the list without crying again, but eventually made it. Just look at this:

I'm scared to go to sleep at night. Why can't we go home and sleep in our own bedroom?

Why are we living with you and Aunt Sue instead of at our house?

Who is living in our house with Daddy?

Why is my brother sucking his thumb so much?

If we move into an apartment, will Daddy come live with us there?

Mommy says that no dogs are allowed at our new house. Where is Sparky going to live? Will Daddy give him away?

Who is playing with my toys at our house?

If we move to a new house, will we have a yard to play in?

Why do I get spanked when I fight with my brother when Daddy and Mommy yell at each other all the time?

If Mommy gets a job, who will take care of us?

If we move to a new house, will I ever see my friends who live next to our old house?

Daddy was very mad when we went to see him yesterday. Does he still love us? Does he still love Mommy?

Does Daddy miss us?

If we don't live with Daddy anymore, are we still a family?

Aren't families supposed to live together?

Why doesn't God make Mommy and Daddy love each other again?

What will happen to us if Mommy doesn't want to live with us either?

Is this my fault?

Are Mommy and Daddy getting a divorce?

While I was reading Tanya's questions, I felt tremendous pressure to go back to Mitch, but I honestly think it would kill me. Every time I start thinking about him, I feel angry, bitter, and so frustrated I could scream. My self-confidence and self-identity are shot, and all of our phone calls still focus on him. Hopefully, this controlled separation will give me time to become the woman and wife I know God wants me to be. I've not been a very good wife so far, I'm afraid, but I'm willing to face that fact and discipline myself accordingly with God's help. I can only pray that Mitch will begin to feel the same way. Do you think he'll ever understand why I had to leave?

I'm reading the book you recommended on emotional abuse, and it explains very clearly what I'm feeling. Do you think Mitch might read it?

Please pray for the children. If only I could snap my fingers and fix everything so they wouldn't have to go through this, but there's so much to fix. I know I need to be strong and submissive to the Lord's will, but I'm feeling so hopeless right now. I could use your prayers, too.

Love to Minnie,
Stacy

FROM: Gerry

TO: Mitch

SUBJECT: Keeping "The Main Thing" the main thing

Sue and I keep thinking and praying for you and Stacy. The situation here is presently very unstable. Stacy came to our house in a state of panic and confusion and opened her heart to us about your marriage. At first, it was difficult to get our bearings because the whole thing was such a shock to us. That's why I have waited until now to respond to you about some of the comments you made to Stacy this past week. Also, I'm sending this as an email because I don't do well with this kind of stuff over lunch. Maybe we can talk after you think about it for awhile.

Having weathered my own marital failure, I consider myself a bit of an expert on certain things. Not only did I mess up my marriage, I also made the process of reconciliation much more complicated by not keeping The Main Thing the main thing. Since I was angry, hurt, and confused when Sue took off, I started building cases against her in my mind. They weren't really true, but they sure made me feel better about what was happening. In other words, I allowed my focus to drift from the main thing into suspicion and defensiveness. Mitch, maybe you can already relate to what I'm trying to say. Let me give you a short list of thoughts you may be tempted to nurture against Stacy.

1. You may be tempted to think this is all Stacy's fault.
2. You may start to believe Stacy doesn't love you any more.
3. You may consider ways to get even.
4. You may drift into fears of financial insecurity and thoughts about losing your new Z.
5. You may be feeling pretty sorry for yourself.

6. You may have contacted some friends and complained about how awful Stacy is treating you.

7. You may think about telling your mother. She'll surely rally to your side against "the enemy" (Stacy).

8. Now that Stacy has exposed your failures to others, you may feel left alone and alienated from your mutual friends (like Sue and me).

9. Speaking of which, since you and I haven't really had a chance to talk, you may already feel Sue and I are partial to Stacy's side of this story.

10. You may even think we're all against you (Stacy, Carter, Minnie, Sue, and me), and that we want to see you lose.

11. You may wonder whether your kids miss you, or whether Stacy has poisoned them against you.

12. You may be blaming God for what's happening to you. Or, you may think Stacy's becoming a Christian has had something to do with the rift that's grown between you. You may even use this to validate your rejection of God.

Mitch, Sue and I would like to help you keep The Main Thing the main thing. The Main Thing is simply this—you have a marital problem. Nothing more. That should be your entire focus. Getting to the root of your marital problem should keep you awake at night, not stewing over distractions like the dozen I've listed above. Your children still love you, your family members will understand, and your friends will all support you both. Just because Stacy came to our home for refuge doesn't mean we have taken her side in this. Sue and I both love you and want to help you through this temporary challenge.

In fact, I want to give you a little piece of advice. Stacy is your wife. You should actually protect her from insulting or accusatory comments from your family and friends. Don't allow others to maliciously criticize her in their attempts sympathize with you. Remember how Carter was always ragging on us to "be men"? One thing he always told me was that a man takes the heat for what's happening in his marriage. Stacy loves you and is worth taking the heat for. Remember, my friend, the restoration of your marriage is The Main Thing right now. It's more important than protecting your image.

Sue sends her love as well. Let's all get together as soon as the dust settles.

Your friends forever,
Gerry and Sue

P.S. What's The Main Thing again?

FROM: Mitch

TO: Gerry

SUBJECT: Your "main thing" is not my MAIN THING

It's like you people come from another planet. Can't you grasp what's happening here? You may think you can relate because of your marital problems a few years back, but you're missing the real issue by a mile. Who are you trying to kid? I'm out, and everyone else is in! Stacy's going around blasting me every opportunity she gets. The more she talks, the more everyone sympathizes with her story and the further away she gets from me. The "main thing" for me is getting my family back together, and I see everyone standing in the way of that happening, especially you and Sue! As sure as I'm sitting here, if Stacy would never have gone over to your house that stupid night she'd be home where she belongs right now. Your interference has not been helpful. You should have brought her right back home the next morning and made her face me straight on. *That* is what a "real man" would have done. Instead, you helped her disregard her responsibility to her family. Marriage is a commitment. You just don't walk out and come back whenever you're dang ready.

Just what am I supposed to be feeling over here, huh? The people I trusted are working against the very thing I consider to be the "main thing." If we have to go through a "controlled separation," neither one of us will want to get back together. It's like my friend told me: "absence makes the heart wander" (NOT grow fonder). Stacy needs to get herself home right now so we can save our marriage. Did you get that? She needs to get home SO WE CAN SAVE OUR MARRIAGE! That's the MAIN THING! Why is that so hard for all of you to understand? I can convince Stacy that I will try harder and be the husband she has always wanted if she comes home. Right now we can't even get five minutes together without her consulting you. It seems to me you've become the "main thing."

You might sense I'm a little upset. No kidding! Unless there is a major change in something or someone, our marriage is going to be over and I don't know what to do about it. I spent the better part of this morning with an attorney discussing the options of a legal separation or a divorce. I'll bet you can understand those kinds of separation. One is legal, and the other is permanent, and neither is "controlled" (whatever that means). My attorney has never heard of such a thing as a controlled separation. He advised me of my legal rights and emphasized the need to protect myself. I was warned about how Stacy could hurt me financially and take my children from me if I wasn't careful. For a couple thousand bucks retainer, he said I could get some action instead of all this hand wringing and talking behind my back. He even thought I could get a court-appointed arbitrator who wouldn't be partial to Stacy's one-sided sob story like everyone else in my life. Furthermore, he suggested a counseling center in town that does "conciliation" work. Sounds like money well spent to me.

Gerry and Sue, I'm sorry for venting at you. I feel like I'm on the horns of a huge dilemma here. Frankly, I'm scared to death, frustrated, and angry as a nest of wasps. I want to sting anybody who stands in my way. I'm guessing you mean well, but I think the legal route might be way better for our marriage than all this one-sided nonsense I've been subjected to so far. I think it's important to work with a counselor who isn't also a mutual friend and sympathetic to poor little Stacy.

Bottom line is I know you're trying to help, but the main thing that should be happening isn't happening. It's been over a week, and Stacy still isn't home. That's The Main Thing around here.

Mitch

P.S. Even though I will be seeking advice from more objective sources, I'd like to stay in touch. You can keep sending emails if you'd like, and I'd be open to a get-together once Stacy and my children are back home where they belong. I might even have my attorney contact you for some background information. Let me know if you'd be open to that.

FROM: Carter

TO: Mitch

SUBJECT: Your angry email to Gerry

Thanks for copying me on your email exchange with Gerry. Before you fly off the handle and do something you'll regret, I thought you might want to read some "fortunes" from the Asian Noodle Co. Generally, I don't counsel people using fortune cookies, but since you seem to be taking anyone's advice I figured, what could it hurt? Here are the Top Ten Wise Words from my fortune-cookie collection:

1. Get to the nitty-gritty of things in all dealings.
2. A friend asks only for your time, not your money.
3. Fortune always helps those who are of good judgment.
4. Good news will be brought to you by mail (or possibly email).
5. Nature, time, and patience are the three great physicians.
6. A friend is something you give yourself.
7. Your principles are worth more to you than money or success.
8. Better to have a hen tomorrow than an egg today.
9. A handful of patience is worth more than a bushel of brains.
10. Time is the wisest counselor.

Mitch, you'd better slow down a bit and think these over. You're getting an awful lot of exercise between "jumping to conclusions," "pushing your luck," and "running everyone down." Listen to the cookies! Use good judgment, take your time, be patient, follow your principles, trust your friends, keep checking your email, and focus on still being with Stacy tomorrow rather than having legal protection today. I've seen hundreds of couples face worse differences than you're experiencing and come through with flying colors. But it takes patience and a willingness to face what brought you to this point. Believe me, you don't need any protection from Stacy right now. You need help becoming better partners for each other. That's something worth investing in.

Now, how about some fried rice?

Ka-ta, your Asian counselor

FROM: Carter

TO: Mitch

SUBJECT: Controlled separation

Mitch, I totally spaced out your question about the "controlled separation" in my email the other day. Maybe it was just as well. Now you can compare and contrast it with the more binding and permanent forms of separation your attorney friend told you about.

Before I get ahead of myself, I want to encourage you in your marriage reconciliation with Stacy. Although changes don't happen overnight, they do happen. People do change their actions and attitudes. Affection can be rekindled and trust restored. However, at the beginning of the reconciliation process you can expect a basketful of negative emotions standing directly in the way of progress. Hurt feelings, anger, bitterness, sadness, grief, loneliness, and anxiety all have a way of stifling any hope of healing in a marriage. That's why I believe Gerry is wise in suggesting a "controlled separation." Actually, the Bible even allows for such a season of separation by mutual agreement (this appears in the book of 1 Corinthians). However, you both need to agree to it or it won't work very well. Two months is long enough for negative emotions to settle down, and it's also long enough for healthy new attitudes and actions to surface and take root.

Gerry and Sue went through a controlled separation when their marriage was falling apart, and I think it would be a good idea for you and Stacy as well. Here's why:

1. It will put a healthy fence around your desire to have Stacy return home before she is ready. You're a pretty good salesman, Mitch, but if she isn't ready to come home things won't get any better once she's there. Probably the opposite.

2. It will also put a healthy fence around Stacy's desire to throw in the towel and reinforce her commitment to your marriage.

3. It will allow time for the Holy Spirit (Whom you don't believe in yet) to work and for the counseling to sink in.

4. It takes time for two people to begin trusting each other again. A two-month controlled separation will give you that time.

5. It will give you the opportunity to intentionally pursue Stacy and the kids as you plan picnics, movie nights, and so forth. You could even spend a night together if you both agree to it.

6. You will be together for counseling and other events, but you will also have the benefit (and protection) of processing time.

7. It will provide an environment where sincerity, desire, and humility can be tested. Your mutual willingness to talk, listen, read several books, and digest lots of insight together will measure your commitment to the reconciliation process.

Controlled separations encourage couples to work on the necessary disciplines of patience, self-control, faith, trust, and honest communication, all of which you and Stacy could use right now.

Do you remember agreeing to follow directions? It might as well start right here. With Gerry and Sue's help, you and Stacy should settle on a defined period of time for your controlled separation, and you'll also want to discuss matters such as weekly dates and family times with the children. Let me know how it's going.

I can almost guarantee that if you will commit the next two months to learning about being a good husband and becoming the man God (yes, I've mentioned Him again) wants you to be, your marriage will be greatly improved. Stacy will certainly be happier than ever before—you can bet on that.

Finally, I have one other thing to strongly recommend. You'd better brace yourself for this one. Is it true that you love Stacy? Is it true that you want her to trust you as her husband? Is it true that you will do anything to make your marriage healthy again? Is it true that you love your little children? Is it true that you can't wait to have them all back together again? Well, then it's time for you to move out of the house and have Stacy and the children move back in. You should want to protect your wife and children from going out on their own. You can't hold Stacy hostage with the house. Mitch, talk of love is pretty cheap. Love needs to be expressed through action. The Bible tells us to love not in word only but in deed and in truth. With you in the house and Stacy and the children out on the street, you're providing a perfect illustration of why you have marital problems in the first place. You have never really set yourself aside and given your wife a special position in your family. Stacy and the children have always been secondary to your work and other activities. But that's history at this point. You will no longer be able to control Stacy with the house or with money. Her anger and bitterness run too deep. She didn't marry you for your house or money in the first place, so why would she come home for them? You need to call Stacy and tell her you'll find an apartment or a motel and that she and the children should return home. Tell her you're willing to go through a controlled separation and that you will join with her in working through your marital problems.

It's time to make sure you're not putting your need to control the situation above Stacy's need for security for her and the children. I have seen many gals head south with only lunch money in their pockets just to get away from their controlling husbands. By demonstrating sacrificial love for your wife (and children!), you'll be giving her a reason to believe in you. Always remember this: your love is what will win her back. Nothing else.

While you're deciding whether to take this advice, try to remember how much you have hurt Stacy over the years. When you can see how you've damaged your relationship, the way to correct it will become clear. When you understand why Stacy left you in the first place, you'll be in a position to understand what it's going to take to win her back. Have you confessed to Stacy how you've hurt her? Have you asked for her forgiveness? Have you repented of your actions against her? This is a good place to start.

With love and affection,
The Rev

FROM: Stacy

TO: Carter

SUBJECT: Learning to "share the air"

Dear Carter,

Gerry has been forwarding all your correspondence with Mitch my way, and when I read your suggestion that he let the kids and me move back into the house it made me cry. I'm sure Mitch will never follow through with your suggestion—he's such a self-centered pig—but it means so much to me that you're looking out for us.

Reading that suggestion to Mitch touched off such a wave of emotion I couldn't sleep all night. It brought to the surface exactly what I've been feeling these past several years. Let me try to explain.

When I was in college, a friend and I decided to take scuba lessons. In addition to learning about fins, wet suits, goggles, and oxygen tanks, we learned what a hoot it is to live underwater for a while. However, we also learned that bad things can happen in a big hurry when you're down there, and when they do, they can be life threatening. That's why divers are taught never to scuba dive alone.

My marriage actually turned into a scuba dive gone bad. Mitch and I started out together with two tanks, but mine gradually ran out of air. Since he always kept his filled to the brim, it became necessary for me to "share his air." That's where both people draw from one tank using the same hose, one person at a time. Each person can get enough air this way, provided no one hogs the hose.

Initially our "share the air" system worked fairly well, but over time Mitch became less concerned about me having any air and more accustomed to keeping the hose to himself. He would swim away and be gone for the longest time without stopping to think about my need to breathe. Holding my breath, I would anxiously await his return. Carter, can you imagine what this was like? How would you like it if you were under thirty feet of water waiting for Minnie to share her air, but she didn't come and didn't come? Sometimes, Mitch would totally forget that the children and I needed any air at all! Did you get that? He would *forget*! How can a man forget about his family?

Over the years, I tried conserving air and even learned how to hold my breath for longer periods of time. I also helped the children learn to get along with less air from Mitch. Together we trained our lungs to breathe in deeply when the opportunity to "share the air" happened. However, the problems got worse and worse. I felt myself fading away many times and began wondering when I would actually drown. I did not know what to do! The water was pressing against me, my lungs were ready to burst, and life became desperate. Being isolated thirty feet below the surface in a marriage with a man who was either unable or unwilling to share his air was literally suffocating me. Finally, I just couldn't take it anymore. The day came when I was completely out of air—and Mitch went right to bed and fell asleep without even caring!

That's when I decided to take my chances. I loaded up the children and started swimming to the surface. It was when I slammed the door of my house, got into my car, and started the engine that I burst onto the surface and took my first breath of fresh air in a very long time. Carter, can you imagine what that first breath of air felt like? I felt waves of relief as I sucked it in. I was so thankful not to still be Mitch's prisoner of the deep that I didn't care what his reaction would be. Still don't. Let him rage all he wants to. At least we can breathe.

Whatever else it does for us, this controlled separation should give me time to breathe and deal with my anxiety. Furthermore, it will allow time for Mitch and me to determine what changes will be necessary for us to return to the "deep sea" of marriage together. I'll tell you one thing. I'm not going back down there until I'm convinced he has learned to share the air. I can promise you that!

Thank you so much for your support!
Stacy

TO: Carter

SUBJECT: Just what I need . . .

You won't believe what happened to Sparky, our "dearly beloved" family pet. Why I ever agreed to allow a dog in our home is beyond me. Stacy and the kids begged me for months, and I suppose their whining and nagging wore me down because I finally gave in. After all, I thought a Lab or Golden Retriever could end up being kind of nice for me on hunting trips. One of my buddies has a female Golden, and she will do anything for him.

Wrong. Within six hours of my giving permission, Stacy and the kids show up all hyper and gushing about "the newest member of our family." Tucked under Stacy's arm—almost too small to see—is a weenie Dachshund. The stupid thing is the size of a whipped-cream can and dumber than a rock. She snaps at me every time I kick her off my recliner, and she growls at me when I feed her. I can't tell you how many times I've almost broken my neck trying to walk through my own house with that mutt nipping at my heels. I hate it.

So I told Stacy, as far as I'm concerned, this is not my dog and I'm not lifting a finger to take care of it. If she wants to keep it around, that's her business, but she and the kids have to take full responsibility for it. I'm not touching the thing. (Actually, I can't touch it without getting a handful of teeth. This thing belongs in a cage, not in a house with children.)

Well, guess who has to take care of Sparky now? Another one of Stacy's "brilliant" ideas—she packs off to a Dog-Free Zone (Sue is allergic to dogs—lucky Gerry). So I'm stuck feeding and walking this wretched thing. I was going to get rid of her when Stacy first moved out, but the kids put up such a fuss begging me to feed her, walk her,

pet her, and buy her treats every week. What can I do? I figure Stacy
has made their lives hard enough as it is. I'd better not make things
worse by getting rid of their dog.

Anyway, this morning I had time to kill, so I grabbed my new
Sports Illustrated, wrestled Sparky into her leash (it's BRIGHT
PINK—you can see it from the space station), and dragged her nipping and yapping down to Hurricane Park. Carter, you've never been
to a park until you've been to Hurricane Park. Most cities name their
parks Washington Park, Centennial Park, Overland Park, Sun Dial
Park, or City Park, right? Well, the city fathers of this town apparently
thought naming the place Hurricane Park would boost the city's image
by advertising our famous Wyoming wind. There isn't any equipment for kids to play on, just snow fences, walls, and small buildings
to provide shelter from blowing trash sacks, tumbleweeds, tin cans,
and airborne small children.

Now, it's tough to manage a crazy dog, a lawn chair, a coffee mug,
and a rolled-up magazine under your arm, so the first thing I did when
I got there was let the beast loose while I set myself up behind a series
of snow fences. (You should see what it's like trying to read a magazine in this wind.) I figured she'd explore a little bit, then settle within
biting distance of my ankles. So I'm sitting there, peacefully reading,
when all of a sudden I hear this huge commotion somewhere off to
my left—people shouting, dogs barking, and this awful shrieking
and yelping. That's when I remembered Sparky. She must have wandered off (or been blown away) while I was reading, and apparently
got "discovered" by the meanest looking pair of Rottweilers I've ever
seen. Carter, it was awful. Those Rotts were going for the kill when I
arrived. Their owner was waving her arms and screaming hysterically,
and some jogger was trying to break things up, but it wasn't a pretty
sight. By the time I was able to get them apart, Sparky was just lying
there, all covered with blood. For the first time in that dog's life, she
didn't even have the energy to snap at me when I picked her up. She
was limp as a dishrag, and I figured her for dead.

My initial instinct, after telling off the stupid woman who let her
dogs get out of control, was to put Sparky in a trash bag and drop her

in one of the litter barrels. I figured I could tell the kids she ran away while I had her at the park. Unfortunately, she wasn't dead, so I had to bring her to the Vet Hospital. I can't even imagine what this is going to cost.

Can you believe this happened to me on top of everything else going on? I can already hear everybody blaming me for it as if I had it all planned this way. I suppose it's better she didn't die—the kids would be heartbroken, and Stacy would be madder than ever. Probably will be madder than ever anyhow, as if I could have done anything about it. I mean, what was I supposed to do? One minute I'm minding my own business, and the next minute Sparky is off getting into trouble. Oh well, what's any different today than yesterday? It's the story of my life lately.

On another note, I had an idea I want to run by you. I'm thinking about buying a really nice diamond necklace for Stacy. You know what they say, "Diamonds are a girl's best friend," right? She's always wanted me to do romantic things for her like fancy dinners, special flowers, or evenings away from the kids. I think diamonds would really impress her. What do ya say, cowboy? She thinks I'm such a tightwad, maybe this will convince her otherwise, huh? Here's my plan. I want to start the evening off with a nice romantic dinner at Elmer's Steak and Ale. Then head to the drive-in in the ragtop. Whoa! After the first feature, it's out with the jewelry. She'll be so surprised when she realizes how much I spent on her. I'm planning this for next Sunday night right after racquetball. What woman could resist such treatment? Let me know what you think, Carter. Who knows, maybe you should do likewise for Minnie. No charge for the idea, friend.

Well, it's off to reality again. Stacy's clunker died, so I've got to make an appointment to have the blasted thing fixed again. It frustrates me that Stacy and I aren't living together. It would sure be a lot more convenient.

Oh, I almost forgot. This might be a good time for you to call Stacy and the kids. They'll certainly need some sympathy when I tell them about Sparky. I doubt they'll want to talk to me about it—they'll probably think I did it on purpose because of how much I despise the thing. What do you think—does God answer prayers about dogs? Does He answer prayers from dog killers?

Your buddy,
Mitch

P.S. Speaking of buying gifts for our gals, have you seen this cartoon? Pretty good idea, if you ask me. Later.

FROM: Carter

TO: Mitch

SUBJECT: Diamonds are NOT a girl's best friend

I only have three responses to your email:

1. Do not—and again I say—DO NOT buy Stacy any diamonds! Trust me on this one. She doesn't give a rip about diamonds, dinners, or drive-in movies. She needs room to breath!
2. Do not underestimate your responsibility for the dog. You should have cared more about Sparky simply because your children and Stacy love her.
3. Your incident in Hurricane Park made me think of a great illustration about why your marriage is failing. However, I don't have time right now to include it in this email. I'll send it tomorrow. In the meantime, I want you to be patient and read the first two chapters of Genesis in your Bible. Is it a deal?

I'll check back tomorrow.

The Rev

P.S. Now that you mention it, I think BRIGHT PINK is definitely your color. Later, you sissy!

FROM: Carter

TO: Mitch

SUBJECT: Hurricane Park vs. Eden Park

Mitch,

I was on my way out the door when your message popped up on my screen yesterday and I couldn't resist reading it. But I couldn't respond without missing my appointment.

Sorry about Sparky. Just this morning I visited with Stacy and understand that, thanks to the dog docs at your local veterinary hospital, she's going to recover despite the beating she took. But what a price tag! I suppose you'll get to use the money you were going to buy diamonds with after all—on Sparky's hospital bill. How does that feel?

I told you in my last email that the events at Hurricane Park made me think of an illustration that explains why your marriage is in trouble. Let me start by describing the events at Hurricane Park as seen through Stacy's eyes. First of all, it was clear from your email that you never took any responsibility for the dog. (Stacy confirmed this on the phone in no uncertain terms.) You removed yourself and refused any role in the dog's life. You never fed her, never pet her, never paid one ounce of attention to her except to mistreat her and "kick her off your recliner." When the day finally came for you to take responsibility for her, disaster was written all over it. What happened at the park was a no-brainer. You didn't care one bit for the dog, only for reading your magazine. The fact that your wife and children adore Sparky makes no difference to you. What matters to you is what matters to you, not what matters to them.

To understand what went wrong in Hurricane Park, I'd like us to look at what went right in "Eden Park." (Did you read the first two chapters of Genesis like I asked you to?) Genesis opens with a description of how everything got started, then lands us in a beautiful place called the Garden of Eden. God really used His imagination decorating and populating the place with animals (elk and deer), fish (rainbow trout) and birds (pheasants and quail). But the crowning glory of His creative blitz was man. (Have you found Genesis yet, young man? If so, look at the first chapter, verse 26, where God says, "Let Us make man in Our image.")

Whoa! What a deal. For a closer look at this, go to the second chapter, verse seven. God formed this guy, Adam, out of dust from the ground and dropped him in the middle of this beautiful garden. But you know something? There was a problem. The garden wasn't enough for Adam. Perfect as it was, something was missing. Notice verse 18. God's perfect man wasn't happy because he was alone.

Can you relate, Mitch? You've been alone for just a couple of weeks now, and you're complaining pretty much nonstop. Thankfully, God was very concerned about Adam's loneliness. He wanted his new man to experience love and companionship, so He went to work.

The rest of the second chapter is about God's solution. First He put Adam to sleep (which explains why men often go to sleep while talking with their wives), did a ribectomy on him, and used invisible stitches to close him up again. Then He used Adam's rib to fashion an absolutely perfect woman and brought her to Adam. How long do you think it took him to remember to breathe when he first laid eyes on her? One can only imagine what their love story looked like during those first few days (weeks, months, years). Two perfect people in a perfect place, naked and unashamed (yup—see verse 25). No marital problems there! Life was good! Just relax and enjoy the scenery!

Naked and not ashamed. How can we even relate to that? As far as "naked" goes, my wife sleeps in a nightgown that has feet in it like my little babies used to wear. And as for "ashamed," my white legs literally glow in the dark. I'm so ashamed of them I'm tempted to wear boots to bed. Bony, ugly, and hairless, they're like two baseball bats attached to a sorry-looking trunk adorned with a head shaped like a muskmelon. But Adam and his new wife were perfect. Wow.

So what we have here is God creating the perfect marital relationship for Adam and Eve to enjoy. And since they were sinless (unlike Carter, Minnie, Mitch, and Stacy), one can assume we might be able to learn something from their relationship. I'll pick up on that thought in my next email. Right now I get to meet Minnie for lunch.

In the meantime, let me encourage you to think about what kind of husband Adam would have been given the fact that God created him perfect. Meditate on it for a while, Slick!

Later,
The Rev

P.S. Is it easier for you to believe that God designed marriage, or that marriage is a purely human invention and has no basis other than human tradition? If you believe humans set up the whole thing, then Stacy has license to go packing whenever she wants to without the slightest ounce of guilt. She has no responsibility to your marriage whatsoever because it's her interests vs. yours. On the other hand, if God set up marriage, He also established its boundaries. If that's the case, you and Stacy need to submit to them for the sake of your happiness. If Stacy violates God's guidelines for marriage, she will need to answer to God, not to you. What do you think about that?

P.P.S. In Genesis we're told that God caused a deep sleep to fall upon Adam, took one of his ribs, fashioned a woman out of the rib, and introduced her to Adam when he awoke. Well, another version of this story came to me over the Internet recently. It goes something like this: Adam is lonely, so he asks God what a good woman would cost. He wants a woman who will do all the laundry and dishes, raise the kids, keep the house clean, and fix three great meals a day. God tells him it will cost "an arm and a leg" for such a woman. Adam thinks about it for a minute, then asks what he can get for just a rib? The rest is history.

FROM: Mitch

TO: Carter

SUBJECT: Too much is too much!

Carter,

I didn't get to your email about controlled separations and handing my house over to Stacy until this morning. When I read it, I just about went out of my mind with anger. I can't believe you would even suggest such things. I even asked my friends at work today what they thought, and they couldn't stop laughing. I was actually embarrassed that my counselor "friend" would propose such a one-sided solution. The whole thing is outrageous. Why shouldn't Stacy simply return home where she belongs? Why should I have to agree to anything? She's the one who moved out. Why should I put myself out to accommodate her temper tantrum? I have bills to pay just to keep the air conditioning working so I can be comfortable in this blasted Wyoming heat. If our marriage is going to make it, she needs to get her rear back home where it belongs, NOT MAKE ME MOVE OUT OF MY OWN HOUSE! As I mentioned before, if it's a divorce she wants, she's well on her way to getting one because I'm not going to put up with this much longer.

I'll be more interested in making the changes she wants when she demonstrates that she still wants to be married to me. Coming home is where that begins. My friend Stu at work says that he dug in his heels and it wasn't very long before his wife ran out of money and came home with her tail between her legs. Stacy is in the same mess. She has no job, no place to live (other than with Gerry and Sue), and no money to work with. Look at what she's doing to the kids. They want to come home—they tell me so every time we talk! At least *they're* not too proud to admit they miss me. Maybe after a couple of weeks of freeloading, she'll see the light, too.

Nobody I've talked to even knows what a controlled separation is. Where did Gerry get that idea? I suppose that's another one of your brainy solutions. Well, the only control I want to talk about is getting Stacy home. Gerry said I sounded like a control freak the other day. Well, if getting my wife to come home is being a control freak, I guess I am one. What kind of a husband wouldn't be? A wuss, that's what.

I talked with Stacy last night, and she was pretty open about her feelings. I told her I wanted her to bring the kids and come home, but she isn't "ready." I don't know what that means. Maybe she's not out of money yet. She wants to work on the marriage, but apparently for spiritual reasons, not because she's in love with me. I'm a bit confused. Why would she come home to someone she doesn't love? For that matter, why would I want to live with a woman who doesn't love me? Maybe coming home isn't the answer after all. I'm getting dizzy thinking about it, so I'm off to the club.

Before I go, I want you to know I read your email about that guy, Adam. It may sound funny, but the thought of what a perfect husband would be like never even occurred to me. It also never occurred to me that God would give my marriage the slightest thought. After considering your question about who designed marriages, I guess I want to believe God did, but my friends think that's the stupidest thing they've ever heard. On the other hand, I have to admit most of them are divorced, so I probably should take their opinions with a grain of salt. Still, this God stuff seems pretty lame when Stacy is off spreading rumors about me all over town.

As mad as I am about your counsel to Stacy and me, we're still friends and I will still read your emails. I do want my marriage back, so any ideas are better than no ideas. But knock off your preaching about this controlled separation stuff and about me moving out of my own house. Agreed? It gives me a headache.

Sorry to be so short with you, but that's the way it is.

Mitch

FROM: Carter

TO: Mitch

SUBJECT: Hurricane Park vs. Eden Park — Part Two

Well, you old hothead, how the heck are you? Can I say that your last email was right to the point? It was nice to see a little heat in the boiler. At least I know exactly where you stand on the subject of a controlled separation. You also made it quite clear how you feel about moving out and letting "the wife you love and the children you would do anything for" move into the safety of their own home. Sounds like your divorced friends have given you pretty good advice about how to avoid a divorce. Just dig in your heels and demand your own way. When you think about it, why would anybody do such an unthinkable thing for someone they loved? Anyway, time is on your side when it comes to staying put in your house because Stacy is drifting further and further away. She has been looking seriously at a condominium on the north side of Cheyenne about twenty minutes away. Your friends are right. Why would you want her living in her own home where she and the kids would be safe and secure? Be the boss and win those battles! Sounds like good advice to me.

Before I continue I'd like to share something personal. Minnie and I had a spat a few nights ago, and I was still feeling depressed about it yesterday morning. I can't believe that after almost forty years of marriage we're still not past this nonsense. What's the matter with us? Mitch, I counsel with couples almost every day, and yet we're not exempt from having marital difficulties just like everyone else. I often find it difficult to express my feelings for fear of her response, yet she has no trouble expressing hers!

Anyway, even after a few days, Minnie and I were just barely managing to live together. Oh, we weren't yelling at each other because we stopped doing that thirty years ago. (I'm not kidding! Yelling seemed so unproductive and hurtful that we couldn't bear it any longer. It was destructive and caused our disagreements to escalate beyond belief. So we agreed not to raise our voices at each other, and we've done pretty well throughout the years. I personally recommend this to every family I counsel with. Not raising your voice helps keep disagreements in check. It also keeps them from escalating into full-scale verbal warfare.) So, like I said, we were having such a tough time getting past this one we decided to work things out over lunch. (Marriage tip: Taking your wife to her favorite restaurant is not a bad idea when you need to eat humble pie together—it helps everything go down more smoothly. Something to think about, young man.) So that's where I was headed yesterday when I so rudely interrupted my email to you.

Now, where were we? Oh yes. Another thing that was clear from your email is that you really don't like the Bible much. You prefer the counsel of your friends. You know something? Lots of people would agree with you. Funny thing is, for all the arguments I've heard against the Bible over the years, nobody has produced a better alternative. Do you think we should follow the advice of a holy book from one of the cults? How about one of the many theories from today's leading therapists and psychologists? Or, maybe we should stake your marriage on the wisdom of your friends. Whose advice are you ready to trust? The choice is yours. If you don't want to hear truth from the Bible, I won't share it. But until you say so, I plan to stick with the Bible.

Now, getting back to the perfect husband (Adam, not me), I think the thing that characterized him was *leadership*. He was commissioned to "rule" over every living thing in Eden Park and told to cultivate it, keep it, and take dominion over it. I've told Minnie many times that fishing and hunting are simply "taking dominion" and that God will be unhappy if I don't obey Him. Following this comment, she usually gags, mutters unintelligibly, and looks for something to throw. Where is her spiritual insight? Do you have these problems with Stacy? If only our women would read their Bibles more.

Mitch, I'm assuming you've read the first two chapters of Genesis by now so you're able to follow my thinking on this. With a God-given mandate to take responsibility for all created things (the idea here is wise and capable husbandry, not self-serving tyranny), it follows that Adam would have taken the lead in his marriage as well. God gave him the responsibility, and He probably also provided lots of valuable counsel during those garden walks. Adam appears to have run with his new mandate. After all, he organized the entire animal kingdom and immediately defined and protected his relationship with Eve as soon as she showed up.

By the way, it's important to point out something. I'm not saying that women can't lead—I know many women who do a superb job of leading. Rather, it's that women wouldn't have to lead in the home if men would do what God intended them to do in the first place.

Can I slip a quick illustration in here? Yesterday I was counseling with a lady who said her lazy husband spends every evening on his computer playing games until the wee hours of the morning. She has to do everything around the house, including caring for the children. In short, she has become the leader of the family and is frustrated about it. She wants her husband to care enough to lead as God intended instead of being the lazy bum he's turning into. What do you think, Mitch? Do you agree with her? What should I tell her husband?

Practically speaking, Adam's leadership must have taken many, many forms. As I said, he named and categorized the animals, managed the garden, modeled a relationship with God, taught Eve everything he knew, and set the course for exploring and developing their brand-new relationship. I'm sure Adam was very busy. I'm also sure he didn't spend his evenings shouting at Eve or neglecting her needs just because he was busy on the coconut phone trying to close a deal on bananas. Rather, I see him as a loving, compassionate, reasonable, understanding, and involved leader who nurtured his new wife, not demanding that she meet all his needs. He might even have been willing to lead Eve through a controlled separation, don't you think?

Check your cinch,
The Rev

FROM: Mitch

TO: Carter

SUBJECT: What's up with all this homework?

I couldn't believe all the books you sent. Do you expect me to read them all? Stacy enjoys reading and somehow finds time to do it, but I'm so busy I can't even tell if I'm coming or going. If it isn't extra hours at the office, time at the club, or trying to figure out this whole mess with my friends, I'm busy doing Stacy's work around the house (not that she seems to appreciate it any). I just don't see how I'm supposed to read all these books. How about I call you and you can summarize them for me over the phone?

I did manage to get through the "personality" test you sent Stacy and me. Do you know it took almost an hour to plow through? Fortunately, I was able to get it done between matches at the volleyball courts. (Did I tell you about that? I joined a coed volleyball league to get me through my lonely evenings. It sure has been hard not having Stacy around.)

Actually, I apologize for not getting to the reading assignment you sent a couple of weeks ago. I find it difficult to concentrate when I'm alone. It seems like I can't read more than two sentences before my mind wanders to this problem with Stacy, and then I'm off in la-la land until the phone or doorbell rings. To be honest, it gives me a headache. Everything reminds me of our problems, and I get depressed. Stacy is making my life miserable enough without you adding all this reading, studying, and meditation on top of it. I know you must be trying to keep me busy so I won't feel sad, but frankly I'm staying pretty busy without your help. You may not understand this, but I'm working as hard as I can to just keep from blowing my stack and leaving town on a vacation. I don't handle this kind of nonsense very well.

Besides, I hate to read. Even when I was in school, reading wasn't one of my strong suits. I could go through an entire chapter of a book and not remember a thing I'd read. I must have some sort of disability. The newspaper is OK because I just skim the scores and market news, but books are another story. Maybe if Stacy would come home where she belongs, she could read them to me. Now there's an idea! Every evening at bedtime, she could read this stuff to me and then we could talk about it.

Carter, would you mind talking to Stacy about that? I'll bet that would help us a lot. By the way, would you do something else for me? Please ask Stacy to contact the lawn maintenance people about winterizing our yard. She has already been in touch with them, and I don't know whom she spoke with. Since she's not taking my calls these days, maybe you could pass along this message. Thanks.

I wish I had more time to write, but I've gotta run. By the way, have you been in touch with Gerry or Sue these past couple of days? The kids seem to be having some trouble adjusting to all this, and I think it would be helpful for someone to talk to them besides Stacy. Maybe Gerry would spend time talking with them if you asked him to. Would you mind following through on that?

There's one other thing. Would you mind encouraging Stacy to read the chapter on separation and divorce in that little book you sent me? I think it would provide a good reality check during this weird limbo thing she's putting us through. Made sense to me, at any rate.

Later,
Mitch

P.S. Have you been fishing lately? I went this past weekend to a secluded little spot on the Platte River and caught some real nice trout. I read something last summer in a book on nymph fishing about how to keep the nymph down deeper in the drift of the river. It really worked! Maybe I should send it to you. It might improve your fishing!

FROM: Carter

TO: Mitch

SUBJECT: Understanding counseling

Mitch, I think we'd better get a couple of things straight before going any further. I'm wondering just what you think counseling is, anyway? Are you under the impression that Gerry, Sue, and I are responsible for making your marriage work? If you are, we've taken a wrong turn somewhere. You're the one who should be working on your marriage instead of playing coed volleyball. If you have a problem reading, I suggest you "fix" it quickly and get busy catching up on your assignments. Incidentally, it's strange that you can learn to catch more fish from reading a fishing book but can't learn to save your marriage from reading a marriage book. If it were me, I'd sure be more interested in rebuilding my family than in filling my freezer with dead fish.

Here's the thing, Mitch. When I do counseling, I see myself as a "coach" or "facilitator" to help you be successful in your marriage. When you place your marriage above everything else, including fishing, volleyball, and whatever else you've joined lately, I'll be available to "help" you with your marriage. If you're too busy to do what the "coach" thinks you should be doing, I guess you'll be sitting the bench while I devote my "coaching" to other people who are willing to give their marriage a 100 percent effort. I refuse to waste my time "coaching" someone who has more important things to do—like playing volleyball or sitting at the local "pub" with his buddies. The reason you have problems is because "other things" have continually cut into your marriage commitment. You have failed to make your marriage a priority and it's dying from neglect. As your friend and counselor, I won't work under these conditions. Until you personally get behind the counseling process, I regret to say you're on your own.

To make sure this is clear, let me illustrate the relationship between counselor and counselee. My children were always in the 4H group that met in our valley. They liked to raise cattle to show in the county fair. One rule of 4H is that the parents are not to do the work. Simply put, the parent's job is merely to "coach" while the child puts in the sweat equity. Let me tell you something. It's plenty tough for a ten-year-old "squirt" to manage a 350-pound steer or heifer. After our kids picked the steers or heifers they wanted to show in the fair (ten months later), the work had just begun. The calf would need to be broke to lead, and would need to learn how to stand properly, be brushed, bathed, and tickled without kicking anybody or running into the next county. The calves needed hay and grain twice a day, plenty of water, and exercise for muscle development.

Our kids worked hard to produce show cattle for the fair. Finished cattle often weighed as much as 1,200 pounds, yet in all the years we were in 4H I never did a lick of the necessary work to get them ready. I "coached" the kids how to do it and encouraged them to do it, but I didn't do it for them because it was theirs to do. There were two sides to this process—coaching and doing. Make sense?

In counseling, my job is "coaching," and your job is "doing." You need to be reading, learning, and doing the things necessary to produce a "blue ribbon" marriage. Right now, all I see you doing is wishing and complaining, and neither one is going to get you an inch closer to Stacy. It's time to get to work.

For your information, the books I sent you were for you to read, not for you to give to Stacy to read. Let me give you a few hints about reading. I find it's easier for guys to read a little at a time. Set small goals and read several times every day. Train yourself to be a learner. Keep a book handy at all times. When you're waiting for an appointment, pull out your book and read. While you're waiting for the waitress to bring your food, pull out your book and read. See your marriage recovery as catching the world's largest trout—the one that got away. Trust me. If you work at this, something great will happen.

Mitch, I want you to give me a phone call so we can discuss this and finally decide whether we're on or off. There have been far, far too many mixed signals up to this point. It's time to decide once and for all. I'll wait to hear from you.

Later pardner,
The Rev

FROM: Carter

TO: Mitch

SUBJECT: Hurricane Park vs. Eden Park—Part Three

Well, Mitch, I'm glad you finally called. After the first several days passed, I figured you'd decided to hang up the gloves and join the ever-growing ranks of the "unnecessarily divorced." Since you finally seem ready to take this process seriously, I'm going to pick up where we left off looking at Adam. But first, I want to tell you about a counseling appointment I just finished.

The guy actually seemed pretty nice. He has been married for three years and has a couple of what he calls "rug rats" (children). However, he is successfully working himself straight into a hole— financially, maritally, and emotionally. More hours in the day would only give this guy more time to screw up. His wife constantly harps at him to become "Mr. Responsible" at home, but to no avail. Does that sound familiar? They're about two inches from a major collapse in their marriage, and he is totally oblivious. Nonetheless, we had a bottle of water together and went to work. You know something? I really like this guy. He's a great businessman, a good communicator, and very self-motivated. Just not at home. Now that's the problem! He's no different from you and me and a thousand other guys like us who struggle with this matter of leadership in our marriages and families. I just hope we can sort it all out. The truth of the matter is, all our marriages need someone to step up to the plate of leadership— and it isn't supposed to be our wives. If you could have been present in the counseling session, we would have sounded like a chorus of three blind mice singing the blues.

I appreciate your honesty about my using the Bible as our frame of reference. Even though you're not a "Bible thumper" as you have referred to me, I maintain it will still provide direction and helpful counsel to your war-torn marriage. The Bible is like a lion. If you turn it loose it will defend itself. During the next couple of weeks, you'll have adequate opportunity to make a personal decision about the Bible. Agreed? OK then. Let's get going.

I need to be brief today because I am going to "take dominion" over the fish in the river as the Bible commands us to do. Minnie and I are headed to the mountains in the RV (we call it the Motel 6) for a week. However, before I leave I want to share with you four basic areas of leadership that are essential for a healthy marriage. In fact, these four areas of leadership will change not only your marriage but also your parenting. So, it's time to wake up and pay attention!

Here's my point—men need to lead their wives in four ways: **spiritually**, **relationally**, **physically**, and **mentally**. I think it would be good for you to take a few minutes to think about this and see if you agree. Should men lead in these four areas? Why or why not? Take your time, but answer the question for yourself. Also, if you were to improve your leadership in these four areas, how would it change your marriage? It seems from Stacy's perspective that she does most of the "leading" in your family. She is all alone in taking care of the house and the kids. She is the one addressing their spiritual needs, taking care of their physical needs, seeing to their mental needs, and arranging opportunities for their relational needs to be met. Yes, you provide money for food and shelter, but in what other ways are you leading your family? Stacy couldn't think of any. (That's not exactly true, right? I'll bet you still run the remote control and the recliner lever.)

Basically, I think it would be helpful for both of us if I did a little overview of these four types of leadership. As usual, I'll be using the Bible. Before I get rolling, however, I need a snack and a cold drink. What do you say?

Back again so here we go! The first type of leadership I'd like you to think about is spiritual leadership. That means taking responsibility for your wife's (and children's) relationship with God. The way God set things up in Eden, Adam's whole life revolved around God. Adam assumed responsibility for the world God created, and every day

Adam enjoyed time together with God, discussing his work and who knows what all. God created Adam for relationship. Adam was created to be a friend. When Eve came on the scene, don't you suppose Adam taught her everything he knew about God? I'll bet it was the first thing he told her about after his ribectomy. Since Adam knew God was the source of life and joy, he would naturally want Eve to know everything he knew so she could enjoy God's company as well. After all, what would happen if she didn't know about Him? What if she had no interest in God—the center of Adam's life? What would happen then? Spiritual leadership was important to both of these garden dwellers.

The second type of leadership is relational leadership. Adam and Eve had a whole lot of relationship building to do. After all, they had a very brief courtship, during most of which Adam was asleep. Come to think of it, most men make a habit of sleeping through their courtship. Why else would I have such an ongoing parade of wives visiting my counseling office wondering who they married? Anyway, relational leadership is very important to a marriage. As husbands, we must continually strengthen our relationships. Don't you suppose Adam would have had to learn how to relate to Eve? To discover what made her tick? He would have been fascinated to discover how they were similar, different, and complementary. He would have experimented with different ways of communicating and found meaningful avenues of encouragement for building her up. Even in a perfect garden, I'll bet it wasn't automatic. Part of God's creative genius is that He allows people to grow, mature, discover, and explore. Those elements were present in Adam's perfect garden. Adam's job was to get to know Eve, mature their relationship, and expand their understanding of each other. As you know, that must have been a huge assignment. Right?

Now, I know you've been waiting for this one. The third type of leadership Adam had to take responsibility for was physical. Of course, this wasn't limited to developing his wife sexually. Sorry! Although that was an important aspect of Adam's leadership, there's a whole lot more to physical leadership than sex. (For example, providing food, safety, shelter, rest, and overall well-being.) But let's go back to the sex thing for a minute. Do you think they both desired the same level of intimacy in their perfect environment? Did they start out knowing everything there was to know about heating up the other's radiator? Was their understanding of stimulation and arousal comprehensive at the outset? I doubt it! As the leader, it was Adam's job to understand Eve's very different sexual appetite, and to help her understand his. He needed to learn how to honor her romantic side, not just focus on his physical interests. The sexual side of marriage needs leadership, and Adam needed to lovingly take responsibility for it, along with the many other aspects of physical leadership. He called his wife "bone of my bones and flesh of my flesh." Eve was "bone of his bone and flesh of his flesh." Meeting her needs was the same thing as meeting his own needs! And the same thing is true for you and Stacy (see Genesis 2:23-24).

Finally, the fourth type of leadership addresses the area of the mind. Husbands are notorious for spending their days learning new things and experiencing new things—and never sharing a shred of it with their wives. I am convinced it wasn't that way between Adam and Eve. She came on the scene a totally clean slate, and I'm sure he considered it his privilege to teach her everything he'd learned about their perfect world. No doubt he wanted Eve to grow strong intellectually, not only for her own sake but so she could be a worthy partner and companion for him. Imagine the conversations they enjoyed. I believe Adam was the smartest man who ever lived outside of Jesus Christ, and I'll bet Eve wasn't far behind him, if at all.

OK, my fellow student of marriage, I have given you four aspects of leadership to meditate on in my absence during the next week: spiritual, relational, physical, and mental. I want you to think about them often. Many of us guys think the most important part of marriage is, "What's for dinner?"! But it's not. It's leadership. Eve didn't want a passive, uninvolved husband any more than Stacy does. She wanted a guy who was a strong and loving leader—a man who would offer protection and safety even when they were separated. What do you think about that? How does a man who is separated from his estranged wife show loving leadership? It's something to think about.

Until I write again, keep your knife sharp, Bwana. Who knows when you might want to carve up an apple or whittle some lovebird initials on a backyard tree. (You do have trees in Wyoming, don't you?)

The Rev

P.S. I'm going to follow the counsel of the great apostle Peter from John 21, where he said, "I go a fishing." Wish me luck!

FROM: Stacy

TO: Carter

SUBJECT: How do I handle Mitch?

Do you know how many times Mitch called me yesterday? I talked to him seven times, but my caller ID indicated that he actually called twenty-three times. I don't want to ignore him, but I really don't have anything to talk about right now. The only thing he wants to discuss is when I am coming home. Carter, it's not that I don't ever want to go home, it's just that I can't face going home right now. I am shot. My nerves are shaky, and my emotions are all over the place. It wouldn't be fair to our reconciliation process. I'm so anxious about what the future holds and very concerned for the children. Sue is adamant that for the time being I should stay right where I am and heal a bit.

Gerry and Sue have been so kind to me, Carter, and I know they're trying to reach out to Mitch, too. I think Gerry is getting together with him on a regular basis so he won't feel cut off from the process or worry that Gerry and Sue have taken my side. To be honest, I've been surprised by their impartiality. Gerry has been very hard on me at times for my negative thinking and unloving comments. I must confess I sometimes talk hatefully and lack the energy to be all lovey-dovey and start working on this marriage again. I probably waited too long to do this because I feel really burned out.

Mitch has been talking a little more openly about our separation. He seems to want you to keep emailing him counseling insights. I know your email about leadership really hit him. Mitch worries only about himself, which means I have to worry about everything else in our lives, including Sparky. (Did you know he has not been to the Vet Hospital even once since dropping her off?) Mitch hasn't the foggiest idea about what goes on while he's away at work or play. I don't think he even cares. Honestly, I just couldn't keep this up any longer. I already feel more like his mother than his wife. All I wanted was for Mitch to become a part of "his" family, but he would just call me a nag and say the worst things about me. I don't know if I can ever forgive him for some of the comments he made. To make matters worse, he just ignored me as if I didn't exist. Made me feel like a "non-person" who wasn't worth even acknowledging—like Sparky. Am I expecting too much? I'm just tired of being the cook, maid, mother of two children and a grown man, prostitute, and brunt of all his crude jokes. Having a nice house isn't worth putting up with all that from a man who doesn't care about me.

The condominium looks like it's going to work, so I'll probably move in a couple of weeks. It sure wasn't easy. Mitch closed all our joint bank accounts. He was probably afraid I would take off with his precious money. That really hurts because I never had any intention of doing anything of the kind. However, I feel he should at least help the children and me with some of our living expenses. I'll need some money to rent the condo and would even like to be helping Gerry and Sue with food right now. It feels so awful to be penniless. Could you ask Mitch about this? If he doesn't want to help, I won't press the issue because my parents have said that they would help. They love Mitch and want to give him room to respond, but they refuse to put me out on the street with two little kids.

I'm in regular touch with my pastor and others at the church. They've helped some with my needs, and they regularly pray for us that our marriage will be saved. When I hear them praying, I feel enormous pressure. Everyone has such great and glorious expectations of me, but I just don't feel able to fulfill them right now. Do you understand? The people who are praying have nice families, but I see no end in sight to my problems unless Mitch begins to understand what has happened between us. I feel frustrated and scared.

I've looked into a few jobs, but as the statistics say, "single parents live below average poverty levels." As I look at what I can make in the job market minus childcare, rent, food, and transportation, I get a knot in my stomach. Hopefully if we get a divorce, some child support will come our way, but even that won't be enough. I know how much Mitch makes and how much the payments are on the house. He'll need to sell the house as well as that fancy "family" car he bought to sport himself around in.

Carter, as I told you before, I am willing to face what I have done to our marriage and work toward getting back together again, but it's going to take time. Do you think Mitch will be patient in the process? I don't think so. If I don't go home like he wants, there'll be a divorce.

I just wish I knew what was around the corner. I guess that's what prayer is all about. We don't know what the future holds, but we know that God holds the future.

I know you're busy and phone calls are expensive, but would you mind giving me a call? I would like to actually talk with you about Mitch. It's been awhile since you've been with us, and he's really different than the person you used to know.

Thanks for your help,
Stacy

P.S. Just one more thing. Do you think you could talk with Gerry about how to set up an orderly visitation schedule? We need some parameters for Mitch's seeing the children. He simply announces his "windows of availability" and shows no consideration for anyone on this end. It's not that I don't want him to be involved with the kids, but he must start considering someone other than himself. He expects me to drop whatever is going on when he decides to see them. It just can't be like that anymore. I have other things to do, and I need to be able to plan ahead without spur-of-the-moment interruptions. Thanks so much, Carter.

FROM: Carter

TO: Stacy

SUBJECT: How you should handle yourself!

Stacy, in your last e-mail you were wondering how you should handle Mitch. Maybe you should be more careful about how you handle yourself. It appears that you want to have your cake and eat it too. In other words, you want a "controlled separation," but you don't want to pay the price for it. Every marital separation has certain consequences. Mitch is anxious, frustrated, and concerned right now. You should expect frequent calls as he attempts to pacify his anxiety. Talking with you will help him transition through the separation. You owe him that consideration. Certainly he doesn't need to call twenty times a day—and I'll speak with him about that—but it could help the situation if you would pick up the phone more often. You might even want to call him from time to time. I know it's tough for you right now because you are hurt, but try to be civil.

Another consequence of separation is tight finances. You'll need to adjust to a much tighter budget—especially if you rent the condo. Part of the financial hardship of any separation is being "penniless," so you'll need to get used to it. Please be patient while we work out the financial details with Mitch. Also, remember that God can use tight finances to draw you closer to Himself. In the meantime, I'm thankful others are willing to pitch in and help. Just make sure you remind yourself that their help is short term. You must learn to live on a lot less income and a whole lot more trust in Jesus Christ. We're all praying for you and Mitch.

Warmly,
Carter

FROM: Carter

TO: Mitch

SUBJECT: Protect your wife at all costs

I can't believe what a great time Minnie and I had camping and fishing together! There's nothing like being out in the fall when the trees are changing, the elk bugling, the fish feeding on dries, and the frost settling on pumpkins. Snuggling with Minnie on those cold nights just can't be beat—unless it's snuggling with her during the day as well. What a party!

I got an email from your lovely wife. In fact, she asked if I would call her on the phone, so I did. We had a great conversation. Mitch, she's a very special lady and seems willing to attempt to salvage your marriage. You and I need to be careful not to hurt those possibilities by pushing her into a corner, or she'll be off like a shooting star. She told me at one point she actually thought you were thinking about what I had written. Congratulations! She was worried about wires being crossed in your attic because of the smoke coming out your ears. (Must have been when you were reading my email about loving her enough to let her and the kids live in the house.)

Actually, she commented on how important your leadership is to her. She really wants to look up to a man who is lovingly leading instead of mooning the recliner all the time. She would be thrilled if your concern for the family would prompt you to take initiative and become involved with your family. Frankly, you have disappointed her by being consumed with your own agenda and ignoring the needs of her and the kids. Your lack of leadership has pushed her to the point of exasperation. Incidentally, that's what causes her to constantly peck, peck, peck at you for everything. Hence we have the definition of a "hen-pecked" husband. If you would offer better leadership by taking initiative around the house, maybe she would stop riding you all the time like a woodpecker on a pine tree.

Mitch, can you see what she is talking about? Do you care that she is frustrated? You spend countless hours thinking about what YOU want but seldom if ever think about leading your family. You know something? Every man should be the leader in his home. That doesn't mean every man should lead in exactly the same way. Just as each man is unique, so each man's leadership will be unique according to his strengths and weaknesses. Some men are "type A" personalities, and some are "type B." Others have virtually no personality at all. Poor guys. No—poor wives who have to live with these boring guys! Some men are task-oriented leaders, and others are relationship-sensitive leaders. In any case, all men are supposed to be leaders. So let's get to work on our leadership skills! Here's a good question for you. How will you lead Stacy back into your marriage? I didn't say "force" or "push" her back—I said *lead* her back. That's an interesting question, isn't it?

Let's take another look at Adam. He's got this new garden to take care of and a new wife to enjoy. Earthly bliss. However, he's also got something to be very concerned about: an enemy. (Don't you think on one of those garden walks, God would have told Adam about Satan?) Now, if you knew there was an enemy "out there," what would you, as the leader in your garden, do for your wife and children?

Protect them! Right?

Leaders always protect those in their charge. The head of any household is also the protector of his household. That's what being a man is all about. There's a catch, however. To protect, one must be involved, not just present. There is a difference between the two. *An uninvolved husband means an unprotected household.*

I don't know what the temptations were in the Garden of Eden, but I do know God warned Adam not to mess with the tree of the knowledge of good and evil. I also know evil was present in the form of a serpent and that it seemed determined to undermine their loving relationship. (See the third chapter of Genesis.) The responsibility to protect everyone against this evil fell on Adam's shoulders. (At least he had shoulders.) The question was, would he protect Eve?

Mitch, let's think for a moment about what this looks like. How would you describe protection? If you were doing your best to protect someone—Stacy, for instance—what would you do? Would any harm come to her? I should hope not!

A few days ago I emailed you about leadership. Do you remember? Good leaders are aware of the spiritual, physical, mental, and relational needs of those they are called to lead. Since good leadership means protecting those being led, wouldn't it make sense that a good leader would be concerned about the spiritual, physical, mental, and relational safety of those under his charge?

Don't you think Adam would want Eve to be in top spiritual condition? Wouldn't her communication with God be one of Adam's top priorities? If so, I suppose he would protect both her time with God and her understanding of God. Surely Adam wouldn't be distracted from his leadership by work or racquetball, would he? Surely he wouldn't leave Eve unprotected, would he? I doubt it! Adam wouldn't want Eve to drift into spiritual laziness or spiritual carelessness (like most of us). Wouldn't it make sense that everything Adam knew about their enemy, Satan, would be passed on to Eve?

It wouldn't stop there, either. Adam would protect Eve physically as well. Diet, exercise, and caution would be everyday conversation between them. I can only imagine what Adam would do if someone tried to hurt Eve. Would he let anyone grab her by the arm and jerk her around, push her down, or shove her out of the way? Certainly he would never do such things to her *himself*. Sexually, he would be gentle and cherishing, allowing nothing to frighten or harm her. Her physical protection would be one of his primary concerns. Agreed?

Protection of the mind is one of my primary concerns in counseling. In our society, we degrade the mind. Our wives and children are constantly exposed to all kinds of corruption. Many wives are forced into things that cause enormous mental and emotional damage, and our children suffer at the hands of a media bent on destroying them rather than protecting their fragile minds. Why is this allowed to happen? Because their leaders and protectors have deserted them. Not Adam! He took his leadership seriously. He delighted in seeing Eve grow in wisdom, knowledge, and understanding. I guarantee that if Adam lived today, he wouldn't leave his family unprotected in the hands of the media or Internet chat rooms. He would help them guard their minds.

By protecting Eve in this way, he was protecting their relationship. Before you read on, think about that statement. By protecting Eve spiritually, physically, and mentally, Adam was guarding and investing in their relationship. She would gladly be his helper and submit to his loving leadership because of the safety she felt (and deserved) under his protection. Since a leader-protector (husband) sees his wife as delicate, beautiful, and deserving of honor and respect, he never uses force or aggression against her. As a result, their relationship can blossom into something beautiful. (Just a footnote here. Husbands who allow their anger and aggression to take the form of abuse aren't men at all. They're cowards. These guys deserve nothing more than a trip behind the woodshed with some real men who hate the abuse of women and children.)

Mitch, I understand Adam and Eve lived in a perfect world without sin, not in Colorado, and certainly not in Wyoming. Reality is much different for our families. However, they serve as an outstanding model of how things were designed to work. You've done some home remodeling, right? Think about a plumb line that tells you what's crooked. In the same way, when you hold your marriage up against the plumb line of Adam and Eve's relationship, what do you learn? You learn that your marriage is crooked. You learn that you've not been a good leader and that you haven't protected your family. What you end up with is a starting point for getting back together with Stacy. You must *lead* her, not force her. You must *protect* her, not ignore her feelings and needs. Believe me, I understand this is not at all easy for husbands to hear, but we must hear it. Trust me, it applies to my marriage, too.

We won't become better husbands by sitting in our recliners stewing about our problems. We have to do something about them. Remember, it takes work to rebuild a marriage. You are committed to working on your marriage, and this is the beginning of that work.

I'm going to leave you with a few (more) questions. Please take some time to answer them carefully.

1. Have you been providing leadership in your family? If not, who has been leading them?
2. Have you been protecting the family God has given you? If not, who has been?
3. How does being your family's leader and protector translate into your present situation? Does being separated give you an excuse to abandon or neglect either role? Why or why not?
4. Take a look at the *Lazy-U* cartoon I've attached to this email. Does this look like leadership? Does it look like anyone you know? I hope not.

Hey, husband of Stacy, I just had lunch with an old friend of yours. Do you keep in touch with Jim? He left me with a parting comment I can't get off my mind. He said, "People don't really want to change; they just want to be comfortable." Do you think we're like that? Is it possible we're floating along the path of life like a stick in the river with no intention of changing directions? Are we just "floaters?" You know something, my friend? If we aren't willing to change direction, we'll end up just like that stick—stuck in the mud in the middle of nowhere. In reality we should be more like fish that are swimming directly upstream, bucking the current with strength and determination. One thing is for sure—change isn't easy, is it?

The Rev

P.S. I just counseled with a woman who complained that her husband always wants her to watch pornographic videos with him. What do you think about that? Good idea or bad? Is he protecting his bride? Is this leadership?

   Here's another thing to think about. Your family needs some of your leadership and protection right now. Your wife and kids are about to rent a condominium. If Stacy decides to make this move, they will need some money. There are a few people out there who have agreed to help her if necessary because they don't want to see your wife and kids out on the street, but they're waiting to see if you'll accept responsibility for them first. As far as Stacy goes, she's reported to me that she's torn between the fear of making this move and her inability to handle the stress of being with you. Nonetheless, she is willing to work on your marriage through counseling. So, Adam-Mitch, what do think ought to be done for Eve-Stacy to demonstrate leadership and to protect her from fear and the attacks of the serpent? Is God speaking to you? You know it wouldn't hurt if you asked Him for some help.

FROM: Carter

TO: Mitch

SUBJECT: Leading from afar

I can't believe it's October already. It seems like we just started a new year, and all of a sudden it's Christmas. I know Christmas doesn't start for another two months for most people, but when you have twelve grandchildren, it starts early. Like April. Problem is, Minnie and I can't agree on what to buy. I think BB guns would be nice. She thinks bed sheets. We're miles apart at this stage, but I can tell where things are headed. They'll get sheets. Poor kids! Think of it, growing up through those difficult first few years without a gun. What can be worse than that? I suppose having cute little animals on your sheets might be worse. After all, you've got to start teaching kids when they're young that you don't sleep with animals, you shoot at them. Don't you agree?

Hey Mitch, I've been thinking about all your phone calls to Stacy. Sounds like there are plenty of them, and they're all about the same thing—her moving back home right now. That dead horse is beginning to stink, don't you think? I have a suggestion.

We've been discussing the role of a leader (husband) in his wife's life. Remember, a good leader takes responsibility for his wife's spiritual, relational, physical, and mental development. Her health and well-being in these areas is his primary concern, and so he makes it a habit to regularly teach his wife. Just as a *leader* (husband) is a *protector*, he is also a *teacher*. You know, Mitch, you could put your phone calls to much better use by teaching Stacy instead of simply replaying that old favorite, "Come Home Right Now or Else." She doesn't need to be "told" what to do. She needs to be "taught" how to live successfully.

When was the last time you explained something to her? I mean something besides "telling" or "commanding" or "demanding" in no uncertain terms that she is to "get herself and those kids back home this instant." Have you ever tried teaching her about what you're learning? You're learning from the books I've sent, aren't you? You are reading them, right? Well then, teach her about what you're learning. Teach her about time management or financial stewardship. Teach her how to fish or throw a Frisbee. Have you ever brought her to "the club" and showed her how to use the equipment? When was the last time you showed an interest in her spiritual experiences or shared your thoughts on God with her? Have you explained to her what you think is going on in the world this week? (I'm assuming you have at least some access to news of the world up there in Wyoming.) Does she understand the financial markets or the economics of oil as well as you do? Can she paint, sing, play an instrument, lead a discussion in her area of expertise, negotiate a better deal on car insurance, grow award-winning roses, or design an award-winning photography exhibit? Are you teaching her how important it is for her to develop a hobby? What about helping her understand the importance of occasional rest apart from the children—like you give yourself regularly? What have you helped her become good at? What do you know how to do that she doesn't? In which areas of life are you thriving where she is starving? Have you picked any wildflowers for her recently or told her all the ways she is beautiful to you?

Mitch, do you teach your wife how to live skillfully, with discernment and understanding, and with a reverence for God? I realize this is a huge responsibility for us feeble guys, but I guarantee it's the truth. Despite our hang-ups, we should always attempt to be better leaders, protectors, and teachers of our wives. Yes, it takes discipline, endurance, patience, and courage, but it also makes for the world's best friendship. What husband wouldn't want that? So how about having something meaningful to discuss with Stacy the next time you call?

The Rev

P.S. Here's another leadership tip: Don't start by "teaching" your wife to clean up after the dog, mow the lawn (do you have lawns in

Wyoming?), or clean the gutters. She already knows how to do those things thanks to your leadership expertise in the areas of recliner operation and remote control pointing. Might be time to balance your leading in these areas with some learning in a few others. For example, get acquainted with the super duper pooper scooper. The future is yours, Slugger.

FROM: Mitch

TO: Carter; Gerry

SUBJECT: Enough is enough!

As I look at my bedside clock, I'm reminded that I haven't slept a wink. My stomach has been churning, I feel tense in my chest, and my nerves are as tight as my belt has been getting. (Yes, thank you all very much for pointing that out, my "friends.")

Since about 1:00 in the morning, I have been reading over all the emails I've received from you people since the beginning of this mess. The more I read, the madder I get. I'm angry with everyone "involved" in my marriage problem except of course my "non-religious" friends who've actually been encouraging me and supporting my position. I'm tired of being a whipping post for "religious" antagonists. None of you have been supportive of my hurts in this marriage. It's like this entire mess is my mess. I thought it took two to tango. Well, does it? How come you constantly ride me and chew at me like a beaver on bark? Do you actually think I'm the only one to blame here?

I get the feeling I won't get my marriage back unless I go through you. Stacy seems to be fixed on a controlled separation because you "counseled" her into it, not because she would necessarily want one. She's determined to listen to no one in the world other than Gerry, Sue, and Carter. Gerry this, Gerry that, Carter this, Carter that. What about Mitch? Oh, he's only the husband—he doesn't matter at all in this situation. As I look back over the emails I've sent, I've tried to be compliant and not run Stacy off. But matters continue to get worse instead of better. I've attempted to be agreeable and to graciously accept all your hammering on me, but nothing I say seems to get us back on track with our reconciliation. So, while you're all resting smugly and peacefully, I'm sitting here bleary-eyed and too tense to sleep at 2:30 AM.

Why is it none of you seem to understand that I hate not being in control of my marriage, my children, my finances, and even myself? Instead, I have to put up with being controlled by my wife, her friends, her pastor, her "counselor," her Bible study group, and anyone else who has an "interesting" opinion about something that's none of their business. How can I make this any clearer to you? If you would all just get out of the way, I could finally move ahead toward putting our marriage back together. WITHOUT ANY FURTHER HELP, I might add. Isn't there someone else out there you could find to counsel? This might sound pretty harsh, but I still don't think any of you get it. My marriage and my family are at stake here, and all I get from you is preaching, sarcasm, and "concern." That's well and good for you—you have nothing to lose. I, on the other hand, have everything to lose! What is it going to take to get you to back off and let Stacy and me work on our marriage together WITHOUT YOUR UNWANTED INTERFERENCE?

Mitch

FROM: Mitch

TO: Carter; Gerry

SUBJECT: Where I've been

You guys never cease to amaze me. After last night's email, I thought I'd never hear from you again, and now I find six messages on my voicemail from the two of you, plus one from Sue. I wish I could retract that email, but I can't. Once you click "Send," the message is gone like a bullet from a gun; there's no getting it back. The damage is done, and I'm so sorry.

You must be wondering where I've been. I'm still trying to process it all myself. When I finally finished railing at you guys last night, it was 3:00 in the morning. Since I couldn't sleep, I switched on the tube and started watching some old movie. The next thing I knew the garbage truck was banging and screeching out front of our house. It was 8:45 and I had to give a staff briefing at 9:30. Well, I showered, shaved, gulped a black coffee, and blasted toward the office as fast as the Z would go, which is pretty fast. Only I never got there.

You (Carter) haven't been to this part of Cheyenne before, but there's this intersection about a mile from our house with four-way stop signs and a new elementary school on the corner. I always cut through there because it saves me about six lights on my way to work. This morning, however, I was still pretty angry (very angry, actually), my head was killing me, and I was freaking out about my meeting. (I haven't exactly been Mr. Manager of the Year these past several weeks.)

So I'm coming up on this intersection going *way* over the speed limit, slowing down just enough to scan for cars, then hitting the gas again to blast through. That's when I noticed this kid crossing the street right in front of me. She must have darted out without even looking. The instant I spotted her, I jerked the wheel to the right as hard as I could. The next thing I knew there was this huge jolt, then the air bag caught me full in the face like a knockout blow. (I know those things are supposed to save lives, but they sure deliver a beating.)

Have you guys ever had this happen to you? During those few moments I sat there, stunned by the airbag and horrified that I'd just killed a little girl, the ugly reality of my life ran through my mind in vivid, sobering detail—the truth of everything you guys and Stacy have been trying to tell me. All I could think was what a horrible, angry, self-centered person I've become.

Struggling against a growing sense of dread, I climbed out of the car and braced myself for what I was about to find. But there was nothing! As it turned out, I hit the curb and a street sign instead of the girl, and no one but her saw it happen. She was apparently late for school and went running off as soon as I stepped out of the car (probably thought I'd yell at her for being in the road or something). I backed off the curb, changed the tire, and did my best to straighten the sign. While I was wrestling with that sign, I was overcome with the feeling of being totally alone and I realized I was going to cry. Leaving the sign at a crazy angle, I got back in the car and barely made it to the Wal-Mart parking lot before absolutely crying my eyes out. Every time I managed to get a grip on myself, Stacy and the kids would come to mind and it would start all over again. I just could not stop.

I'm not one for emotional fanfare, but I want you guys to know how sorry I am for sending that email last night. I also think I understand what you've been trying to tell me this past month. What can I say? To be honest, I don't know. That's why I'm not calling yet. I need time to think this through. What I do know is that I want more than anything to make it up to Stacy and the kids. I've been a terrible husband and father, but I want to make things right. I only hope it's not too late.

Please keep working with me and tell Stacy I love her. I'll call you as soon as I can. Thanks for being my friends.

Mitch

FROM: Carter

TO: Mitch; Gerry; Stan; Robert; Mike; Justin; Phil; Jim D.; Jim P.; John; Brad; Rich; Doug; Andy; Dan; Scott; Harv; Brent; Pete; Jack; Don; Manny

SUBJECT: Egotistical, angry, impatient, misdirected, and childish dads

Every now and then even a guy who counsels with other people needs to vent. I am so ticked off I just have to let fly at someone. Incidentally, I'm sending this email to all you guys in my address book. None of you need to take it personally, although we all need to take it seriously. To be honest, I hope every man in the world reads it. So when you're finished reading, pass it along to your buddies, OK? Furthermore, I need to apologize in advance and say I'm sorry if I offend anyone. I'm not trying to be offensive. I guess I'd rather ask your forgiveness than keep this all bottled up inside of me. Some will probably think I am overreacting and that this guy I'm going to tell you about has "deep personal issues" that need to be "uncovered in an understanding way." Whatever. Everyone handles things differently and that's cool. For now, please forgive me, but here I go anyway.

You know I was recently up in the mountains for a week—camping, fishing, looking at the fall colors, watching for elk, and chasing Minnie all around an empty campground. (Remember, fall is the rutting season.) It was a great week in all respects. However, when the weekend rolled around you wouldn't believe what happened. What appeared to be a nice little family arrived and pitched their tent right next to us (instead of in one of the forty other empty sites). I should have known the guy was a dipstick by how long it took him to put up the tent. Outdoorsman he wasn't. In fact, it took him about an hour to do the ten-minute job. You could tell he was a weenie by the size of his hatchet. I've seen beavers with bigger teeth. After he set up the tent, he went out and got a "load" of firewood that couldn't have amounted to more than five or six twigs. Not even enough to dry wet socks.

They stayed most of the weekend, and this "male" endlessly ripped his young son to shreds. He called him names, made fun of his efforts to help, and verbally attacked the little guy all weekend. His abuse just broke my heart and made me madder than I can describe without using foul language. What in the world gives this guy the right to treat his boy so badly? What kind of "man" does stuff like that? You guys don't treat your kids that way, do you? Do you scream and attack them in anger? Do you order them around like dogs? You'd better not! Whatever parenting is, it isn't what this guy was doing. He needed to be taken out to the woodshed and have his tongue nailed to a stump. The way he was talking to his son was so out of line I wanted to go right over and slam his knuckles in the tailgate of his truck, but I couldn't because Minnie had my leg chained to the picnic table. You know something? I wouldn't talk to my worst horse that way, let alone my son! What a pathetic excuse for a man. He needed a good thumping by an old cowboy who's meaner than a junkyard dog when it comes to abusive men.

I've been writing emails to my friend, Mitch, about what it's like to be a real man. I've used Adam (from the Bible) as my example. Adam was a real man whereas this guy was only a male of the species. Unlike Adam, this guy wasn't a real leader. If he were a leader, he wouldn't need to push and shove his little guy all over the campground. Real men don't do that! What kind of "protector" of his household would inflict wounds on his own child's heart? What kind of leader would intentionally cause his wife to lose all respect for him like that? What a sorry father he was. Nothing but an impatient, self-serving, egotistical child in a forty-year-old body. A "male," not a "man." Do you remember the old saying that "if it walks like a duck, swims like a duck, has feathers like a duck, and quacks like a duck chances are it's a duck?" Well, it might be true of ducks, but it's not true of men. Just because a male walks like a man, talks like a man, grows hair like a man, and has bodily functions like a man doesn't mean he's a man. He can still be a mouse. Or a rat. What makes a man is godly character, integrity, and self-control. Real men are patient and kind. They are the leaders, protectors, and teachers of their families, not abusers, bullies, or overgrown children with tiny hatchets.

I kept wondering what his wife must have been thinking. I know what Minnie would have been thinking and doing. She would have been all over me like a swarm of hornets the first time I ever talked to one of our four children that way. As the saying goes, "Behind every successful man is a strong woman." Don't forget it! Anyway, Minnie would never have tolerated my acting like that. She would have sown my lips together with bailing wire after leaving six or eight boot marks on my backside. She protected our kids like a sow bear protects her cubs, and rightfully so. After all, what child deserves that kind of treatment? I expected the wife of this bum to defend her boy—especially after the seventh, eighth, or fifteenth episode, but she didn't say a thing. What would your wives do? What kind of woman doesn't respond to something like that? Come on, guys! Encourage your wives to get in your face about things like this. If they don't know how, have them call Minnie for some pointers and the local hardware store for some equipment (duct tape, vice grips, wire, toilet plunger, huge axe, etc.).

What if this sorry father had been a real man? Like all young boys, his little guy was probably a little preoccupied, lazy, or overexcited. No kidding—that's what campgrounds are all about! Sure, there might have been cause for some correction, training, or discipline. Every little person needs to be taught how to work and how to be more focused. After all, kids will be kids. But that's no cause to become a bully (coward). So, what would a real man do?

First, get a real axe and throw that puny hatchet in the trash. Then learn how to put up a blasted tent. Finally, talk with the boy. Don't scream at him or smack him around! Take him by his hand and lead him—don't shove him! Model what you want him to become. You don't want him to grow up and become an abusive weasel with a weenie hatchet and a few sticks of firewood, do you? Rather you want your son to become a real man who has character, integrity, patience, gentleness, and a double-bitted axe for producing a stack of real firewood that'll dry out every sock in the campground.

Let me throw this at you guys. If any of you have problems acting abusive like this with your kids, for goodness sake get some help. Get some anger management counseling. Let your wife help you correct your disposition. Invite her to be an accountability partner. If she hears you mouthing off to the kids, allow her to pull out the duct tape and shut you down. Then, find yourself a Bible-believing man who will knock you around a little and hold you accountable for your unacceptable behavior. Your kids are depending on you. Get tough with this problem! In the meantime, read and think about what Ephesians 6:4 says—don't exasperate or provoke your children to anger.

OK, this was a good email for me to read after I wrote it. Pass this message on to your buddies. What do you say? Let's get on the bandwagon and fight like crazy against "males" who abuse their little kids.

Until we meet again, throw out your sissy hatchets and get yourselves double-bitted axes.

The Rev

P.S. Your children are depending on you to be the man God wants you to be. God offers His Holy Spirit to you, and He will empower you to become men of character, integrity, and self-control if you ask Him. Make sure you take Him up on His offer.

FROM: Mitch

TO: Carter

SUBJECT: How do I trade in my tiny hatchet?

Well Boss, you really know how to put together a thunderous email. I'll bet there's not a guy in the country who'd want to camp near you. Stacy and I actually laughed over all that indignation when I showed her your email. It was nice to be on the same side of an issue. Thanks.

I've noticed some pretty weird things going on in my head lately. During the past couple of weeks, it feels like I'm gradually getting a little past my anger and selfish feelings. Actually, I've been able to stop long enough to consider why Stacy moved out. Doing an overview of our marriage has allowed me to see my failures more clearly. In fact, your last email about Mr. Tiny Hatchet hit me right in the heart. I can see myself doing the same things to my own dear children. I have been so rude and cruel to them. They've run to me for attention, and I've ignored them and sent them away. So many times I just couldn't be bothered by their petty problems. For the first time in years, I just wept over my insensitivity. Whether or not things work out between Stacy and me, I'm really going to try to be more involved with the kids. It's so important that they don't suffer because of my stupidity.

I've been thinking a lot about how to put my marriage back together again. The question is, can "Humpty Dumpty" ever be put back together again? I'm afraid that if I don't come to understand what pushed us off the wall in the first place, all our efforts to reconcile will be a waste of time and energy. What if we patch things up for now and then fall off the wall again in a year? Won't that just make matters worse? I'm doing my best to really understand where our marriage got off track in the first place. Your emails about being a leader, teacher, and protector of Stacy have helped me clarify things.

I think I started taking Stacy for granted right after we got married. Other things captured my attention. I wanted the respect of my peers at work and wanted to look successful to others. I can see now it has been a major ego trip. When we had our first child, everything came into focus again (for about two weeks), then my attention shifted back to my personal needs and wants. It was exciting to leave home in the morning and boring to return in the evening. Think about going to the theater. You know what I mean—there's the first act, the intermission, and then the second act. Well, I think I've been viewing my marriage and family as the intermission to my life's drama. When I came home, it was like an intermission from what was really important. I can see now all I wanted was to rest and relax so I would be ready for the second act starting first thing the next morning. (Did you see yesterday's *Lazy-U* comic? I've attached it for your viewing pleasure. Talk about too close for comfort—who draws those things?)

Stacy, on the other hand, saw our marriage and family as the main drama and the rest of her life as an intermission. My intermission was her drama. Our marriage and family was the most important thing in her world, while to me it was an unwelcome delay. No wonder we fell off the wall. We were pushing from two different sides, and I pushed harder. She tried to keep us in place, but I was too indifferent. After all, it was intermission!

I have neglected Stacy and my children. I know that in time I will see more of my failures and have more regrets, but for now I'm just trying to understand what happened. I read those sections in the Bible you talked about. Adam must have been totally nuts over Eve. I'm sure he didn't view her as an intermission. Stacy and I had something similar to what Adam and Eve enjoyed years ago, but it slipped through our fingers like sand. I want very much to rebuild our marriage, but there are still huge hurdles to get over. For example: money, who lives where, and that ugly phrase "controlled separation." I bristle at the thought of any of them. (Guess I'm still working with a pretty small hatchet.)

For some reason I have a greater interest in God than ever before. I want to believe He has a design for marriage, but when I watch TV or read the newspaper or hear about the fun my friends are having, I start to wonder. Most of my friends are divorced, and their lives are an absolute mess, but they don't seem to mind. When you talk about God He seems real, but when I'm around other (regular) people, He doesn't seem so real at all. This is tough.

However, I *am* interested in continuing with your "counseling," so get with it and send me another email, you lazy sluggard.

Mitch

P.S. Stacy and I are going out to talk on Thursday. How do I lead, teach, and protect a woman who doesn't want anything to do with me? My plan is to listen, ask questions, and try to understand. It seems to me if I'm going to learn how to lead, I have to know more about who I'm leading. She has become a stranger to me lately, and that makes me nervous. Please pray for us. Thanks.

FROM: Carter

TO: Mitch

SUBJECT: "Can two walk together unless they be agreed?"
(Amos 3:3)

Mitch, I was pleased to read your most recent email. You seem to be going about this in a healthy way. You are precisely correct in realizing that you must learn, understand, and feel what Stacy is experiencing before you make corrections. Remember, she no longer sees you as her leader, protector, or teacher. In fact, you have hurt her deeply and she sees you more as a threat than a person she can trust. You must be willing to take the necessary time to rebuild her trust. Actually, I think you hit the nail right on the head. You have been into your own intermission.

Incidentally, I loved your illustration of the theater. It was very fitting to the attitude most of us men have at times. Home is our castle, and we're the kings. Kings do what they feel like and leave tending the castle to others. Ouch. I know I've been there, and unfortunately you've been there, too. In fact, the queen in your castle no longer respects the king and sees no future in the kingdom. Put another way, she's no longer interested in fluffing the pillows on your throne (recliner) or polishing your scepter (remote). Now, Jesus once said the one who wants to be great in the kingdom should be the servant of all. Do you suppose it's time to fluff the pillows on her throne for a change? Just a thought! I know you realize the seriousness of your situation.

When I arrived at my office this morning, I noticed a bumper sticker on the car next to mine that read, "I'd rather be golfing." The question that immediately popped into my tiny mind was, "What would I rather be doing?" I really couldn't come up with any staggering ideas. I wouldn't mind being in my tractor bailing hay or fishing for big rainbows up on the river, but I don't think I'd rather be golfing. What about you, Mitch? What would you rather be doing?

To be honest, the question itself is discouraging to me. Our lives have come to revolve around what "I'd" rather be doing. What about what Minnie would like to be doing? What should we be doing together? The trouble is, we're so different in what we like to do. I like racquetball, and she likes Nerfball. She likes bicycles, and I like Harleys. I like fishing fast rivers, and she likes fishing quiet lakes. She likes going for walks, and I think that's as boring as crocheting. She likes veggies and fish, while I like steak and taters. Are we different or what! Actually, we have more things in common than I'm letting on. For starters, we've got four kids and twelve grandkids. Plus, we share the same cars, water heater, well, and checkbook. We sleep together, eat together, and grow old together. We live in the same house and cook on the same stove. No, that's not right. She cooks on the stove most of the time. I can boil water and pop popcorn, but that isn't exactly cooking. We even complain at the same time. I once told a friend that we open the cattle gates together, but she reminded me she's the one who opens the gates while I sit in the truck. I stand corrected. The point is, we should be doing things together instead of going our independent ways all the time. Wouldn't you agree?

I'll bet this was no trouble for Adam and Eve. Remember, Adam was alone for the first part of his life. Then God gave him Eve as a companion and friend so he wouldn't be alone. Picture Adam the day Eve was created. He's running around the garden thinking, "What would *I* (emphasis on *I*) like to do today?" Suddenly, God introduces him to Eve. Adam takes one look at her and does what? Head to the golf course? Not on your life! His bumper sticker now reads, "I'd rather be with Eve." I'll bet the biggest struggle for Adam was to keep his marriage from being both the drama *and* the intermission.

Being a good leader-protector-teacher (husband) is rooted in trust, and trust is usually won through loving companionship. You know something? The Bible says it was "not good for the man to be alone."

I'm going to tell you something else. It's not good for the woman to be alone, either. Make no mistake about it; a woman whose man is out "doing what he'd rather be doing" is a woman who might fall in love with a snake. (Check it out in the third chapter of Genesis.) She might even be a woman who would go live in a condominium somewhere, if you follow my drift.

OK, I just figured it out. "I'd rather be building my relationship with Minnie!" How about you, Mitch? What would you rather be doing? How about trading in your "Mr. Alone" attitude and building a meaningful relationship with your wife and companion? Maybe if your wife doesn't feel so alone, she'll be more apt to trust your leadership, be thankful for your protection, and gladly seek out your companionship. Your effectiveness as a husband is in direct proportion to how successful you are in building a relationship with Stacy. No relationship, no effectiveness. How about that relationship? Maybe you can go on a snake hunt together.

Come to think of it, all this talking about that bumper sticker has put golf on my brain. What would you say to eighteen holes here in Colorado sometime soon? Maybe in light of what I have just written, we could get our wives to join us! Actually, they'd probably have more fun at the mall. The mall!!! Now this is getting painful! Better polish your putter.

The Rev

P.S. I'm shocked at how weak most marital relationships really are. It's surprising how couples who can't stay away from each other before their wedding can't wait to get away from each other afterward. But it doesn't have to be that way, young man. There has never been a better time to be creative than right now. Why not get started today?

FROM: Carter

TO: Mitch

SUBJECT: What went wrong in Eden Park?

Golly, my dear old friend, you will never believe what happened to Minnie and me last night. Let me give you the background to what has planted my sleepy backside in front of my computer at 4:30 AM thinking about your marriage and writing this email.

It started off as a terrific night, actually. First, we had an elder's meeting at church. (Every Tuesday evening at 6:00 I meet with the elders of my church.) After a time of prayer that melted the ceiling tiles, we discussed the weightier matters of church life like "Who did what to whom," "What did who do to what," and of course, "What is God doing to whomever." After that, it was off to my office for three counseling sessions. It's amazing what God does in the lives of people He loves. One couple was thinking about getting hitched up, the next couple was thinking about breaking up, and the final couple was already split up. The whole gamut of marriage in one evening. It's truly amazing that God can actually use a goof-up like me to guide those who want to be hitched up, to help those who are split up, and to confront those who are broken up—all in the same evening.

Anyway, I arrived home about 11:30 and found Minnie lying in bed wide-awake waiting for me to arrive home. What I mean by that is she was *only* waiting for me to arrive home and nothing else. After telling her how beautiful she looked, I reluctantly rolled over and went soundly to sleep.

At approximately 2:30 in the morning, I jumped out of bed and landed on my neatly heaped pile of clothes and boots. I'm pretty sure what triggered my flight was the sudden screaming and flailing that erupted just a few inches away from my face. Apparently, a big ranch insect landed somewhere in Minnie's beautiful, graying hair. Getting bugs in her bonnet has always been quite unsettling for Minnie, especially at 2:30 in the morning. Talk about a rude awakening. Trying to find the light switch was like looking for a paper clip in a cow pie, and by the time we were both safely tucked back in bed we were more wide awake than a plane full of tourists landing at Denver International Airport in the midst of our typical Colorado wind.

So here I am writing you, my good buddy, instead of snuggling up with my lovely wife. How boring! Something is wrong with this picture. Oh well! Thanks for your phone call yesterday. You were right about one thing. It's no fun being king of a deserted castle. You were right about another thing, too. The husband has a tremendous responsibility for keeping a family healthy. I like the way you put it when you said, "How goes the husband, so goes the marriage." I have discovered during more than thirty years of counseling that men are the major contributors to failed marriages. Why? Because they are careless about their leadership, they don't protect their wives, they are consumed with other things (mainly themselves), they seldom teach their wives anything, and they forget they're in a relationship, not a service contract.

There's one more thing you are right about. Your wife does deserve a better husband, and that's precisely what we are trying to work towards together.

Before I started this email, I was thinking about the seven wonders of the world. (Don't ask me why!) I guess it's because one of the seven wonders is that I am still alive after the bug-in-bed routine. Actually, it was because I read an article about them in my doctor's waiting room last week. Did you know there are ancient wonders, natural wonders, and modern wonders? Pretty cool. I'll have to teach Minnie about this.

Anyway, in the spirit of all this wondering, I've come up with my own seven wonders. Here they are:

1. I wonder why Minnie married me. Was it for fame, fortune, or my good looks? (Maybe she just wanted my saddle.)
2. I wonder why God loves me.

3. I wonder why God gave me such a great family.

4. I wonder if Adam had a navel.

5. I wonder who took care of David's sheep while he was off slaying Goliath.

6. I wonder why Jesus Christ was willing to sacrifice His life for the likes of you and me.

7. I wonder what happened between Genesis 2:25 and Genesis 3:1. (The Bible doesn't tell us.)

Let's think about this last "wonder" for a minute. I wonder what happened between Genesis two and three. At the end of chapter two, we're told the man and woman were both "naked and unashamed." Sounds wonderful to me! Then, at the beginning of chapter three, things are suddenly quite different. The serpent (evil) is talking to Eve. Notice how subtle and real his temptation is. Eve is being led down the garden path, and it's the serpent who's doing the leading! What's going on here? I thought "leading" was Adam's job! Why is the serpent teaching Eve about God? I thought "teaching" was Adam's job! Eve is inches away from the biggest mistake in the history of humanity—and where is Adam? I thought "protecting" was Adam's job! How do you get from total, uninhibited nakedness to Mr. Leadership Vacuum in less than one chapter?

Let me offer something for you to consider. The Bible doesn't tell us what happened, but we can use what theologians call "sanctified imagination." I'm assuming that between these two chapters there was a period of time where Adam began living a life of unbelief and neglect—unbelief in God and neglect of God's perfect gift (Eve). The bottom line seems to be this. Adam and Eve were living in perfect conditions but they weren't robots. They must have had the ability to exercise their free wills. They could choose to follow God or yield to their own self-serving desires. At some point between these two chapters, I think that's what happened to Adam. He became self-centered. At some point, he began to fail as a husband, much the same as I often do. Tragically, his failure as a husband led to the ruination of his marriage and all of his descendants. Then again, so does ours.

Mitch, I've run out of gas. My eyes are getting heavy, and my brain is slowly turning into mush (even more than usual). It's now 6:00 in the morning and I've only slept two hours. If you don't mind picking up this thought later, I'm going back to bed! Until then, keep wondering!

The Rev

P.S. I wonder if any parts of my marriage have gradually deteriorated over almost forty years? Am I fully aware of what's happening to us? Is the evil one sneaking up on us? I think I'll ask Minnie these questions after breakfast. On second thought, maybe I'll wait and ask her after dinner. But that could mess up our evening together. Probably it would be better if I asked her the first of the week. Then again, that could get our week off to a bad start. Maybe that's a good question to start next month off with. Or to end next month with. Or next year. What do you think? There really isn't a good time to ask such a question, is there? "Hey Minnie! Where are you? I have a question to ask you!"

FROM: Carter

TO: Mitch

SUBJECT: Where the buck stops

What a crazy night that was last night. Wasn't there a movie called *Sleeping with the Enemy?* With all Minnie's screaming and thrashing around, I sure thought I was sleeping with the enemy. I wonder how many couples go to bed every night and think of it as sleeping with the enemy. Now there's a sad thought.

Do you know how many people I have married? No—not me personally! Rather, do you know how many marriage services I have officiated? Many, many, many! I have taken countless couples through eight or nine sessions of premarital counseling and then to the altar where they have said their vows and committed their lives to each other. Do you remember doing that, my friend? Of course you do, and so do I. Take a minute and listen to your vows in your head while I run to the kitchen for some orange juice.

You know something? There's orange juice and then there's orange juice. I just love the stuff, so Minnie tries to keep a pitcher in the fridge. Now, some orange juice is thick and filled with pulp from the oranges—it pours like motor oil and you almost have to chew it to get it down. It's like a meal in a glass. I love it! Then there's the yellow-water type. Kind of reminds you of yellow antifreeze. Orange drink. I can't stand it! Well, what I have in my hand is neither because we apparently ran out of orange juice, leaving only purple fruit juice. Maybe I'll dump some coffee grounds in it just to simulate the sensation of real OJ.

OK, back to weddings. Have you noticed that wedding vows are pretty overwhelming? They give away the farm and promise the moon. Heavy stuff. Too heavy, apparently, for the frail-shouldered men our culture seems to be producing these days. You'd be astonished how many couples I see in counseling within a few short weeks after reciting their vows. So often, by the time a couple returns from the honeymoon, their disagreements have gotten louder and their patience with each other has completely evaporated. What was once wrapped in understanding and care is now tossed about in a brown paper sack. The thrill of the hunt has turned into the dogged endurance of a marathon.

The whole thing is like elk hunting. At first the mighty hunter moves silently through the timber, ever so careful not to break a twig or make the slightest sound. No sacrifice is considered too great when measured against the chance to score. This is called *courtship*. Then the target is in sight, the trigger is pulled, and the hunt is over! This is called *the wedding ceremony*. All of a sudden, the hunter couldn't care less about making noise or breaking sticks. He runs through the forest firing his gun into the air and screaming for his friends to come help. This is called *marriage*. The hunt is over! What's next?

Why do the romance of courtship and the commitments of wedding vows evaporate so quickly? I'll tell you why! Because they're no match for everyday self-centeredness.

That's what I was attempting to say early this morning through the fog of sleeplessness. Somewhere between the end of Genesis two and the beginning of Genesis three, Adam began failing as a leader. Over time, he found something else he'd "rather be doing." Self-centeredness. What a costly enterprise.

Mitch, have you ever heard of the two types of sins? No, I'm not talking about tiny hatchets and pink leashes. I'm referring to sins of commission and sins of omission. Sins of commission are wrong things we do; sins of omission are right things we don't do. Although the sins of commission receive far more airtime, both are equally dangerous—especially to a marriage.

Take the ultimate downfall of Adam—eating the forbidden fruit. That was an outright sin of commission. God forbade it, but Adam ate it. Boom. Instant consequences. But it was Adam's sins of omission that got him into trouble in the first place. Not believing God! Not leading his wife! Not being the husband he should have been. Think about it, Mitch. If you are too preoccupied to properly care for your wife, you, too, might be guilty of the sin of omission.

The big sin in the garden was not charged to Eve's account, but to Adam's. The apostle Paul, who wrote much of the Bible's New Testament, places full responsibility for what went wrong in the garden squarely on Adam's shoulders. Adam was responsible. God made him the leader, and he failed at it. (Paul refers to Adam several times in the New Testament books of Romans, 1 Corinthians, and 1 Timothy, in case you care to explore this yourself.)

Marriage is a huge assignment for a man. Courtship may have seemed like a "walk in the park," but it's peanuts compared to the challenge and thrill of leading a household. Only real men should apply. Or reapply, as the case may be. (Many of us undertake the reapplication process at some point in someone's counseling office.)

Well, Sport, I've written enough for one day. Your brain cannot contain any more wisdom right now, so go get an orange juice, moon the recliner, flip on Monday Night Football, and veg. Hold on a second—your wife might be dancing with the serpent. Maybe you should pick up the phone and have a pizza delivered to Gerry's house for her and the kids. (Be sure to pay for it, you penny pincher.) Here's another idea. Now that your Z is all fixed up again, why not go have her car cleaned and washed? While you're at it, take the kids to the park so she can go shopping or something. In other words, be creative with your God-given responsibility for a change! Remember, the serpent is after your marriage.

By the way, please have your sweet little wife send me another email. I would like to know what she thinks about all this. She'll be sure to tell me how you are doing. Until then, remember to check around the house for snakes.

Love ya,
The Rev

FROM: Stacy

TO: Carter

SUBJECT: Something is happening in Wyoming (besides the wind)

Dear Carter,

Mitch and I went out for coffee the other night after the kids went to bed, and we had quite the conversation. It seemed so different than ever before. We didn't necessarily agree on everything, but we were actually pretty nice to each other. I'm not sure what's happening, but it felt like the first positive step we've taken in the direction of reconciliation. It's been about a month since I left Mitch, and something is definitely different with him. Of course, I'm skeptical because he has been such a chameleon our entire marriage. However, it did feel like he was genuinely interested in the children. He has missed them a lot and would like to take them overnight two weekends from now.

When we returned to Gerry and Sue's, he came in, and we all talked for over an hour. We discussed getting together each week for the purpose of keeping communication open, and I brought up several other things because I didn't feel safe discussing them just with Mitch. It's not totally because of *his* reactions, but also because of *my* reactions against him. He surprised me by seeming to understand the importance of having someone else mediate our discussions. I hope this will be helpful in the long-run.

Supported by Sue's counsel, I agreed to have her watch the children so Mitch and I can go out for dinner and a movie next week. I hope we're not moving too quickly. I take comfort in the fact that Mitch has been more considerate lately of how fearful I am and how unsure I am about the future. The absence of his demands has been refreshing. I still feel subtle pressure to go home again, but nothing like before. Gerry tried to talk to Mitch about setting a specified length of time for our controlled separation, but they couldn't agree on anything. I told Mitch I was emotionally unprepared to return and that if our marriage was going to work I needed to change my terrible attitude. I also told him that God was convicting me about this and that Sue was helping me work on it. We all agreed it would be foolish to throw two screwed-up people back into the same situation that screwed them up in the first place.

Then, all of a sudden, the strangest thing happened. Mitch took the lead in the conversation and suggested our separation last three months. He said he felt completely responsible for what happened and that he needed time to rebuild my trust. He actually blurted out that he couldn't understand why I would even want him back. I was shocked because I'd been thinking the same thing. "Why do I want him back after all that has happened between us? Am I just a sucker for punishment?" It was sort of awkward until Gerry broke the tension by standing up and announcing, "I'll drink to that." He went into the kitchen and returned with four glasses of ice and a six-pack of Pepsi. We had a little party with chips and dip, then Mitch left.

My head was still spinning thirty minutes later when the doorbell rang. When I opened the door, there stood Mitch. He had tears in his eyes and said, "I just can't do it, I just can't do it. This separation has been too long as it is. We just can't keep it up this way." It was so much his style. I knew when he agreed to three months he'd never go through with it. I knew he'd get into his car, realize he was no longer in control, and back out of his promise. I knew it! "What a loser," I thought.

I just stood there looking at him, feeling waves of disgust, when he said, "Where's Gerry?" I moved aside so he could come back in, and he walked straight through the living room and down the hall to Gerry's study. I could feel my blood pressure skyrocketing and knew I was getting madder by the minute. This was *so typical*!!!

Finally, he and Gerry came back into the room. Mitch was crying his eyes out. He crossed over to where I was standing, gave me a big hug (you can't imagine how repulsive that was to me—I wanted to beat on him with my fists!), then he left without a word. It was too much, Carter. I broke down in sobs, and Sue had to come hug me. All I could think about was how much I hated him. And then Gerry asked if I wanted to know what that was all about. I told him I didn't care, but he insisted. He said Mitch was overcome by remorse over our whole situation, and that he felt three months was way too long for me and the children to have to live out of suitcases. So he made arrangements to move in with a friend for "as long as it takes to put this marriage back together." Gerry said Mitch would be moved out by tomorrow morning, and that he and Sue would help us move back in to the house right after lunch. Talk about emotional ups and downs!

Oh Carter, I'm so confused. What have you been telling my husband? All of a sudden he's out, and I'm home. He's agreeing, and I'm disagreeing. He's remorseful, and I'm hateful. Do you suppose God is working on him? Or do you think this is just one more of his schemes to manipulate me? Is he going to show up any minute with his suitcase and force his way back into my life? What is happening up here?

Pray for my terrible attitude.

Love,
Stacy

P.S. Do you think I should ask him to trade cars, also? That would test his sincerity, don't you think? Relax, Carter, I'm just kidding. You've been counseling too long!

FROM: Carter

TO: Mitch

SUBJECT: I wonder if divorced people ever look back
with regret?

I feel my heart jumping all over my rib cage with excitement. I received an email from Stacy telling me you moved out of the house. Congratulations! What in the world caused you to do that? Was it something in the water, or do you just love Stacy and the kids more than you love yourself? It must be the latter. Mitch, I am so proud of you and glad I am a witness to such a courageous act. Even though you're struggling with the "God thing," I still think God will bless such a "selfless" act. Proverbs 16:7 reads, "When a man's ways are pleasing to the LORD, He makes even his enemies to be at peace with him." Aren't you glad you moved out?

When I finally got control of my emotions, I began wondering what your divorced friends might be thinking. As I remember, they thought "moving out" was the stupidest thing in the world. Maybe that's why they're all paying attorney fees, court costs, spousal main-tenance, and child support. Unlike yourself, your divorced friends may never have learned how "self-centeredness" destroys relationships. I'll bet they have regrets about their own divorces, and since "misery loves company" they wanted you to join them.

Well Mitch, if you and Stacy end up divorced it wasn't because you moved. On the other hand, it could be that moving Stacy and the kids back into the house is the first major step toward the healing and rec-onciliation of your marriage. Trust me, you'll never regret humbling yourself and putting your family first.

Let me ask you something, Romeo. Do you love Stacy and the kids? Well, you don't even have to tell me because your actions speak louder than your words! Way to go!

Sorry to be so short today, but we're calving at the ranch so I'm vaccinating calves this afternoon. You'll be hearing from me soon enough.

The Rev

P.S. Why not tell your friends "talk is cheap?" Then give them this Bible verse from 1 John 3:18: "Let us not love with word or with tongue, but in deed and truth." Just kidding. I'll bet that would send their heads spinning! Who would ever dream of doing such a thing? Someone who really loves his wife, perhaps?

P.P.S. I had a great experience yesterday when I read the *Lazy-U* comic. It didn't remind me of anyone I know! (Not that I showed it to Minnie, or anything.)

FROM: Carter

TO: Stacy

SUBJECT: Your role in this drama

Dear Stacy,

Well, my dear friend, how does it feel to be married to such a sincere and understanding husband? I sure have enjoyed emailing him. He has a great love for you, and he's willing to make whatever changes are necessary to improve the quality of your marriage. It will take time, but he is definitely trying to be the man you want him to be. (I'd also like for him to become the man God wants him to be, but that's God's business, not ours.) I'm certainly praying that both of you will submit to God's design for marriage.

It was absolutely wonderful to hear from you, though to be honest I was a bit surprised by your email. Your side of the story is understandable, of course. Mitch has been hurtful to you in many ways, and I can appreciate your reservations. So let's not be naïve. Changing bad habits takes time. We'll be patient and watch for what God is doing in everyone's life. After all, He has His side of the story as well, and that's the one we really need to hear about. If we don't hear from God, we will never truly deal with the spiritual aspects of our marriages.

So, though you were right about one thing (your marriage being in the dumper), you were also wrong about something. It doesn't need to stay there. People do change their attitudes and behavior for the better. God can and does bring restoration and renewal to broken marriages, making them better than ever in the process. My marriage testifies to this truth, and so does Gerry and Sue's. The covenant you made before the Lord is at risk and your children are at risk, so you need to work yourselves out of this mess ASAP.

There's no hocus-pocus about solving marital conflict. It's not nearly as complicated as you might think. It is my unprofessional opinion that marriage counseling has far exceeded its natural boundaries and often makes resolution more difficult than is necessary. Solving marital problems isn't really that hard—wanting to solve them is the hard part. Most of the time, the two people involved don't want to make the necessary changes in their lives. They don't want to get rid of their sinful self-centeredness. They want to stay just as sinful and selfish as they have always been, and they expect everyone around them to change to accommodate them. You wouldn't believe how many disgruntled couples I see who refuse to acknowledge their sinful behavior and selfish attitudes. The thing is, it doesn't work that way. Sinful, selfish people make lousy spouses. In fact, sinful and selfish people are miserable to deal with no matter where you find them, but especially in marriage. So how hard is it to improve a marriage? The answer is, it's easy! All you have to do is get away from your sinful, self-centered attitudes and begin the process of serving your spouse. How hard is that?

Frankly, it's impossible. Unless, of course, you're both willing to engage in self-sacrifice, discipline, and plain old hard work. Stacy, you've been hurt and mistreated. It grieves me to know what you've gone through. At the same time, your own self-centeredness and its many tentacles have reached into every area of your marriage and that is what has nearly killed your relationship with your husband. Just think about that for a minute. I'll bet if you look back over the past several years of problems in your marriage, you can see self-centeredness dripping off the walls. Your marriage is infected with it because you and Mitch are both infected with it.

Let's take your husband as an example. You said he really doesn't carry his load in the family. Rather than helping out with the kids, he drops his buns into the recliner and tunes out the needs of the family. What's the problem with that picture? God knows what's wrong with it! He would confront your husband about his self-centeredness.

On the other hand, let's take you as an example. Your husband feels like you mother him and that you don't respect what he does. In other words, you constantly pick at him. He wants to enjoy a sexual relationship with you but says you are regularly cool and reluctant. What problem do you see with this picture? Well, I think God would say the same thing to you that He would say to Mitch. Your self-centered behavior is hurting your marriage in the same way Mitch's is. How hard is that to understand? It might be hard to swallow, but it's not hard to understand. No need for any one-hour counseling sessions at one-hundred dollars a pop, no pills to swallow, and no seminars to attend. Just a simple suggestion from God Himself. If the two of you will commit to selflessly serving one another from now on, your marriage will spring to its feet like the family dog when the mailman comes calling. Now how would you like that?

Can I take you to Genesis for a minute? I know you've been reading what I'm writing to Mitch, but that has all been focusing on his role in your marriage. This has more to do with you. God brought Eve to Adam to be his helper. That's really all we know. She was to come alongside and assist him. Helping him be all that he could be was her God-given responsibility. After Adam took her under his wing with the "bone of my bone and flesh of my flesh" commitment, what do you suppose Eve did? Did she start ordering Adam around, telling him how to pick fruit and how to cultivate mushrooms? I seriously doubt it. Rather, I picture her encouraging him, supporting him, and partnering with him in the great adventure of pioneering life on this planet! How great would that have been? What a fantastic marriage! Adam loving Eve selflessly, and Eve responding to Adam selflessly. Holy cow! Think of it!

We both know that didn't last. Adam took his lovely wife for granted and grew self-centered, and Eve responded in kind. The Bible doesn't say what happened between Genesis two and three, but I don't believe the events of chapter three happened overnight. Something was going on between those two lovers that gradually pulled them apart. It seems to me their unwillingness to believe God led them down the slippery slope of self-centeredness. What do you think?

Husbands have been selfish ever since, and women have been responding selfishly for just as long. That's how you and your husband arrived in the place you're now standing. Rather than being the partner God meant you to be to your husband, you have turned your attention, love, and respect to the children and to others who are better at fulfilling your needs. Understandable, yes. But sinful nonetheless. So the question on the table now is not, "How did we get here?" The question is, "Are you willing to do what it will take to get to a better place in your marriage?"

I look forward to hearing from you again. Until then, go buy yourself a brand-new dress and send the bill to your understanding husband!

Love to all,
The Rev

P.S. Go ahead and also pick out a nice pair of shoes to match the dress.

FROM: Mitch

TO: Carter

SUBJECT: Life is good!

For the first time in I don't know how long, my life is totally messed up—but I feel great! I'm sleeping on the couch in a filthy, one-bedroom apartment (I can even write my name in the dust on the shelves), but life is good! As you probably heard, I finally agreed that Stacy and I need to be separated for a while longer. We just can't be together without falling back into our old habits and destructive tendencies. I still want to push my agenda, and she still wants her independence. I get defensive whenever she says something I don't like, and she gets mad almost every time I open my mouth. If we want this marriage to survive (which I do!) I think a separation with some structure might be in our best interest. (Did I say *controlled separation*? I didn't think so!)

Carter, I finally realize the importance of getting my mind off of Stacy and onto myself. It has been so natural for me to blame this whole thing on her while dodging the guilt connected with my own actions and attitudes. I do want us to be together, but not at the risk of an even worse breakdown later. There are still nice opportunities for us to get together even though we aren't living together. Gerry and Sue kept our kids last night, and we had dinner at Stacy's favorite restaurant, followed by a movie. After the movie, you guessed it. I dropped her off at my house and left like a good little boy. She did give me a quick hug good night, but that's all. I could feel her reservation, and I needed to respect that. I'm not saying it was easy, but it somehow felt good.

You know something, Carter? This lady loved me at one time in history. She thought I was Prince Charming, and we had blast after blast goofing off together. I remember going "pool hopping" late one night with another couple. That's where you sneak into a swimming pool and play around in it until the apartment manager catches you and calls the police. It was the middle of February and colder than ice. We decided to sneak into a heated outdoor pool in downtown Denver. It was great! We splashed around for about twenty minutes before the security guard showed up, then we jumped the fence and ran for the car. Except for me, that is. I lost one of my shoes on the other side of the fence, and by the time I retrieved it and got to where the car was supposed to be—it was driving away! So there I stood at 1:00 AM in the middle of downtown Denver, in February, in my wet swimsuit! I ran after them for almost an entire block before realizing they weren't going to stop, then I ran some more when I heard the security guard yelling at me from the front of the hotel. The trouble was, the more running I did, the less likely it was that my ride would know where to find me—and I desperately needed to be found! I can't even describe to you how cold I was, or how many people stopped to stare at me. By the time they swung by with the door open, laughing at how red I was, my suit was frozen stiff and I could hardly move. It took about a forty-minute hug from Stacy just to thaw me out. Oh man, was that ever great. The best hug of my life! What a memory. I want so bad for us to get back to that place in our relationship I'm willing to do anything necessary to get us there. Even sleep on a smelly couch.

Stacy says she's a Christian now and that I'm still a sinner. Do Christians have forgiveness for sinners? Do you think she will ever forgive me? I know she reads her Bible occasionally, but do you think she'll ever do what it says? I sure hope so. The thought of divorce just kills me. Do we still have a chance?

Your good friend in Cheyenne,
Mitch

P.S. Do you know how long it has been since I lived in another guy's place? You should see the sink. I'm convinced aliens live in the drain. All of this serves as a constant reminder of what I used to have and took for granted. What a bonehead I was!

FROM: Carter

TO: Mitch; Stacy

SUBJECT: Snake hunting

Little did I know, Stacy, that you would actually go out and buy a new outfit—including shoes—and blame it all on me! Go figure! I should have known better. You women love it when you can blame someone else for what you were going to do all along. But what the heck. I'll bet you look great and are all set for a romantic evening with Mitch. So what's the big deal, Mitch? I turned her into a party animal for a mere $127.86 and you're complaining? Hey, isn't this what marriage counseling is all about? So what's with the phone call about your finances being so tight? Am I to understand that you can't afford this new outfit because you have so many more important things to spend money on? Hey, wait a minute. Aren't you the guy who went out a couple weeks ago and bought yourself a new, double-bitted axe when you already had a perfectly good hatchet in your garage? What's up with that? Remember, what's good for the goose is also good for the gander! So, knock off the complaining, get out the ostrich boots, put on the fancy Wrangler jeans with the big belt buckle, squeeze into a flashy shirt, and hit the town! It's time to bring a little fun into your relationship with Stacy. Who knows? It might even turn into a really, really long night! Whoa, it's getting exciting in here. Always remember the word *relationship*! Think relationship! Relationship! Relationship!

Wait a minute—did you hear that? Shhhhhhhhhh . . . Can you hear it? You know it's in there somewhere. You've seen it before. Down in the grass near those rocks. Can you see it now? Just barely! OK, use the shovel to separate the grass . . . slowly . . . not too fast. Be careful! You don't want to miss him again! You know the consequences. Listen carefully . . . stay focused . . . get ready, and . . . oh no! Son of a gun, he got away again. That rattlesnake slipped right back under those rocks.

Rattlesnakes are the biggest pain in the neck at the ranch. I don't know how many I've killed over the years, but I know one thing—I'm a big sissy when it comes to snakes. I'd rather tackle a bear with a hay hook than hunt down a lousy rattlesnake. Though I've never been bit, I'm convinced I'd probably die from fright before the venom got to me. If I weren't such a weenie, it would be another thing, but I am what I am. Even my kids used to dangle snake-looking ropes over my shoulders just for the fun of seeing me jump into orbit. Then they'd laugh and laugh. Those sorry kids! I should have sent them packing long before I did. I can only hope their kids will be as considerate toward them.

I was thinking about you two earlier today and it occurred to me you might profit from thinking about that serpent for a few minutes. Better to know about a snake than to be surprised by one, right? Have you ever seen the kid's movie *Jungle Book*? I've seen it about fifty times. (Just wait—someday you'll have twelve grandchildren!) Anyway, there's a snake in that movie, and he is determined to get the little boy into his deadly coils. He uses a snakelike trick of gradually hypnotizing his victims. When they look into his eyes, Kaa has them. He even has a little song he sings while lulling them to sleep. This snake is sharp as a tack and deadly as can be. Even when Mobley tries to resist temptation, the snake is more cunning and eventually lures him in.

That serpent in Genesis is just like the snake in *Jungle Book*. He lulls his victims to vulnerability with soothing notions of self-glorification. No matter the snake is lying, exaggerating, deceiving, and making impossible promises, it's what we like to hear and it works more often than I care to admit. Throw in a man who is placing his interests above his leadership responsibilities and a woman who is shopping around for new opportunities rather than partnering with her husband, and you've got a real dangerous situation brewing.

Can you see this? You need to see this! If you can, you can understand how simple it is to solve marriage problems. Simply return to your God-given responsibilities and take a shovel to those self-centered impulses that infest the pastures of your heart. It's no secret where they come from. Where did they come from in Genesis three?

It really is in your best interest to pay attention to this. Want to know why? Just consider the alternative. When Adam and Eve ate the forbidden watermelon, or whatever it was, all hell broke loose. The joys of open intimacy evaporated, their eyes were opened to each other's inadequacies, and they were plunged into shame. So much shame that they had to abandon all that wonderful scenery for a tangle of fig leaves.

Now, instead of enjoying God they became terrified of Him. They actually tried to hide themselves. How laughable is that? Read Genesis chapter three again. God showed up for their daily walk, and they cowered (rhymes with *coward*) behind a bush. What kind of leadership was that? So God called to Adam (not to Eve—remember, the man holds the responsibility to lead), and Adam started doing the shameful shuffle in front of his wife. (How much respect do you think she felt for him while that was going on?) Then God started asking questions, and the finger-pointing began. "Don't blame me—*You* gave her to me in the first place!" (Oh my! Could this be a case of being married to the wrong spouse?) "She fell first—she's the one who got me into this mess!" (Oh my! Is she the leader now?) The woman wasn't far behind. No sooner did Adam point her way than she pointed to the serpent: "He tricked me!"

How much sense did it make for them to be finger-pointing? How much sense does it make for us to blame others for our failures? When two people spend their time looking out for themselves, it's not a pretty sight. I should know. Minnie and I did it for years, and I counsel with couples every day who do the same thing. Christian couples are divorcing just as fast as people who don't even believe in God. We may hide our marital sins behind religious fig leaves, but God is not fooled. How many families do you know that live in anger, abuse, and emotional separation all week long, then 9:30 Sunday morning rolls around and out come the fig leaves to "hide" their selfishness from everyone else at church? What a joke! How deceived can we be?

Mitch and Stacy, I know you know this already, but I felt it was worth repeating one more time. The basis of marital success lies in obeying God's Word, taking responsibility for our failures, and casting off the spirit of self-centeredness. We can actually get closer to an "Eden Park" experience in our marriages by developing our relationship with God. We can stop blaming others for our sin and quit listening to "soothing" advice from questionable sources. With God's help, you can become far more healthy and happy in your marriage than either of you can possibly imagine at this point.

Think about it, my dear friends. Until we talk again, sharpen your shovels, hoes, picks, rakes, and whatever other tools you might need to kill that lousy snake. Come to think of it, the Bible is sharper than any two-edged sword, shovel, or hoe. It wouldn't hurt you both to become better acquainted with it. You never know when you might need something sharp around the garden.

The Rev

P.S. I just finished meeting with a man who is separated from his wife. Do you know what he said to me? He said the separation was his wife's fault. He sounded just like Adam. I had to silently ask God to quiet the "raging volcano" that was burning within me. I know what I told him was pretty blunt, but nowhere near as blunt as what I wanted to say. So what about you? What would you tell him? What do you say to a man who blames his wife for his problems, or a woman who avoids responsibility by blaming a serpent?

FROM: Carter

TO: Mitch

SUBJECT: When Adam fell you fell

You know something, Mitch? I really enjoy hearing from you. You are a fine snake killer. You have tremendous potential to be a great father and a terrific husband, especially since you now see the importance of putting self-centeredness to death. Your growing interest in spiritual matters also excites me because at that level positive changes in your marriage will begin.

You asked a difficult question at the end of our phone conversation yesterday. Remember? I couldn't get into it just then because I had to meet with my accountant, but I'd like to pick up on it now. Your question went something like this. "Why are all marriages infected with self-centeredness because of Adam and Eve?" Tough question! I'm going to answer in part with a rather flimsy illustration, but first I need some suds. Pepsi, for short.

OK, I'm back. A few years ago, my oldest son wanted to coach a baseball team made up of underprivileged ten-year-old kids. He approached the league and got their approval, then arranged for sponsorship so the kids could have uniforms. (Their parents couldn't afford anything.) Even though these kids had never played ball in their lives, they did amazingly well. In fact, they ended up in the championship game. Surprise, surprise! It was almost like a Disney movie in which the underdogs trounce the rich kids. Who would have guessed they'd get as far as they did?

Like most Little League games where there's practically no defensive play, the score was something like ninety-seven to ninety-six by the time they reached the bottom of the ninth inning. My son's team was ahead by one run, but now the other team was coming up to bat.

There was no way our little guys could win. They knew it, the parents knew it, and the other team knew it. To make matters worse, my grandson, who was the pitcher, walked the first three batters. Grandpa was having a meltdown! Can you picture this? Championship game, bases loaded, no outs, bottom of the ninth. It was hopeless. I felt terrible for them.

The coach from the other team could hardly stand still. His team was about to win the championship! It was in his hip pocket, and his excitement was spilling out all over the place. In his mind, I think he was already busy polishing the trophy and planning what he'd say to his team during their victory celebration. Up and down the baseline he ran, telling his three base runners to take off the instant the ball was hit. Up came the next batter. He didn't even bother swinging for the first two pitches, and then my grandson did an amazing thing—he threw a strike! Stunned, the batter got ready to swing on the next one. You could see it in his face. All eyes were on my grandson. No pressure here! He went through his little wind-up routine and flung the ball with all his might. Smack! Now, get this. The ball went straight up in the air like the St. Louis Arch, crested somewhere over the pitcher's mound, and began to descend toward the centerfielder who was standing completely out of position—on second base. As the ball approached him, he lifted his glove into the air to protect his head and caught the ball! Unfortunately, following the instructions of their overly excited coach, the three little peewees on base each took off pell-mell toward the next base as soon as the ball was hit. So when the kid who was on first base reached second, our centerfielder was standing there with the ball. They looked at each other like neither one of them knew what was going on, and then our little centerfielder tagged him with the ball as if to say "hi" instead of "you're out of here, you little peanut!" Instantly the game was over with an unassisted triple play, and the parents from my son's team erupted with cheering like there was no tomorrow. Nobody could believe what happened. The ragtag ball team actually won the championship! The look on the other coach's face was priceless. He looked so confused standing there in his "Baseball is Life!" T-shirt that the umpire actually walked over to explain to him what had just happened. I think he had to run through it four or five times before the poor man realized they lost.

When I left the field twenty minutes later, the other coach was still trying to explain to his crying team—and their angry parents—why they had lost the championship, and my son was still trying to explain to his dumbstruck team why they had won! The other team was surely better and should have easily won, but it didn't work out that way. The winning team lost and left the field dejected, discouraged, and defeated. The underdogs won and whooped it up with pizza and root beer at the local Pizza Hut. (I think they were going to do that anyway. Winning just confused things for a while.)

The same thing happened to Adam and Eve. They were made to be winners but turned out to be losers. They were caught in a "triple play" by the serpent, and the game was over. No replays, no second chances, and no next year. Once sin entered the family genes, there was no getting it out. Their self-centeredness became the family defect that has been passed on to every one of their descendants, right down to the present generation. Including Minnie, me, you, and Stacy.

Notice something important here. God didn't put Adam and Eve into a corner of the garden for a time-out. Nor did He discipline them by giving them the flu or a car accident. He didn't ground them for a thousand years of hard labor or slap a curfew on them. Rather, their sentence was permanent expulsion from the garden, along with spiritual and physical death. In short, the game was over! The consequences were staggering. You cannot minimize the holiness of God or trivialize His justice. Adam and Eve were not the only ones punished. All of mankind must suffer the ultimate consequence for Adam's sins of unbelief and self-centeredness.

Picture in your mind's eye Adam and Eve making their way through the garden gate—heads lowered, shame written all over their faces, and Adam not bothering to hold the gate open for Eve. They had rebelled against God, and now the consequences had begun. Shut out forever and ever, they were irreversibly corrupted by the events. As I said earlier, their sin actually polluted the entire gene pool. Even their children and their children's children would be corrupted and punished eternally. From then on every human being has been born with a sin nature that God must punish. That's the tragedy of Adam and Eve's story and the reason behind Jesus Christ's death and resurrection. Christ's death paid the penalty for our sin and broke sin's control over our lives. We can enjoy His power in our lives if we receive Him as our Savior. Only then will we be free from the penalty of sin and the consequences of Adam's self-centeredness in our marriages.

I wonder what Adam and Eve's conversations sounded like the first week after their exodus from the garden . . .

Adam: "Way to go, Eve! This is your entire fault, you know."

Eve: "Oh sure—it's always my fault! You blame me for everything."

Adam: "Well, if you hadn't listened to that snake in the grass, we wouldn't be in this mess right now."

Eve: "I seem to recall your eating some of that fruit, too, Mr. Self-Righteous. Am I not right?"

Adam: "Yeah, but you gave it to me!"

Eve: "Since when do you do anything I ask you to do? Hey, I was just delighted to have you around for a change. Since you started training the elephants, you've been more interested in them than in me."

Adam: "That's because they don't constantly criticize me."

Eve: "Well, then, maybe you should go live with them. In fact, you can sleep with them as well. I'm going to bed."

Adam: "I'll bet they'd be more affectionate than you ever are."

Eve: "Maybe if you paid me the slightest bit of attention, you'd find me more affectionate as well."

Adam: "Yeah, right. Like that ever works. Listen, I don't want to talk about it any more. Besides, I'm hungry. Where's my dinner?"

Eve: "Fix your own dinner."

Sound familiar? Minnie and I can sure relate. Our marriages are all affected by self-centeredness because of the sin natures we inherited from these first two parents. That's how Adam's troubles became my troubles and your troubles. On the other hand, remember the little underdog ball team that won the championship? Not a hope in the world of winning, then all of a sudden they're champions. Same as us. Our marriages have the sentence of death upon them, but we can be champions if something miraculous happens. Hello? Hello? Christ dying for our sins and empowering us to live selflessly is the miracle of the ages for marriages—as well as for every other area of our lives. You see, Mitch, God has a great plan for restoring not only your marriage but your broken relationship with Him.

Well, the Pepsi has run out and so has my free time for today. Until we talk again, get your glove ready. I think it's time to catch that fly ball.

The Rev

P.S. Here's a little reading assignment from the New Testament of your Bible. Ready? 1 Peter 5:5 and Colossians 3:12-14. Read 'em and weep!

FROM: Mitch

TO: Carter

SUBJECT: What's with all this psychology?

For an old cowboy, you're writing about pretty heavy stuff. You better be careful, or you might just blow a fuse. I've never bought into the psychology that we blame our ancestors for our problems. So often I hear people complaining about problems in their lives, and next thing you know they're blaming their mothers, fathers, sisters, brothers, uncles, aunts, and babysitters. Rev, I've always taken responsibility for what I have done and left my ancestors out of it. I don't see any reason to start blaming poor old Adam and Eve for my marital problems at this point. It just doesn't make sense. How could Adam and Eve have anything to do with Stacy and me? The ball's still in your court, Dr. Rev!

I've started reading a little book Gerry gave me on becoming a believer. It's called *Ultimate Questions* and has apparently sold millions of copies. Thankfully, it's short so I won't get bored. Carter, I am interested in spiritual questions like "What happens when we die?" "Did I live before this life?" "Is mankind basically good or bad?" and "What is God like?" But how can you say you're right and everyone else is wrong? Thankfully, Gerry is taking a shot at answering these questions. I feel like I'm on a spiritual journey. If all of this will help my marriage, it's well worth the time and energy. I only wish I could conduct this spiritual investigation without the baggage of a troubled marriage hanging over my head. I don't want to say "I believe" just to please Stacy, because this decision seems bigger than that. Plus I don't want her to think I'm just doing it to manipulate her to get back with me. She's still so distant and skeptical of me I don't want to add fuel to the fire. To be honest, her attitude is really starting to bug me. For the first time in my life, I'm trying to be what she needs me to be, and she's blowing me off!

Last night was a good example. Stacy and I had a seemingly good time at dinner and a movie. She was pleasant but wasn't there emotionally. When I talked to Sue this morning, she said Stacy has had a lot of things on her mind. In fact, Sue thinks it's probably because of the pressure Stacy feels about having me move back into the house. Even though we all agreed to a three-month break, Stacy is apparently having a tough time with that. I'm glad Sue is staying in touch with her.

On the bright side, something else was rather interesting. She had her nails done. I have asked her to get her nails fixed for months now, and all of a sudden they were beautiful. I asked her why, but she wouldn't say. I could tell that she went out of her way to get all dolled up for our date. Can you imagine how thrilled I was? You know something, Rev? I want to believe so badly that we're heading in the right direction, but I can't get any readings from her. What does it seem like to you?

I keep replaying our evening. You know, the most difficult part of it was when we started talking about getting together more frequently. I don't see the harm in meeting more often for coffee or something, but she didn't seem interested in seeing me any more than our previous agreement allows. I understand she's been hurt, but I wonder if she knows how her indifference hurts me? After the movie, I took her back to my/our/her home and that was that. I wanted to kiss her goodnight, but for some reason I only gave her a hug at the front door, (which she didn't return). When she said good-bye, her eyes got moist and she started to say something but stopped in the middle of the sentence. She said we'd have to talk later. Carter, for some reason I'm afraid of that conversation. What if she isn't willing to work on our marriage anymore? What if she wants a divorce? Deep down in my heart, I believe Stacy wants a divorce, but her belief in God won't allow her to go through with it. That's why I think she's acting so sad and impersonal. On the way "home," I wondered if she should maybe get a physical. Do you think she's depressed? Is she getting enough rest?

Maybe I need to back way off again and let her relax and heal? What do you think, Cowboy?

I can hardly wait for your next email.

Mitch

P.S. When I had the kids overnight, we went to a little "pay" fishing hole and had a great time. Both of the little ones caught fish. Maybe after this is all over, you and I could take our families up to the Fryingpan River and catch some lunkers. I'd be happy to show you how it's done.

FROM: Carter

TO: Mitch

SUBJECT: A long obedience in the same direction

How are you, my friend? I was moved by your last email. I know you're working very hard on this marriage stuff. I can hear it when we talk and read it when you write. The pain of caring without reciprocation is one of the hardest challenges we face in life. Mitch, I'm with you on this. What you're going through is difficult. It'll require a decision to keep at it even though you don't feel like it. Stacy is apparently burned out from your years of mutual self-centeredness. She'll rebound, as long as she remains committed to doing what's right, but it's not going to be as soon as your newfound resolve would wish. You're in for a different kind of hunt than you're used to. It'll require a decision to keep at it. To undertake "a long obedience in the same direction." (I borrowed that phrase from a book in my library by Eugene Peterson. He makes the point that good things don't happen instantly; rather, they're cultivated over time through faithfulness.)

So hang in there, young man. You'll be glad you did. In the meantime, I think I'll give Stacy a call and see how she's doing.

The other thing I could sense from your email is that you were not that moved by what I wrote recently. I suppose those are tough concepts to get your mind around when you first read them. Maybe it would be better to just look at it this way. You know that genetic diseases are passed down from one generation to the next, right? It happens that way in cattle, and my doctor friend fascinates me by the hour with stories of how it works with us human types. Well, spiritual disease is passed on in the same way, except there are no exceptions because it started with the very first couple. Their "disease" (unbelief) instantly contaminated the entire bloodline and has been passed on to each and every descendant ever since (except one—Jesus Christ— which we'll get into later).

Maybe it'll make more sense if we look at what that contamination does to us—its symptoms. I'll throw out a few initial thoughts here, then describe things in more detail later. First of all, I've called the "disease" unbelief because God explained how life works to Adam, and Adam chose not to believe Him. God said, "Don't do this, for in the day you do it you will surely die" (spiritual death—like a divorce from God). Adam considered God's input, weighed it against the benefits laid out by the serpent ("You can be like God!"), and decided to put his money on the serpent's word. An interest in self, motivated by unbelief.

If you're willing to chew on this some more, read Genesis chapters three and four a few more times. You can see the symptoms clear as a red pepper on a white plate. Guilt. Shame. Fear. Blame. Denial. Anger. Jealousy. And so on throughout the book. Not just in Adam and Eve, but in their kids. Their contamination was passed on as a spiritual genetic defect, manifesting itself in self-centeredness. This is obvious not only in the book of Genesis but in life all around us (not to mention in our own lives). Here are a couple more things for you to read. (Calm down, Mr. I Hate Homework—they're all short!) Read 1 Corinthians 15:21-22 and Romans 5:12, 15, 17-19. Sin and selfishness are simply in the gene pool. Did you have to teach your kids how to fight or lie? Me neither. They do a great job of taking after their dads without ever having to be told.

On a far less noble topic, I'm not feeling too hot today. I can't quite put my finger on it—I'm either totally exhausted or depressed. Even my daughter thinks I'm moving a little slower than normal. A bunch of things have gone wrong at the ranch lately. I have cattle to move and endless repairs to make on dilapidated corrals and outbuildings. I poured about five yards of concrete last Friday for some feed bunks, and possibly that's what really washed me out. Maybe I'm a little depressed because one of my employees quit. I don't know. Do you ever get this way? Maybe one of my circuits is fried. Since I only have two circuits, that means I'm operating at half of normal (which is none too swift to begin with). When I got up this morning, my body threatened mutiny. Hopefully, as the day drags on things will improve.

Nah, I can already tell—things aren't going to improve. I'm going back to bed. Maybe my body will be ready to try again tomorrow. In the meantime, keep on loving and leading your wife. It's the right thing to do, and it will bear fruit one day soon. It's already bearing fruit, only none of it is ripe yet. Hang in there.

The Rev

P.S. Sure, I'd love it if you'd "teach me how to fish." I'll bring the safety strap to keep your pole attached to your belt for when you get swept downstream. After all, you don't have the money to buy any new equipment right now—or at least that's what you told your lovely wife when she bought her new dress, right? Later.

FROM: Gerry

TO: Carter

SUBJECT: Update from Cheyenne

Sue and I have sure been praying that God will use your emails in the lives of Mitch and Stacy. Actually, Mitch has been forwarding them all to Stacy and us so we are up to speed on your counsel to them. This brings back memories for Sue and me. I remember so well your use of biblical principles and illustrations. Now that we're both Christians, those principles mean more than ever to us. We have been praying that God will restore their marriage, that Mitch will come to faith in Jesus Christ, and that Stacy will continue to mature in her faith.

Our personal frustration in all this is that God isn't working as fast as we would like Him to. Our desire is to get Mitch and Stacy back together as soon as possible. However, we've had to concede that God, in His sovereignty, is likely to have very different goals and a different timetable. Thankfully, the success of this ordeal isn't measured in terms of what we can or can't accomplish by inadequate human effort, but rather in terms of what God is doing in the privacy of their hearts. I'm reminded again and again that the Bible says in Psalm 127:1, "Unless the LORD builds the house, they labor in vain who build it." As I read your emails, I often wonder what "secular" counselors say to hurting people. I know I'm sure in over my head trying to deal with Mitch and Stacy, so I'm glad for your guidance and support.

Sue and I need to bring you up to date on how things are going here in Cheyenne. You can email back if you have questions, but my plan is to call you tomorrow.

Mitch seems to be doing well outwardly. He and I are going through that study book you recommended (*Evidence That Demands a Verdict*, by Josh McDowell), and I think many of his questions are being answered. He reads his Bible occasionally and has even come to church once during the past month or so. God seems to be working in his heart, but Sue and I have some concerns about what Mitch is doing in his spare time. I know he has always been committed to his exercise program and that his job is a top priority, so that accounts for at least some of his busyness. However, he seems to be out late almost every night with his friends. When I was with him the other day, I think I smelled alcohol on his breath. It puzzled me because Mitch has never been one to drink.

The other day he did a nice thing for Stacy. He traded cars with her so he could shovel hers out, vacuum up the scraps and candy wrappers left by the children, and give the old thing a bath. I was pleased by this, and I could tell Stacy was surprised. Unfortunately, it didn't turn out so well. Her purse spilled out on the floor, and when she was picking everything up she found a pack of matches peeking out from under the floor mat. They were from a local strip club. It took a moment for this to register with her, and then she went absolutely ballistic. Sue and I happened to be there when she made this discovery. (We were taking the kids out for ice cream so she could have a little breathing room.) Her language and behavior reminded me of that first night when she showed up on our doorstep. There's no better word to describe it than ranting. For almost thirty minutes, she charged around the house, slamming doors, throwing things, and tearing through all of Mitch's belongings. Finally she dropped into the sofa, turned bright red, and went totally silent. I was stunned by the whole thing. To say she was a bit angry would be the understatement of the decade.

So that's one part of it. The other part has to do with Mitch's roommate. He's a big guy named Stu. He works with Mitch and spends a lot of time at the health club where Mitch works out. I play a little racquetball at the club, and I've gotten to know Stu fairly well. Carter, this guy is the consummate ladies' man and has a "partly cloudy" reputation at best. Does this make you think what I'm thinking? To make matters worse, I stopped by Stu's place last Saturday to take Mitch out for lunch, and I couldn't help but notice a whole pile of very inappropriate reading material on the coffee table. Satan seems to be on a real headhunt for Mitch, and I'm very concerned. Do you think I should confront him about any of this?

After Stacy regained some composure, Sue and I tried to talk with her about the situation. She was surprisingly unwilling to discuss the matter. When she did begin to talk, it was all reflections on their marriage. It seems Mitch was gone many nights even when they were together, often getting home late and smelling of smoke. She confided that their sexual relationship was almost nonexistent, and that she has suspected him of having an affair for the past two years. She told me Mitch was so hard to live with that sex was the furthest thing from her mind as well. To make matters even worse, Mitch apparently is the life of the party whenever he's out with his friends. He flirts with every attractive woman and shows no interest in Stacy when she is present. When she stopped talking, we all sat there looking at one other. She asked me what I thought, and I just smiled like a dummy and said, "I really don't know what to think." What do you think, wise one?

As you know, Sue keeps in daily touch with Stacy. Sue is convinced these past years have devastated her. It's plain as day that Stacy's emotional reservoir is empty and her spirit is broken. She told Sue that she has completely lost her identity. She has no close friends and seems to be starving to death socially. All she does is raise the children and talk to her mom. Apparently she applied for a part-time job over at the grocery store to generate a little spending money. She knows Mitch's salary was never intended to support two households, so she has been hesitant to ask him for help. The thing is, when Mitch found out he got pretty angry. He's still paranoid and controlling, and he doesn't want her out of the house. That's wrong, isn't it? Why can't she get a job? Mitch says her cell-phone bill has gone up so much he's going to have her service cancelled. All of these little disagreements add fuel to the fire and keep both of them on edge. I'm trying to work through these matters each week when the three of us get together, but it's getting tough again. For a while it was much better, but I can't help thinking we're now heading downhill and picking up speed.

The more I think about Stacy, the more concerned I get. I think she's struggling spiritually, too. She says she feels like God is a long way off and that her prayers get no further than the bedroom ceiling. She cries when she tells us she had dreams as a little girl of having a beautiful family and a cozy home with lots of gardens and a white picket fence. "Now look at the mess I'm in," she blurted out the other day. "My relationship with the Lord is at an all-time low, and my marriage is hopeless." Having confessed that, she pounded her fists on the armrest of the sofa and then left the room. Sue and I just looked at each other. Our hearts break for her because her dreams and commitments seem pretty much shattered.

I don't know what to make of all this, Carter. Something significant must be going on in her mind because she told Sue she is determined to send Mitch "the email of his life." Of course she's afraid of his reaction, but says the time has come. Another day of reckoning has apparently arrived for Mitch. Sue politely asked what the contents of that email might be, but Stacy wouldn't disclose her thoughts. Instead, she assured Sue that we (and you, Carter) would all be copied.

This has been hard for me because it seemed like we were making such progress for a while. Ever since Mitch's accident, he has appeared to be bending over backward to do the right thing by Stacy. I asked her the other day what she thought about the improvements Mitch has been making. She said, "What improvements?" So I reminded her about some of the nice things he has done—moving her back home, taking her out on dates, cleaning her car, doing things with the kids, and so forth. She told me those weren't improvements; they were just the way Mitch manipulates her to get his own way. She said all he wants is for them to get back together so he can stop being embarrassed and inconvenienced by all this nonsense. She said it has always been about him and that it's still all about him. "He probably wanted to clean my car because he was feeling guilty about spending all his free time at the strip club. Trust me, he'll never change," was her parting shot. "Especially once he gets my email."

Can I ask you something, Carter? How do you counsel with people day after day, week after week? I'm working with just one couple, and they're about to drive me crazy. Pray for Sue and me while you're at it.

I'm going to call your office for a phone appointment tomorrow. Please have your secretary give me twenty-minutes sometime during your busy day. I think it would be good for you and me to be on the same page as we deal with this couple. Is that cool with you?

Your friend and brother,
Gerry

P.S. Be prepared for the email from Stacy. Whatever it is, it should be interesting.

FROM: Carter

TO: Gerry

SUBJECT: Confronting Mitch

Gerry,

In your last e-mail you raised some good questions. Should we confront Mitch about the "questionable" reading material at Stu's house? And what about Stacy's comments concerning Mitch's possible relationships with other women?

The answer to your first question is, "Yes!" But be careful.

Your second question isn't so easy. I'm not sure what I think about Stacy's comments. Maybe and maybe not! I really don't know.

As you proceed, remember what the apostle Paul wrote in First Corinthians 2:14: "But a natural man [or worldly minded man] does not accept the things of the Spirit of God, for they are foolishness to him; and he cannot understand them, because they are spiritually appraised." Gerry, always keep in mind that Mitch doesn't need to simply "clean up his act." He needs Christ to enter his life and change him from within. Mitch and Stu are acting unsaved because they *are* unsaved. Let's be careful with judging their unsaved behavior. Rather, we need to keep presenting Christ as the ultimate solution.

The Rev

P.S. I'm going to send Mitch a couple of emails dealing with his self-centeredness. Hopefully they'll help get to the root of his escapades.

FROM: Carter

TO: Mitch

SUBJECT: We self-centered guys

Hey Mitch,

Not long ago I watched an interview with some important movie star on TV. Don't judge his popularity by the fact that I've never heard his name before—I just don't follow movie stars that much. He probably doesn't know my name either, so we're even. Anyway, he has had many difficulties in his quest for stardom, and made reference to his "setbacks" several times during the interview. Finally, the woman doing the interview picked up on it and asked him which three things he hates most about himself. (How'd you like to answer that question on national TV?) His response was unbelievable! Without even taking a moment to think about it, he announced the number one thing he hates most about himself is his selfishness. I almost choked on my bratwurst. Then, as if that wasn't enough, he listed number two as his self-centeredness. Needing a swallow of juice, I ran to the kitchen and missed number three.

All this was pretty flattering for me, seeing as I now have something in common with a famous person. We're both self-centered. Wow! Seriously, I think that was a bold confession to make. He certainly gained my respect, and I hope people watching were likewise confronted by his boldness. Most of us do everything humanly possible to cover up our self-centeredness, but he confessed it publicly. That took guts.

Self-centeredness isn't just an isolated condition. It has been rearing its ugly head for thousands of years. Trouble is, self-centeredness has been packaged in such soft and "understanding" terms that we completely miss its destructive significance. Unlike my new movie star hero, most of us don't hate our self-centeredness—we cater to it. Although none of us want to be called selfish, self-centered, self-righteous, self-absorbed, self-indulgent, self-deceived, or any other derogatory "self" term, we make every effort to ensure that our needs are properly met. We're "overworked" so we deserve a break. We're "important" so we demand respect. We're "distracted" because of all the important responsibilities we're shouldering, or "uncommunicative" because of how much we've got on our minds. What's wrong with any of that? We even justify fantasizing about and flirting with other women because it "feels so good" to our midget-sized egos. "Cut us some slack," we tell our wives. Do you see anything wrong with this type of thinking, Mitch?

Counselors often elect to diagnose the problems of hurting marriages in terms that imply misunderstanding rather than by naming the sin of self-centeredness. Even churches have fallen prey to unbiblical diagnoses. I doubt if that movie star is a counselor, but he sure expressed the condition of mankind more accurately than most of us who ought to know better.

The Bible certainly doesn't mince words about self-centeredness. Have you read the first dozen chapters of Genesis yet? My goodness, what a mess! We've already discussed Adam and Eve, but what about their kids? Talk about sibling rivalry! Adam and Eve's boys didn't mess around with bickering or shoving. One of them jumped straight into murder. What's worse, it was rooted in how to worship God. Cain brought vegetables to the big sacrifice; Abel brought a lamb. God preferred the lamb to the veggies (I can relate to that), and the next thing you know Cain whacked Abel.

If you spend a few minutes reading this story for yourself (Genesis 4:1-15), you'll see a lot more than murder going on. There's anger, depression, jealousy, envy, stubbornness, lack of self-control, hate, denial, and disrespect. Where'd all that come from? A polluted bloodline, that's where.

By the sixth chapter of Genesis, the earth is crawling with Adam and Eve's offspring. They have at least obeyed *that* part of God's command.

So how are things going? Genesis 6:5 says, "Then the LORD saw that the wickedness of man was great on the earth, and that every intent of the thoughts of his heart was only evil continually." Wow. That's quite a departure from the perfect garden of their great-grandparents. This tells us that self-centered thinking leads to evil doing. Evil actions are produced by evil thoughts. When the mind is focused on what I want, what I feel, what I think, and what I intend to do about it, my life will become a reflection of what I think is best for Mr. Number One. The guy in the lawn chair (see today's attachment from *Life at the Lazy-U*) is me.

God hates self-centeredness for many reasons. He created people to be God-centered, God-focused, and God-obedient. That's why Noah was spared from the destruction of the flood—he placed God's will before his own. The rest of Adam's children were quickly destroyed.

What about the human weenie roast in Genesis 19? God was fed up with the self-centered people of Sodom and Gomorrah. Just imagine all the men of your city routinely raping anyone they felt like, anytime, anywhere. (I'll bet there were strip bars and porn shops in those two cities.) All of this was an expression of self-centeredness and godlessness, and God didn't allow it to go on forever. He never does.

You know something? These little case studies demonstrate how self-centeredness can take individuals, families, cities, and world populations captive. Anywhere you find someone with a pulse, you find self-centeredness. What about you, Mitch? Remember, this is a heart issue. How's your heart doing these days? Even as you read this, self-centeredness is attempting to destroy your marriage from the inside out. Look at your divorced friends and others who have unhappy marriages. Can you see that self-centeredness is at the root of all their problems? It's everywhere.

Well, gotta run. Meanwhile, let's learn what we can from my new favorite movie star, whatever his name is:

1. We are selfish.
2. We are very self-centered.
3. We are always hungry.

This third point is optional. You might want to put something else in there like, "I don't want to sleep on a couch for the rest of my life." That sort of thing. Amen, and Amen.

The Rev

P.S. I was distressed to hear from Gerry that your self-centeredness might be expressing itself in behavior not consistent with trying to heal your marriage. You've emailed me about your attitudes. They've been changing, and you're sorry for the way you've treated Stacy. I've been encouraged by what God is doing in your heart, and I believe you are sincere in what you tell me. However, what does it say to Stacy when she finds matches from the local strip club in your car? It says you're a bunch of hot air. When you spend late nights flirting with sensuous women, it communicates you have a whole lot more on your mind than your marriage. Is the shortage of money in your accounts due to the rising expenses of your separation, or to the cost of lap dances and drinks? Do you want to talk about it? I'd appreciate a phone call from you ASAP.

FROM: Carter

TO: Mitch

SUBJECT: Fighting self-centeredness

Mitch, since you haven't called since my last email (or taken any of my calls), I'm not sure whether you need more examples to convince you of the danger of self-centeredness or whether I offended you. Are you still on board? Or do you not know what to do? For now, I'll assume "yes" to both.

So let's talk about terrorism. All of this talk of fighting terrorism seems a good analogy for fighting self-centeredness. You can get only so far by bombing "strategic targets." Beating terrorism requires good intelligence, hand-to-hand combat, and the eventual elimination of its source.

So it is with self-centeredness. You can't bomb it out with sermons, speeches, or New Year's resolutions. Self-centeredness is a far more insidious enemy than we realize. The only way to fight it is by digging out the driving thoughts, attitudes, and motives that fuel it from the secluded caves and bunkers where they hide. They tunnel deeply into our egotistical infrastructure and blend in with the normal patterns of our personalities. In fact, without the penetrating power of Jesus Christ's death and resurrection, and the discernment we gain from God's Word, it's impossible for us to root them all out.

The Bible contains a huge collection of examples, from King David's adultery with Bathsheba to Ananias and Sapphira's fatal mistake of faking their piety. If you need specifics, I can give you hundreds of them. If you could learn one thing from reading the Bible, it's that God hates self-centeredness.

Have you ever stopped to wonder why He hates it? First, it robs God of His rightful place in the hearts of His people. We were created to be God-centered, not man-centered. Second, He knows how harmful it is to us. Why do you think He wants husbands and wives to love each other selflessly? Because that's what's best for them. Self-centeredness destroys people, destroys relationships, and destroys intimacy. God loves us too much to want us harmed in that way. That's what the Ten Commandments show us, as well as the book of Proverbs, the teachings of Jesus, and the writings of the apostle Paul. It's all about protecting us from the devastating effects of self-centeredness. It also happens to be the reason Christ died and rose again—to break the grip of sin on our hearts.

Mitch, your marriage suffers from the effects of self-centeredness. For that matter, so does your separation. You are not placing anyone else's needs above your own, and neither is Stacy. Let me ask you a question, my friend. Have you confessed your sin of self-centeredness to Stacy? Are you willing to turn away from self-centeredness and seek to become selfless? I have great hope in God's ability to help you understand these principles and ultimately turn your sorry marriage into something that will be pleasing to Him, Stacy, and you. However, before He can do that, you need to see your sin in contrast to His Holiness. Mitch, you stand against God because you haven't surrendered the rule of your life to Him. Put first things first. Ask God to save you from your *self* (sin).

One thing I know for sure. It's time for hand-to-hand combat! We need to dig the self-centeredness out from the hidden recesses of our lives and, with God's supernatural power, be delivered from its continual terrorism. They say soldiers should never fight alone. Are you with me, my friend?

Before I go, where are you going hunting this year? It's getting to be that time again. I just talked with a friend who prefers duck and goose hunting to elk hunting. I've never done that before, have you? Sitting in a duck blind sounds like a guy could freeze his tail off, but I'm ready to give it a try. I've got an old twelve-gauge Winchester that shoots pretty well, some arctic overalls, and two pairs of warm gloves. What do you say? Let's go! Oh, wait a minute. Can we barbecue steaks in a duck blind? Maybe I'd better check into that first.

Until then, make sure your spotlight is charged. Down in the caves where self-centeredness lives, it's darker than the inside of a cow.

The Rev

P.S. Mitch, read this next paragraph very thoughtfully. I'm asked the question all the time: "Why are we always disagreeing and fighting?" You and Stacy are asking the same question. The answer is actually very simple. It's found in James 4:1-2, "What is the source of quarrels and conflicts among you? Is not the source your pleasures that wage war in your members? You lust and do not have; so you commit murder. You are envious and cannot obtain; so you fight and quarrel." Self-centeredness is behind all the destructive bickering and fighting of every unhappy marriage. It's the source of all abusive behavior and cannot be ignored while solving marital disputes. No, it's not personality differences, ancestral baggage, or a bad environment. It's self-centeredness that's at the core of family heartache. So get this through your thick skull my good friend.

TO: Mitch

CC: Gerry; Sue; Carter; Minnie

FROM: Stacy

SUBJECT: The collapse of our marriage

Mitch, I guess you've probably been expecting this email. I told Gerry and Sue it was coming. They've been wonderful to me, and I think they deserve to be informed so I'm sending them both a copy. I'm also copying Carter and Minnie because they've been counseling and supporting me these past several weeks. I'm sorry I've not been truthful with any of you about my struggles. This will change all that.

Mitch, I've wanted to send this to you for a long time, but for one reason or another I've never managed to do it. I'd get angry and lonely and commit to write everything down, then I'd get depressed and frightened and never send it. In fact, I've wanted to send this for more than nine months but couldn't muster the energy or courage. I'd write things down, delete them, write some more, then delete them, too. However, as I sit here at 3:30 AM in front of the computer, I'm thinking the time has finally come. I've been rereading my journal entries from the past nine months, and my heart feels even darker than the night outside my window. I need to tell this to you.

My life has been nothing more than a blur of headaches and heartaches. All I have to show for our years together is disappointment, despair, broken promises, broken dreams, and, of course, a *big* empty house. The woman whose sorry history is recorded in my journal was a woman who had learned to hate her husband. She was a woman filled with anger who had grown so tired of living alone, hiding her feelings, and walking in fear that she wept every day for months on end. She was totally worn out from being controlled and consumed by her husband.

What you're reading now is being written by a different woman. The woman writing this email has come to the end of her ability to care and to the end of her marital commitment. The woman at this keyboard has disconnected emotionally from her husband. She can't even find the energy to hate him anymore. Instead, she is simply allowing him to exist as part of her disappointing history. (A very unpleasant part, I might add.)

Mitch, your need to control me has caused me to completely lose track of the person I once was. How would you like living with a person who controlled your every move? I couldn't even open the curtains without your barking about it. When I tried to vacuum the house, it would interfere with your TV programs and you'd yell at me to stop. If the children left toys outside their room, you'd threaten to throw them away. When the dog barked, you'd threaten to get rid of her. If I used too much water in the bathtub, you'd complain about the water bill. Even my attempts to fix fancy dinners were met with whining and criticism. They were either too expensive, took too long to eat, or weren't what you wanted. And when I fixed meals the kids would like, you demanded I fix something special just for you. Can you imagine what it's been like living with a person who has robbed me of every freedom and pleasure I ever had? You even wanted me to keep a logbook of my comings and goings. It got so bad I felt like my life was one long game of hide-and-seek. Hiding nickels, dimes, and dollars so I'd have a little something to spend on the kids and myself. Hiding time with friends and relatives so you wouldn't feel jealous or suspicious. Hiding my emotions so you wouldn't lash out at me. And vainly seeking your affection so I wouldn't feel like the worst wife in the world. A lot of good that did me.

Gerry and Sue, would you respect a man who wouldn't allow you to visit with your parents or talk with your siblings? Would you? I have been living with a man who wouldn't let me have anything to do with my family. When I wanted to talk with my mom, I'd have to do it on the sly with secret signals so she'd call me back. Otherwise he would see her number on our long-distance phone bill and hit the roof about it. His family was the only family we needed. Mitch's mother thinks her son is the greatest thing since sliced bread and that I'm the wicked witch of the north. Mitch, you've done so much whining to her about how mean I am she actually believes you and endlessly strokes your little ego. Has she ever pressed for the truth? Don't make me laugh. She wouldn't believe it even if she knew it to be fact. She's too deep in denial for that. In her opinion, I'm responsible for everything that's wrong with her poor little son's unhappy marriage. I almost feel sorry for her.

Sue and Minnie, how would you feel if every time you wanted to invite some of your friends over for lunch your husband wouldn't allow it? How would you react? If our house wasn't clean 100 percent of the time, especially when his buddies showed up unexpectedly, I was called a lousy wife *right in front of them.* When the kids misbehaved, I was called a terrible mother. I couldn't win an argument or get a compliment if my life depended on it. He was all that mattered. The only one whose opinions counted. The only one whose needs were important. Mitch, to you I was just one more piece of property to be used or discarded as you saw fit. Thankfully, those days are over. As I said before, the woman writing this email is a different woman. She doesn't care any more. She's lost all respect for her husband and has no interest in putting up with his pathetic childishness.

Mitch, I've tried to cover up for you through the years. Now I no longer care. When you would order me around, I would do everything I could to make you happy. "Why fight?" I reasoned. It wasn't good for the kids to hear us constantly arguing. Every day I would hate it when you arrived home from work. The minute you walked through the door, I knew I'd need to be very careful about your feelings or you'd blow up about something. Actually, you'd blow up anyway. I could count on one hand the number of times you came home and were pleasant to me. Well, I have been embarrassed and humiliated for the last time. Your degrading remarks about my body, mind, and spiritual interests will no longer be tolerated. Try them out on the poor wretch who ends up being your next wife. See how long she puts up with them. You might think me stupid, but I'm smart enough to get out of a destructive relationship before it kills me. I only wish I'd done it sooner. My body may have seen better days, but I'm sick and tired of being the brunt of your caustic comments and crude jokes. Carter, what kind of man makes fun of his wife to all his friends—in her presence? A small man, that's what kind. Mitch, you've called me lazy, undisciplined, overweight, stupid, mindless, irrational, and many other names that aren't worth repeating. It might surprise you to know that even your friends have reached out to me because they feel sorry for me. Some of them have reached out in ways you wouldn't like if you only knew. At least they like me and think I'm a nice person.

Mitch, you kept me powerless by giving me no personal worth. You always had the final word and second-guessed everything I said. What I did was never good enough. When it came to kids, cars, finances, family, or clothes, I couldn't do anything right. You had a stranglehold on everything I thought, everything I did, and everything I am. I just want to be free from your oppressive, controlling nature. Who needs to live under that? Not me anymore.

Now, I know you're currently on a spiritual journey of some sort. Carter, Gerry, and Sue are all praying for your faith in Christ. Well, that journey had better take you right through those first three chapters of Genesis as Carter has been emailing you. You may become a Christian, but unless you learn how to love your next wife you'll be right back where you are now—only with two divorces and even less of your precious money.

In all fairness, I will concede that our failed marriage isn't entirely your fault. It's my fault as well. I've made my share of mistakes. As I look back over the years of our marriage, I wasn't a very good wife because a good wife would never have allowed you to treat her like you did me. *Did you get that?* A good wife would never have put up with your abusive ways. I've been such a fool. So many times I asked for us to get counseling, but no, you said you knew how to fix our problems. "Counselors put their pants on one leg at a time just like I do," you used to say. I should've gone ahead and sought counseling by myself. When you whined to your mother, I should have given her the real story. When you called me the things you did in front of your friends,

I should have told them what you called them when they weren't around. But I was a fool and afraid. When you screamed and yelled at the kids, I should have packed them up and gone for help. But no, I just kept trying to protect you and make excuses for you *just like your mother does.* That's right. My worst fear has come true—I've become just like your mother!

Mitch, I didn't want to face the truth about our relationship. Carter sent me an email some time ago about the role of a wife. He showed me from Genesis that a woman is to be her husband's helper. That was God's role for Eve. She was to come alongside Adam and help him be a man of honor and integrity. Maybe that's why I finally found the courage and determination to write this email. Mitch, I failed at that, and I'm sorry. Like the wife of an alcoholic, I became your enabler. I permitted you to be an abusive bully. I allowed you to control me, use me, and engulf me. I only wish I had it to do all over again. I can assure you things would be a whole lot different.

Which brings me to something else I must tell you. Earlier this evening I was wondering what exactly I would do differently next time. As I read through my journal, lots of things came to mind. None of them matter now, except for one. I would definitely change what happened at the mall four months ago. While sitting on the bench near the fountain, I began to cry. The kids were with a couple from church, so I was alone. After a while I heard someone say, "Ma'am, are you all right?" It was a man about your age, and I told him I was fine, just having a tough day. When he asked me if there was anything he could do to help, I just started sobbing again and had to go rummaging through my purse for more tissues. He actually went over to the soda shop and got me some napkins, then went back and bought me a cold drink. We ended up talking for an hour, then he walked me to my car and told me if I needed anyone to talk to again, here was his number. He understood because he'd gone through a divorce about a year and a half earlier.

I left the mall that day a different person, and after two or three days I called his house and left a message. I was really nervous, but I couldn't wait to talk with him again. There's no need to go any further with this except to say that Mr. X and I have been seeing each other for some time. His touch of compassion and words of understanding ignited a fire within me that I cannot quench. I realize my relationship with Mr. X is nobody's fault but my own, but your treatment of me during these past years sure made it easier to disregard my commitment to you. Again, I take full responsibility for what happened, but I also feel like it saved my life. That's why I chose to call him back. The trouble is, now I don't know what to do. I'm suffering over this because I know it's wrong, yet I can't seem to let go. Getting to know him has opened the floodgates of love, care, compassion, and understanding in my heart. Do you realize how long it has been since a man has treated me with kindness and respect? He actually wants to know what I think about things. He also cares about what I'm doing and isn't ashamed to hold my hand when we go for walks. I've even taken up tennis. Funny, you haven't even noticed, have you Mitch? That's been the story of our marriage.

Gerry, Sue, Carter, and Minnie, I'm so sorry to break the news to you this way. I know you'll be very disappointed in me and this will probably end our friendship. I know what the Bible teaches, so you can save your breath telling me how wrong I am. Carter, maybe your emails will help me sort through the confusion I feel. Please keep me in your address book and send me messages from time to time if you ever think of something to say. But don't make me sit down and discuss this with Mitch. I won't do it.

Mitch, please don't call to spew out all your vile accusations at me. It won't do any good. What you think doesn't matter to me any more. I guess it's over now for sure. You don't need to forgive me because I don't care to be forgiven by you. Now you can go to the strip club with your friends and have something really juicy to laugh about. Have fun. And while you're at it, you'd better start thinking about selling the house. It brings back too many nightmares.

Stacy

FROM: Minnie

TO: Stacy

SUBJECT: A "P.S." to our conversation last night

Carter and I were happy you received the bouquet of flowers we sent. We just thought you needed a little encouragement. It's always good to know someone loves you and believes in you, especially when you're so down. When we talked with you on the phone last night, you sounded like your world was coming to an end. By the way, weren't those roses beautiful? I asked the florist to set them behind the cactus plants so you would remember that behind every sticky situation there's a beautiful rose. We believe in you, Stacy! Carter and I closed out our day praying that God would comfort you and give you clear direction from His Word.

But Stacy girl, it's time for you to take charge of your life. You're jumping from a burning dock into a sinking boat. Can't you see that? I didn't want to say this with Carter on the phone, but *isn't one man enough headache for a lifetime?* Believe me, Carter is enough headaches for two lifetimes! (Go ahead and laugh—it's all right!)

Stacy, on the serious side, I'd like for you to consider three little thoughts I've had since reading your email about Mr. X. The first thing you must keep in mind is that, if you are truly a Christian, God's Holy Spirit is busy convicting you about your relationship with this man. You haven't told us whether your relationship is physical or just emotional, but either way it's a sin against the covenant you and Mitch entered into some years ago. You are a married woman, Stacy, and your emotional attachment (if nothing else) is a violation of your marital vows. God will not forgive you or ignore your sin until you confess, repent, and break your relationship with Mr. X.

Second, from a practical standpoint, you must consider what you're doing to the children. Try to explain your way around this kind of behavior! You are continually telling your children to obey and do what is right, but then you turn around and disobey God and do what is wrong. What will they think of this? Children need to grow up in the safe environment of a secure and loving home and not be tossed back and forth between Mitch and Mr. X. Carter and I are very aware that your home has been anything but secure and loving. But let's fix one problem before creating a whole bunch of new ones.

Third, I've always felt that life and marriage are similar to a game of Scrabble™. When you start the game, you're given seven letters from the alphabet. The challenge is to form the best possible words from the letters and place them on the board. You and your spouse get to build on each other's words. Believe me, I know it's not always easy to do this! Whenever Carter and I play, he comes up with words that aren't even in the dictionary! Anyway, the object is to play more letters and make better words than might seem obvious at first. However, there is one important rule. You must build on each other's words—you can't just go off and start your own words somewhere else on the board. You may not like the letters you draw, or the words your partner is playing, but you can't just build anywhere you want. Nor can you use words that aren't in the English language.

Stacy, you and Mitch entered into a game of marital Scrabble, and you're not finished yet. Together, you both decided to build on each other's lives. The going got tough. Your letters weren't the best. It became difficult for you and Mitch to build on each other's words. In fact, Mitch started using inappropriate words and words that didn't even exist! Things got even worse, and now you've started playing on someone else's board. Not good. Both of you broke the rules! Both of you are cheating! And if you're not careful, you'll both end up losers!

I have a challenge for you, Stacy. Here are seven letters: L-D-Y-R-T-A-U. Which words could you build into your game with these letters? You could spell LADY, YARD, RAT, TRAY, or a whole range of "safe and sensible" words. But what if Mitch's last word was

LOSER? You might be tempted to follow his lead and use his "E" for ADULTERY. Don't do it! Trust me on this, you don't want to build with that word! That's cheating! Use your head, girl, and come up with a better word. How about using his "R" for TRY? My challenge to you is to *try* and keep trying. *Try* confessing your sin. *Try* reading your Bible. *Try* forgiving Mitch. *Try* praying about your whole situation. *Try* calling Carter for help (or Sue, or Gerry, or your pastor, or your support group, if you have one at church). TRY.

I love you Stacy. And I believe in you.

Minnie

FROM: Carter

TO: Mitch; Stacy

SUBJECT: After the crash . . .

I was so sad to read Stacy's email. I know it must have been terribly difficult to write just as it was devastating to read. Although I was unable to reach you, Mitch, on the phone, I have talked with Gerry and Sue, and we are all concerned about the future of your marriage. We also feel grieved for the children. Is reconciliation even possible at this point?

Mitch, what are you going to do now that you know Stacy is involved with another man? What about the fact that you haven't been a good husband? What do you plan to do about that? Is it finally time to "split the blanket" forever?

Stacy, what are you going to do about being involved with a man who isn't your husband? And what about the (formerly) abusive and controlling man who happens to be your husband? Is it time for a divorce?

Folks, this is where you find yourselves after years of unhappiness and indifference. I know you're both angry at each other, but I also hope you're just as angry with yourselves. This is not only about Stacy's sin against God and Mitch, but it's also about Mitch's sin against God and Stacy. We'll be talking more about this in the near future. For now, let this be a season of reflection, not accusation. It should be a time for confession of sin, not blaming each other. For now, let's focus on the subject of rebuilding a marriage. What do you say?

Rebuilding is never easy. I have corrals and barns that are falling down, and I'm always attempting to prop them back up. What can I expect? I've lived on this ranch for more than thirty years. The posts are rotting off, the rails are cracking, the barns are falling apart, and what the horses don't eat the cows knock over and the pigs go under. As I look around the barnyard, I feel a kinship with it all. It looks like I feel. Everything needs to be rebuilt, yet rebuilding takes so much energy. I'm not sure I can pull it off. You know what I mean? It's tempting to keep the whole place patched up with more nails, bigger nails, bailing wire, and duct tape. However, while these things may help me get to next week or next month, the day of reckoning is steadily approaching. If the rebuilding doesn't start soon, there'll be nothing left for the windstorms to blow over. Barns don't rebuild themselves. I've got to get in gear and commit the necessary time, energy, sweat, and resources to get things done.

You two are in the same place, and what you're looking at is just as huge. (Think of the massive rebuilding project at the former site of the World Trade Center towers in lower Manhattan.) All around you lies the wreckage of what once was a good marriage. Now all you have left are piles of twisted morals, melted conscience, missing convictions, and lost hopes and dreams—all covered with the ashes of failed expectations. What on earth can be done about such a colossal marital meltdown? I can only quote the president, governor of New York, and mayor of New York City: "We will not give up! It is time to rebuild!" Do you think the God before Whom you took your vows has any less determination or intention to rebuild your destroyed marriage? I can assure you He has what it takes and is presently determined to *rebuild!* What about you, Mitch and Stacy? Are you going to "throw in the towel" or commit yourselves to rebuilding with God's help?

The only requirement for an effective rebuilding project is self-denial. There's no such thing as self-centeredness at the site of any "Ground Zero" rebuilding project. Rebuilding demands dying to *self*. Why? Because self-centeredness brings devastation and destruction. That's how you two got to where you are in the first place. In contrast, the rebuilding and rescue of your broken marriage will have to be built upon Jesus Christ and His example of selflessness. There will be no room for your pride, fear, or grievances. They'll have to be hauled away with the rest of the rubble and replaced with new materials that will stand the test of time. Are you ready to get on with this? It'll be dirty and dangerous at first, but far more rewarding than you can imagine right now.

I am so thankful that Minnie and I started rebuilding our marriage thirty years ago. Our marriage was in the dumper because I was a self-centered egomaniac. Now, that's a problem for any wife. Rebuilding changed our spiritual and marital relationship. It especially changed Minnie! Made her a better woman! Helped her to finally come around and see her many faults! No, I'm just kidding. Rebuilding changed us both in big ways (especially me). And you know something? Hard as it was, I've not regretted rebuilding our marriage one bit. Nor has Minnie. Was that an "amen" I just heard from the kitchen? (I wonder whether she was praying or agreeing?)

Before you start to rebuild your marriage, check the First Aid Kit for bandages to cover emotional wounds, aspirin for headaches, antacid for upset stomachs, splints for broken hearts, and tourniquets for loss of love. You'll also need some hard-hats to protect those hard heads of yours, you stubborn rascals.

Until next time, get some rest. You're going to need it! This rebuilding stuff will plum tucker you out. Trust me, I know—I've got an entire ranch to rebuild! Now, where's my dinner, Minnie?

OK, it looks like we're going out tonight. I'd better get ready.

The Rev

P.S. Mitch, early on in our marriage I gave Minnie every reason in the world to "go packing" and divorce me. However, she believed in the covenant we made together and refused to "abandon ship." I think you've got one just like Minnie, and you'd better learn to appreciate her a whole lot more than you have. You're one lucky guy. Most women would have left you long ago. Stacy, deep down inside of me I believe you're a woman of commitment and will remain committed to doing what is right. Think about what your marriage could be, not what it has become. Tomorrow could be totally different if you both dig in and start rebuilding.

INSTANT MESSAGES BETWEEN MITCH AND CARTER

5:30 PM

MITCH: Hey Carter, I was just going to write you an email but noticed you online. Do you know how to use Instant Messaging?

CARTER: Just how old do you think I am?

MITCH: Sorry, Cowboy. All this talk of cattle fences and dilapidated barns made me forget what a high-tech guy you really are. Hey, can we talk about all this for a little while? I'm really angry right now. I can't believe Stacy would do this to me.

CARTER: Well, my dear friend and fellow screwball, every marriage has its ups and downs, and for the time being yours is definitely on the down side. You didn't think marriage was going to be a joyride did you? So many couples forget that it actually takes effort to keep a marriage working well. Other things (work, children, faith, hobbies, money, extended family, etc.) get in the way and keep them distracted. Pretty soon they become lazy about their love and make assumptions they shouldn't make. Assumptions such as "We'll work on our marriage later," "Time will heal all," "He'll get better with age," or "She'll quit nagging if I ignore her long enough." Why would you be surprised that your marriage is derailed when you've done so little to take care of it?

MITCH: Thanks for all the "sympathy," Rev. You're a real tender one. Hey, do you know how long Stacy has been seeing Mr. X? I called her and started asking questions but she didn't want to talk about it. She actually cut me off in the middle of a sentence and told me I'd never understand. Then she said good-bye and hung up. I was furious and called her right back, but she didn't answer. She seems to have totally forgotten that I'm her husband! I need to know what's going on. In fact, I have the *right* to know what's going on! So I'll ask you again. Do you know anything about Mr. X?

CARTER: As a matter of fact, I really don't. From her email, it sounds like they've only known each other for four months. One thing I know is that you'll never find out if you don't learn to control your anger. It's far easier for her to hang up than to endure your bellowing. Maybe you need to find a better way to talk with her. She's not likely to share details about her affair with anyone she's not comfortable with. Generally that person will be someone she trusts and someone who will speak to her with love and understanding. Until you fit that description, I'm guessing you'll be in the dark. You may feel you have the right to know, but you apparently haven't given Stacy reason to feel that way. Mitch, your anger seems to be blurring your vision.

MITCH: How would you like it if Minnie had sex with another man? Would you be Mr. Calm & Tender? Would you wave it off as if it were nothing? No way. I know you better than that— you'd be a raging bull. Carter, I can just see that guy swooping my wife off her feet with smooth talk and gentle caresses. I'll tell you what. If I knew who he was, he'd be meeting his Maker right now.

CARTER: I can understand your anger. What has happened is a very serious sin against you. Should Minnie do such a despicable thing, I'm sure I'd be very angry, too. Left to myself, I'd probably castrate the guy. And that's why I've worked hard to surround myself with a few wise and godly men. I always want people in my life who will help me keep my wheels on and not end up in jail. If I were in your shoes right now, I'd need someone to tell me that getting Stacy back was far more important than abusing her with my anger or trying to find Mr. X. Mitch, don't loose track of the goal here. The prize is winning Stacy back, not revenge.

MITCH: How does a woman with "Christian" values and morals end up in the sack with another man? I'm so sick of Christian people talking like they're perfect while acting like everybody else. They're all such hypocrites. If God is so important to Stacy, why is she doing such a thing? Here I've been thinking we were working on our marriage, and she's been sleeping around like a whore. You know what? She can just go live with that guy for all I care. Let him put up with all her nagging and ungratefulness. Let him put his money where his you-know-what is. They deserve each other.

CARTER: Mitch, I suppose what troubles me most about this situation is what you just said. The name of Christ has been tarnished because of what Stacy has done. On the other hand, I have to keep reminding myself of all the things I've done to tarnish His name. That's precisely why I need a Savior. Christ forgives my sin and cleanses me. Stacy will need to confess her sin to Christ if she ever wants to move forward in her relationship with God. You're right about Christians not always "walking the talk." However, I think you're losing sight of what has gone on in your marriage. When you allowed Stacy to return to the house and you moved to Stu's apartment, that was a kind thing to do and I commend you for it. However, that one act of kindness hasn't erased all the emotional damage you've inflicted over the years. Not hardly. What Stacy is doing is wrong, but from reading her email I can see why she did it. It wasn't about wanting to have sex with another man. She wanted to be loved and appreciated. She longed to be cared for. Generally speaking, when a woman has an affair, it's more about her emotions than about sex. Your concern for your own interests says a great deal about why Stacy is so comfortable with Mr. X. From what she writes about him, he appears more concerned about her than about himself. What do you think?

MITCH: Well, I can't be with a woman who has been unfaithful. What man would trust her? Every time I think about it, I get madder and madder. I can just see her going to the mall in high hopes of picking up some guy. No wonder she had her nails done. I'll bet she wore the fancy dress and shoes I paid for, just like a hooker. Only she didn't do it for the money, she did it to "have her needs met." It makes me sick.

CARTER: Now you're just being abusive. You seem to have forgotten about your own unfaithful deeds. Maybe I should remind you about the matches Stacy found in your car. You've been visiting strip bars for some time. I knew about this long before Stacy found the matches. Gerry works out at the same club you do and has met Stu. It may surprise you to know that Gerry has been talking with Stu about spiritual things, including his need for salvation. (What have you been talking to Stu about, Mitch?) Stu has been somewhat receptive to discussing God's love for him, and the issue of sexual sin has been the topic of several conversations. Gerry has even brought up Stu's sexual escapades. I don't have to remind you that Stu is not always flying solo on those adventures, do I? How is it that you are able to be so condemning of Stacy? The Bible says in Matthew 5:28, "Everyone who looks at a woman with lust for her has already committed adultery with her in his heart." When you watch a woman take off her clothes and dance on your lap, doesn't that constitute a "sin" against Stacy? I should think so! It seems to me that your fidelity isn't any better than hers. Stu told Gerry that some of the "material" on the coffee table in your shared apartment actually belongs to you—a "faithfully" married man. Is that true, Mitch? If so, the Bible has another good question for you. In Matthew 7:3 Jesus asks, "Why do you look at the speck that is in your brother's eye, but do not notice the log that is in your own eye?" Why has Stacy's affair taken center stage in your thinking when you've been visiting strip clubs and viewing pornography on a regular basis? When are you going to be honest with yourself? If you would start being as hard on yourself as you are on Stacy, maybe something more positive would happen.

MITCH: Having a sexual affair is a lot different than a little fantasizing over pictures of women or watching them dance.

CARTER: Oh really! Would you be content to stay married to Stacy if you knew she was habitually lusting after other men, watching them get undressed, comparing them to you physically, and having them dance in her lap? Would you enjoy knowing she was so hungry for such things that she was paying for them? Be honest with yourself, Mitch. Your life is just as sinful as hers, right? You're angry at Stacy because you're hurt by what she did. What about how much you've hurt her? Reflect on that for a while, and your perspective will clear up dramatically. I guarantee it.

MITCH: I need to sign off for a while. I'm supposed to meet Stu and some other guys over at you-know-where. We're going to hang out for a while and try to relax. This whole thing is such a disaster I'm at a total loss over what to do. What do you say we continue our conversation a little later, say around 10:00 PM? I'll make sure I'm back online by then.

CARTER: I'll be here.

CARTER (10:00 PM): Mitch? Hello, Mitch, are you there? I just had a bowl of ice cream and poured root beer over it. Whoa! It was great. Now I'm all set to wrap up our great conversation.

CARTER(10:10 PM): Hey, Mitch, you there yet?

CARTER(10:30 PM): Hello? Hello? Anybody home?

CARTER(11:00 PM): Mitch, are you there, old buddy? How's Stu doing? Hello? Hello? OK, let me guess. You're still sitting at the strip club feeling sad about what Stacy has done to you. All your married friends are with you, and their wives don't mind because they know being at a strip club has nothing to do with sex, it's just about friendship and relaxing together. Oh, wait. Your friends are all divorced. Sorry, I forgot. Well, never mind.

- - - - - - - - - - - - - -

CARTER (11:30 PM): You haven't forgotten your old friend, have you? I wonder what Stacy is doing right now? Maybe I should call her cell phone and see if she knows where you are.

MITCH: Your sarcastic comments aren't appreciated. You know this is nothing to laugh about. However, I do understand what you're saying. I'm sorry to have missed our appointment. You may not believe this, but I've been experiencing a real sense of conviction for the first time since that day I almost hit the little girl.

CARTER: Sorry for the sarcasm. No harm meant. Well, not much, anyway. Conviction of sin comes from the Holy Spirit of God who draws our attention to our lost condition and also points us to Christ for salvation and forgiveness. The fact that you are experiencing conviction tells me God is working on your heart.

MITCH: Maybe so. Here's another surprise for you. I didn't spend the whole evening at the club. While I was there, things you said kept coming to mind and making me uncomfortable. Stu thought I must be getting the flu, but I told him it was more like "swine flu" for being so pig-headed. After about two hours, I finally left at 8:30 PM. I got in my "family" car and drove around town for maybe thirty minutes and then I did it. I dialed Stacy on my cell phone. I was so anxious to tell her what I was learning about myself, and how miserable I was without her. When she answered the phone, my heart stopped—I couldn't believe she actually answered. She seemed pleasant but distant, as usual. It was so weird to feel awkward talking to my own wife on the phone. We were meant to be talking in person, not by phone all the time. I wondered what it would be like to see her, so I said,

"Would it be all right if I dropped by for just a few minutes? I won't stay long." She told me tonight wouldn't work, but she'd meet me at the little restaurant near our house tomorrow evening. Carter, I couldn't understand why tonight wouldn't work. Was she with Mr. X? I was trying to be nice and polite, but my suspicion started getting out of hand. I pictured Mr. X in the next room (my bedroom!) listening in. Finally, I asked her if Mr. X was there and if that was the reason she couldn't see me tonight. She bristled and told me it was none of my business. At that point I started losing it. How could she invite Mr. X right into my house and sleep with him *in my bed*? I was so angry the only words that came to my mind are not fit to print here. I'm afraid I started shouting at her and calling her every name I could think of. Somewhere in the midst of it, she hung up. By that time, I had the old Z pointed toward the house and was wasting no time getting there. Almost habitually I hit redial and was preparing to leave a blistering earful on her voicemail, except she picked up on the first ring. I was so surprised I didn't say anything for a moment, so she cut right in and said this was not the time to discuss the matter and could we please talk later. I shot back that, unless she wanted an immediate divorce, she'd better start telling me exactly what was going on that instant. She started crying and tried to speak, but couldn't. I thought maybe she was coming to her senses. I told myself that sometimes you just have to get tough. Then I waited for her to start explaining. After about thirty L-O-N-G seconds, she said, "Mitch, you'll never understand." I just exploded, "No, *you're* the one who doesn't understand!" Then I lit into her with a nonstop stream of accusations. Suddenly I heard this guy's voice on the line saying, "Is there something wrong here?" Without skipping a beat, I tore into Mr. X harder than I've ripped into anyone in my whole life. I told him what he was doing to my marriage and threatened his life if I got to the house before he was gone. I called him every name in the book and then demanded he give me his name so I could make his life the hell he'd made mine. When I finally paused for a breath, the voice on the other end said, "Mitch, is that you? This is Gerry. Sue and I and a few others from the church are over here for a midweek Bible study. What's going on?" Oh, Carter, the anger drained out of me in an instant. I just wanted to die. Once again I had to pull over and cry like a baby. I can't get away from what a terrible person I've become.

CARTER: Wow. What a classic story. You sure know how to turn the heat up on a situation. Gracious. I'll bet Gerry will never let you live this down. Tell you what. I've got to hit the sack now (Minnie just finished the book she was reading), but I'll write again tomorrow. In fact, I think I'll send you a great email about how to overcome being a fool. I'm sure you feel like one right now, so maybe it'll be of some help to you. You know what else? We should try this Instant Messaging thing again soon. No long waits for the next email. Till then, take care.

FROM: Carter

TO: Gerry

SUBJECT: Tell the truth, the whole truth, and nothing but the truth

Have you ever found yourself crying your eyes out and at the same time laughing your guts out and at the same time grieving with great sorrow while at the same time rejoicing with unbelievable praise to God? Well, last night it all happened to me simultaneously. My face hasn't recovered, and my heart has been in overdrive since then. This is the first moment I've had to pass on my experience to you.

Last night Mitch and I were doing the Instant Messaging thing, and he told me about his phone calls to Stacy, which you eventually intercepted. As I mentioned, all those emotions happened to me during the course of three minutes. First I felt sorry for Mitch because this whole marriage thing is killing him. But I instantly switched to gut-wrenching laughter because you caught him by surprise right in the middle of his temper tantrum. Then grief and sorrow gripped me as I felt the hopelessness of this crippled marriage and Mitch's lost spiritual condition. As if all these emotions weren't enough, I began rejoicing in praise to our great God who arranges "all things" after the counsel of His will and according to His divine purposes. There in Mitch and Stacy's home, God's people were gathered together ministering to Stacy, loving her, and praying for her and the man on the other end of the phone who was madder than a cranky old boar. Can you believe it? I grieved for Mitch as he felt conviction and guilt over his unacceptable behavior and yet laughed at God's incredible sense of humor and perfect timing. I was almost overcome with sorrow as I wondered if Mitch would ever receive Christ as Savior. Then I felt terrible over my lack of faith.

Gerry, in all of this I am so thankful for you and Sue. Truly you understand the road to spiritual and marital recovery. Marriages aren't saved through strategic counseling alone. Reconciliation doesn't happen because a trained person manipulates a couple's behavior. Victories are won by God for people who understand that the real battle is a spiritual battle. That's why the apostle Paul reminded us in Ephesians 6:10,12 that we are to "be strong in the Lord and in the strength of His might," because "our struggle is not against flesh and blood, but against the rulers, against the powers, against the world forces of this darkness, against the spiritual forces of wickedness."

Gerry, I was so happy to hear of your Bible study and prayer at Stacy's home. It reminded me again that the *truth* will set Mitch and Stacy free as we *pray* for God's work in their hearts. That's the whole story. So keep praying! Keep truth-telling! Keep mentoring!

Let's remember that this marriage is at a critical stage. It's my prayer that Mitch and Stacy are at the end of themselves and their foolishness and on their way to a new relationship. However, you and I know for that to happen Mitch must put his faith and trust in Jesus Christ and Stacy must repent of her sin. Only God can get those things done, but He's using you and Sue in a big way as we press on. So keep up the good work in Wyoming!

You are a faithful and loving man, Gerry. I respect you and thank God for you.

The Rev

FROM: Carter

TO: Mitch

SUBJECT: The fool has said in his heart . . .

Hey Mitch,

Let's start with something important for once. Ready? OK, here we go. How do you eat a nice big steak? Three words. Often, medium, and small. Eat steak often! Cook steak medium! Take small bites! When eating a nice T-bone, it's best to cut it down into small pieces so you don't choke to death. Then every little piece of steak can be mixed with a few taters and a bit of onion. Now that's a meal to fire your rockets! We're talkin' food! A man can make it through any day provided he gets a little steak under his belt. After all, men need lots of protein. Don't you agree? Add a little gravy, another helping of taters, and you're well on your way to a night in the recliner with the remote in hand. And how about some cherry pie for dessert with an ice cream chaser and a cup of coffee? There you have it—a meal set for a (rather large) king. Hang on for a second, I need to talk with Minnie about what's for dinner!

I'm back. So here's the deal. Getting around a big subject like self-centeredness is just as tough as slamming a big T-bone. You need to break it down into bite-sized pieces, mix it with gravy, and add taters. That's what I'm trying to do with this subject. Self-centeredness can't be devoured in one big bite. It's important to eat the whole thing, but you can't do it all at once. The more you understand self-centeredness and its ugly nature, the more changes you'll be able to make in your life and marriage.

Is the smell of steak distracting you? Maybe some chips and dip would help you stay with me!

Do you know any fools? After what happened last night, I'll bet you know at least one. Well, you know me, so that makes two. In fact, we both know lots of people who act foolishly. They're everywhere. The Bible devotes sixty-six verses to describing the fool, his character, and his actions. I've listed a few of the phrases found in these verses below. Be sure to keep your recent marital experiences (especially the ones from last night) in mind as you look over the list.

__The fool says there is no God
__The fool lacks understanding
__The fool hates correction and discipline
__The fool slanders others
__The fool loves to do mischief
__The fool is always right in his own eyes
__The fool exposes his foolishness
__The fool is arrogant and careless
__The fool appears wiser when he keeps his mouth shut
__The fool hates understanding
__The fool is perverse in his speech
__The fool always quarrels
__The fool has no honor
__The fool trusts in his own heart
__The fool loses his temper
__The fool walks in darkness
__The fool is a sluggard
__The fool has a big mouth

Pretty descriptive, huh? Whenever I think about this list, I just about hyperventilate. I can't believe how accurately it describes some of my actions and attitudes. How about you? I'd say you hit most of them last night. If you want to know the truth, this list pretty much describes all of us self-centered guys. What do you think about that? Can you see the correlation between a fool and a self-centered person?

Nabal, a self-centered fool mentioned in the Bible, lost a beautiful and intelligent wife as a direct result of his bull-headed ways. I'd like you to read his story for yourself. It's only two pages long, so it shouldn't take more than ten minutes. It's in the Old Testament of your Bible, in 1 Samuel 25:2-42. Please read it right now.

Are you finished? Here's the question: who was foolish, and who was not? The guy who had everything and lost it through brute self-centeredness? Or the woman who made great sacrifices to redeem a devastating situation? (We'll let that be a rhetorical question.)

Now, assuming you are still with me, I'd like to ask you a few more questions. Feel free to review the list to find your answers. Ready?

1. Was Nabal a fool because he didn't have anything to do with God? (Yes or No)
2. Was Nabal a fool because he mismanaged his riches? (Yes or No)
3. Was Nabal a fool for raising sheep? (Yes, Yes, and Yes!)
4. Was Nabal a fool because he was harsh and evil in his dealings with others? (Yes or No)
5. Was Nabal a fool because of his anger? (Yes or No)
6. Was Nabal a fool because of his big mouth? (Yes or No)
7. Was Nabal a fool because he really didn't understand his wife? (Yes or No)
8. Was Nabal a fool because he was arrogant and careless? (Yes or No)
9. Was Nabal a fool for not controlling his drinking? (Yes or No)
10. Was Nabal a fool because he continually put others down? (Yes or No)
11. Are there consequences for being self-centered? (Yes or No)

Before I sign off, I want to give you one final test. This one isn't about Nabal, it's about you. It's designed to help you get your arms around your foolishness. I'd normally recommend asking Stacy to help you with it, but I don't want her input to skew your test results, if you know what I mean. Besides, this should be easy. I'll ask only simple questions requiring simple answers. After all, we guys don't have patience for much more than a few words. Here are a few warm-up questions to help get you into a testy mood.

a. Two plus two, minus one, times zero, equals three. (Yes or No)
b. Which would you rather have stuck in your nose: a barbed fishing hook or a piece of barbed wire? Which would hurt more to pull out?
c. Is a rainbow trout known by the rainbow stripe on its side or by its rainbow-colored spots?
d. Does "navel orange" refer to a fruit or a belly button disease?
e. My wife is the lucky, luckier, or luckiest woman in the world to have me as her husband. (Circle as many as you want—she'll say they're all false.)

You must be exhausted after such a grueling warm-up. Better get your second wind because here comes the actual test. Make sure your puny male ego has a bullet to bite on, and remember to consult my "characteristics of the fool" list during this test.

1. I am like Nabal in these three specific ways:

A.

B.

C.

2. My wife would say I'm like Nabal in these three specific ways:

A.

B.

C.

3. My self-centeredness expresses itself in these three ways:

   A.

   B.

   C.

4. The description of a fool fits me at times because I occasionally find myself doing these things (you may refer to my "characteristics of the fool" list at the beginning of this email for help answering this one):

   A.

   B.

   C.

   D.

   E.

Don't overdo it—you can stop at five.

Well, that's it. You have completed the test. I hope you and your marriage will both be helped as you recognize some of the self-centered behaviors that make you a fool. I know you're self-centered, your wife knows you're self-centered, and you know you're self-centered. But now we've identified some tangible behaviors and attitudes you can work on. What do you say?

Until next time, keep your test pencil sharp and lubricate it often by drawing on your tongue. That will also help keep your foot out of your mouth.

The Rev

FROM: Carter

TO: Mitch

SUBJECT: Calling people fools

Hi Mitch!

Thanks for the phone call. Glad you enjoyed my last email. Sorry it was a little corny—corny is as corny does.

Hey, a comment you made stuck with me today—the one about there being plenty of loving and intelligent people who don't believe in God. Of course, your point was that it seems arrogant for me (or the Bible) to call people fools just because they hold different religious convictions than I do. Let's have a heart-to-heart discussion about this soon. I think it's the most important issue on earth. For now, I'd like to throw out two simple illustrations.

First, picture a universe created by an all-powerful, good, and loving being. He sets life up so it functions in a good and rational way. He puts people in his universe and says, "Here's how I've designed it to work. Live according to these guidelines and you'll thrive. You'll also get to know me better, which is important because when you're done here you'll get to come live with me in my perfect world. By the way, I'll make you perfect, too, so you'll fit in when you get here."

Then picture most people in his universe mocking and ignoring him, trashing the place, and violating one another in devastating ways. Consequently their journeys through life are destructive, and their eternal resting place is in a horrible land populated by evil beings whose only desire is to torture and torment.

Assuming this little description is totally true, who is wise and who is foolish? The ones who believe in the Creator and do what He says? Or, the ones who don't? The Bible says that this is reality. We can believe it (wisdom) or suffer the consequences (foolishness).

Let's say there are two identical Z's in the showroom the day you go shopping. You buy one of them, take it home, pamper it, and keep it fully serviced for five years. The other one is acquired by an arrogant, lazy, reckless teenager who has been spoiled rotten by his parents. From the moment he drives the car off the showroom floor, he beats the living daylights out of it (as only a young adolescent male can do). Now, which Z is still going to be in prime condition and fetch top dollar when they both go up for resale in five years? Which owner is the fool—the one whose attitudes and actions reflect what is best or the one who gives his undisciplined attitudes and actions free reign as if money grows on trees and there's no tomorrow? (By the way, which one of these characters has been driving your marriage around for five years? Just curious.)

Speaking of your marriage, if God designed marriage, which He did, and He has a list of "best practices" for making marriages thrive, which He does, it follows that the closer you and Stacy get to God the better your marriage will become. Minnie illustrates this principle with a triangle. Picture a three-sided "Yield" sign like they have on highway entrance ramps. The two lower corners represent the husband and wife, and God is at the top corner. The closer the husband and wife get to God by moving up the sides of the triangle, the closer they get to each other. It's a nice way of saying that true intimacy in a relationship is measured by our spiritual progress individually. When God becomes the third member of the marital relationship and His Word has the authority to correct, reprove, rebuke, and instruct in righteousness (2 Timothy 3:16), the self-centered tendencies of both husbands and wives are held in check by God's guidelines for a wonderful marriage. (Remember the "owner's manual" illustration? Same thing.)

Mitch, there are plenty of colorful symptoms taking center stage these days as reasons for divorce: poor communication, financial tensions, in-law trouble, sexual misconduct, relational gridlock, career conflict, and so forth. However, behind the scenes lurks an enemy of gigantic proportions—the real enemy responsible for failed marriages.

Self-centeredness. Blaming marital failure on "sexual misconduct" is like blaming the dashboard warning light for brake failure. There are many symptoms out there, but only one real cause. Self-centeredness. My needs first, your needs last. (Check out the attached *Life at the Lazy-U* and then repeat after me: NOT!)

The bottom line is this. For us to persist in our self-centered ways when we know they're ruining our marriages is just plain foolish.

Well, I promised Minnie I'd take her to her favorite restaurant for dinner, so off we go. Keep polishing that Z of yours, and keep investing in your marriage. It will be worth it.

The Rev

P.S. How's it going with Stu? Do the two of you ever talk about Stacy? Have you been able to describe her in such attractive terms that he encourages you to try to work things out with her? Just wondering.

6:15 PM

STACY: Hi Carter. Do you have a few minutes to "chat" right now? I've wanted to talk with you so badly since my email about Mr. X. I know you and Minnie *told* me you loved me the next day when you called, but I can't stop feeling awful for letting you down. Do you really still love me?

CARTER: Of course Minnie and I love you. Our love isn't based on what you do but on who you are. We've all made wrong choices, Stacy. That's no reason to stop loving someone, only to be more grateful for God's wonderful gift of forgiveness.

STACY: Boy, I sure am thankful for that. What I've gotten myself into certainly has tested my faith in His unconditional love. This happened with lightning speed. I never planned or expected anything like it. Of course I've read about affairs everywhere, but I never thought it would happen to me. I'm so thankful for Gerry and Sue. They came over to my house the very next day. It was an amazing experience. They just allowed me to cry, talk, cry, confess, cry some more, explain, and talk some more. When it was all over, I couldn't even remember what I'd said, but Sue told me they completely understood. Then they prayed for me and left. Carter, there wasn't one word of condemnation. I knew they didn't approve of my behavior, but they didn't rub my nose in it either. I really felt the presence of God because of them. On the other hand, I received a memorable call from Mitch's mother. She couldn't stop accusing me, condemning me, and judging me. Remember that woman in John 8:3-11 who was caught committing adultery and all the religious leaders wanted to stone her? If Mitch's mother would've had stones in her hand, they would have been flying my way. But Gerry and Sue were just like Jesus, saying, "I do not condemn you."

CARTER: Stacy, friends are very important, and Gerry and Sue are the best. We are all thankful for them. The Bible tells us that "better are the wounds of a friend than the kisses of an enemy." Gerry and Sue will need to confront you about what you've done and what you must do in the future, but they'll do it because they love you. You need their friendly affection as well as their loving discipline and leadership. They do love you, and this will be their way of proving it. On another subject, how are the children though all of this? Also, have you broken off your relationship with Mr. X?

STACY: The kids suffer with all my emotional up and downs, and believe me there are more downs than ups. As you know, I spent quite a bit of time with Mr. X, and during that time my neighbor was watching the children. Of course Mitch has them several days each week, but they are still my main concern in this whole situation. Picturing them being raised by a single mom really concerns me. As for the affair, I'm still emotionally involved with Mr. X, but not physically. I'm hooked on the way he loves me just the way I am. He is understanding and kind. Do you remember your first emails to Mitch? In them you talked about the significance of leading, protecting, teaching, and being a friend to your wife. Mr. X is that kind of a man. I don't think he's a Christian, but he's supportive of my beliefs. I understand he led me to commit adultery, but he leads me in positive ways as well. I feel his protection and know he cares for me a great deal. He is wonderful, and I wish I could be with him permanently. In fact, I really wish you'd pray for me about this. Even though I'm involved in Bible studies with Gerry, Sue, and others from my church, I'm still in love with Mr. X. Yes, I broke off the relationship with Mr. X simply because I couldn't live with God and myself. But the emotional side of our relationship is very much alive inside of me. I don't know what to do.

CARTER: You have no idea how many times I've heard this type of story. Believe me, I understand when a woman says another man has won her heart. An affair often cuts a huge canyon right through the center of a woman's soul. I'm glad for everyone's sake that Mr. X is no longer a physical presence in your life. Ending your physical involvement will help you clear up some of the collateral damage. There is public damage and private damage. Both will remain for some time. As you know, Stacy, those close to you who have found out about this have been affected. People who believed in your commitment to Christ have been discouraged, others disillusioned, and others have questioned their own faith. You need some strategy of confession and forgiveness. Remember what the Bible counsels: "Therefore if you are presenting your offering at the altar, and there remember that your brother has something against you, leave your offering there before the altar and go; first be reconciled to your brother, and then come and present your offering" (Matthew 5:23-24). Have you asked for Mitch's forgiveness? When you do, remember that the affair is only a part of the bigger picture. As a wife, you've failed your husband. I know you told us this in your email, but I want to call your attention to it again. Correcting your relationship with Mitch will diminish your emotional connection to Mr. X. If you fail in rebuilding your marriage, the relationship with Mr. X will simply go underground. Eventually, it will come up again with either Mr. X, Mr. Y, or Mr. Z. Stacy, you vowed "till death do us part," and that should be your present goal. That's what is best for you and for your children. Your friends who love you will be patient, but you must work toward the goal of saving your marriage.

STACY: Carter, I understand I'm Mitch's wife on paper, but that's all. Please be patient and believe me, I'm not jumping into another relationship with any man. I feel the most important thing for me is to stay close to my church family for accountability. I've met with the elders of my church, and they're aware of everything. Please continue to send me your "teaching" emails. I'm learning so much about my self-centeredness.

CARTER: I'll do that. The next several will be specifically about the various "faces" of a self-centered life. I hope God will use them in your life. Now I will sign off. May God bless you as you seek to do His will in your life.

FROM: Carter

TO: Mitch

SUBJECT: Your family tree

Well, Mitch, the boys and I just got back from climbing around the mountains here in Colorado. The hunting season hasn't started yet, but you know how it is. Getting into the high country and snooping around is not only lots of fun, it's great exercise. The problem was, we didn't see a single track. Pretty disappointing!

Still and all, it was gorgeous. There was a fresh blanket of snow on the ground (about three inches), and the country was steep as the dickens. We couldn't have gotten a saddle horse to a downed elk if we had to, but we did find a great spot to camp a few miles back with running water and plenty of wood. I suppose three feet of snow would cramp our style, but what the heck. The boys could always carry me out.

They razz me a lot these days, which sometimes gets under my skin. After all, like most hunters I like to think I'm tough as nails! And I am tough, provided I have enough foam to sleep on, steaks in the cooler, and bullets for my pea shooter. And provided my sons get up before dawn to fire up the stove. (I like it warm in the tent when I climb out of *my* sleeping bag!) But it's not like I'm turning soft in my old age. On the contrary, I'm into exercise (three daily repetitions of knife, fork, and spoon lifting), and more than once I've walked nearly a quarter mile with a steak-filled cooler. That's right. I'm just as tough as any other hunter, provided the boys do most of the work and I get fed properly and often. And provided they cut all the firewood and stack it without knocking me out of my lounge chair or causing me to drop my cinnamon roll. And provided I don't wander too far from the pickup or get too hungry between meals. (Does the fact that my sons gave me a fluorescent orange pillow for Christmas tell you anything about how tough I am?) I may not be able to leap tall buildings in a single bound, but I can sure leap from the supper table to the recliner pretty fast. Stay clear of me, Weenie! I'm one tough cowboy.

Speaking of being clueless in the woods, I've attached a couple of family trees to the end of this email. Please print them out and tape them to the bathroom mirror. (Be sure to throw away whatever is currently taped to the bathroom mirror.) They'll get us ready for what we'll discuss in my next series of emails. It might be hunting season in Colorado, but it's planting season up in Cheyenne. It's time to clear that deadly tree of self-centeredness out of your marriage and replace it with the fruit-bearing tree of selflessness.

We're talking family trees, here. Remember them? You put a set of grandparents in the trunk, their kids are the limbs, and the grandchildren are scattered throughout the branches. More elaborate family trees even have the ancestry of the original grandparents displayed as the root system. I think about family trees every Christmas when Minnie and I are surrounded by my grandmother who is over one hundred years old, our two mothers who are only in their eighties, our own four kids, their spouses, and twenty or thirty grandkids. (Really it's only twelve, but it sure feels like more when we're all in the same house!) Everywhere you move, you're stepping on somebody, and it takes a school bus to go anywhere together. Every now and then, I'll spot Minnie through the crowd and shout across to her, "Where did all these people come from?" She usually wags her finger at me and shouts right back, "Hey, don't blame me—you started it!" (Have you ever noticed how women never take the blame for anything? Now, whom does that remind you of?)

My point is this: you can't choose the "family tree" you were born into, but you *can* choose what kind of "family tree" your marriage leaves for future generations. What'll it be? The tree of self-centeredness with its ugly branches and deadly fruit? Or the tree of selflessness with its sheltering branches and life-giving fruit? The first one will destroy your life and ruin your marriage; the second one will bring blessing to your life and pleasure to your marriage. Both you and Stacy get to choose between the trees. Which one would you like to be growing in your home? Maybe a better question is, "Which one would you like to see growing in your spouse's life?" It's worth serious consideration.

Take a quick look at my sketches. What you're used to is the family tree of Mr. and Mrs. Self-Centeredness. As you move up the trunk, you get into the large, primary limbs. These are their sons and daughters—Self-Will, Self-Absorption, Self-Righteousness, Self-Seeking, Self-Pity, and so on. Just like their parents, these kids look out for themselves and use others to further their own self-centered purposes. As you get up into the branches, you're surrounded by grandkids and great-grandkids of self-centeredness. There are hundreds of them, every one uglier than the last. They've got names like Communication Breakdown, Financial Selfishness, Sexual Misconduct, Deceit, Jealousy, Anger, Slander, Withdrawal, Verbal Abuse, Bitterness, Criticism, Covetousness, Envy, Drunkenness, Malicious Thoughts, Adultery, and too many more to list. Just like their parents and grandparents before them, they're all as self-centered as can be. What a mess! What a sick family tree! Somebody get a chain saw, quick!

On the other page, you see the family tree of Mr. and Mrs. Selflessness. It's just as large as the tree of Self-Centeredness, but far more healthy. Its limbs are also made up of sons and daughters with names like Honesty, Virtue, Humility, and Integrity, to name a few. Its branches of grandchildren fill the sky. They are named Love, Joy, Peace, Patience, Kindness, Goodness, Faithfulness, Gentleness, Self-Control, Respect, Compassion, Sensitivity, and so on.

Mitch, can you see where this is going? Can you imagine a marriage and family rooted in love, kindness, and joy—the fruit of selflessness—rather than anger, lust, and jealousy? Would you like your marriage to Stacy to be characterized by commitment, compassion, loving devotion, and respect? Then it's time to think about the tree you're cultivating.

When Minnie and I were having problems in our marriage, it was because I was planting, fertilizing, and nurturing the wrong tree. Self-Centeredness and its ugly offspring—Self-Focus, Self-Pity, and

Self-Will—were reproducing in my life faster than rabbits. I thought only of myself and used my wife for my personal gratification and convenience. Just think of it—living with a beautiful cook, housekeeper, dishwasher, laundrywoman, and sex partner, all in one! Someone to bear my children and to raise them as well—all without the slightest inconvenience to my personal schedule or interests. Clean socks in the drawer and hot food (steak!) on the table, exactly *how* I want it *when* I want it. And while she cleans up the dishes (after bringing my dessert and coffee), I can moooooon the couch and relax from my hard day of minding my own business. It was wonderful! It was beautiful! It was just the way I liked it!

It was a sick joke, and I was a sick jerk. Just thinking about it fills me with shame. Of course, I never would have admitted I was self-centered, but my actions spilled the beans. I was up to my neck in selfishness, and it was ruining our lives.

Got the picture? Giving self-centeredness room to grow in your own life and in your marriage will eventually lead to destruction and divorce. Mitch, it's your decision. You and Stacy get to decide what your family tree will look like. What do you say we cut down that tree of self-centeredness and chop it into firewood? Sounds like a manly project to me. So keep the chain saw sharp.

The Rev

P.S. I just had the tree doctor out to our ranch to inspect one of the beautiful rows of pine trees that serves as both a snow fence and a wind-screen. The middle tree has been looking dry, brittle, and just plain sick. The doc said it appeared to be dying a slow death, so Minnie asked me to cut it out and replace it with a healthy new tree. Out with the chain saw and down with the tree. It's a done deal. If your family tree is not protecting your family and looks sick, cut it out! What are you waiting for? Let's make some noise!

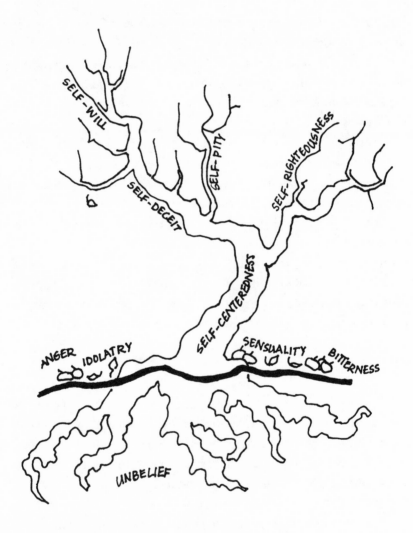

Mr. & Mrs. Self-Centeredness

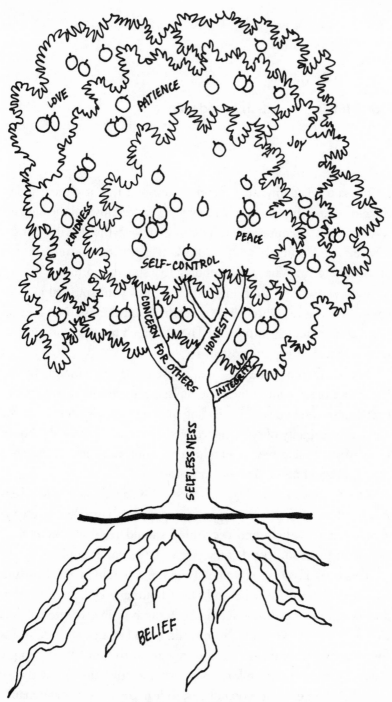

Mr. & Mrs. Selflessness

FROM: Carter

TO: Mitch

SUBJECT: The self-absorbed man

I'll tell you what, my dear friend, I sure had fun at church today. Imagine that—fun at church! I saw my great friends and the message was terrific. It was unbelievable! I didn't even sleep through it! After the service, we had something to eat. It was like putting hot fudge on top of the ice cream. What a great ending to a superb morning.

So how was your morning, Mitch? How's your spiritual journey going? Are you ready to believe that what God thinks about life and marriage is extremely important? That it's much more important than what *we* think? Keep me posted.

As I wrote in my previous email, we're going to be carving up the family tree of self-centeredness and replacing it with the tree of selflessness. Just so you know, I'll be sending these emails to Stacy because she also has been guilty of self-centeredness. I recommend that the two of you discuss what comes to mind after reading each one. Remember, your goal is reconciliation, not blame-casting.

The first ugly son of Mr. and Mrs. Self-Centeredness is Mr. Self-Absorbed. Men often have this disgusting quality. They think everyone should cater to them and everything should revolve around their needs. Surprise, surprise! Let me give you a recent example.

This week I counseled a couple and the wife told me her husband has the notion that since he works forty hours a week, everything that goes on around the house should be her responsibility. After all, he's tired when he comes home from work. (The fact that she also works forty hours a week doesn't seem to register with him.) What's more, they have three young children who demand constant care, and they own their home. It's not brand new, so it needs regular maintenance and repair. But don't forget, he works forty hours a week, so he expects her to get the lawn mowed and the leaves raked. Now, working forty hours a week makes a man real hungry, so he expects gourmet meals to be ready every day at 6:00 PM sharp. And it's not easy to put up with misbehaving children when you work forty hours a week, so he has strict and vehement opinions about how she needs to manage and discipline the children. However, since he works forty hours a week, he's not at liberty to help out with the children as much as he would like to. (Is your pot boiling yet? Mine certainly was!) By the way, a man must be properly dressed when he works forty hours a week, so his wife had detailed instructions as to how his laundry was to be done and how his socks and underwear were to be folded and arranged in the drawer. And a man who works forty hours a week deserves to come home to a clean, well-vacuumed, neat and tidy house. He would show her how it should be done, but after forty hours each week he's just too fatigued to help. The poor man. (By this time I was fidgeting in my chair and rubbing my temples to make them stop throbbing.) Then came the grand finale. This exhausted man would like to quit his forty-hour-a-week job and relax for a while. After all, it takes a lot out of a man to work forty hours a week, and a lengthy sabbatical every so often is good for the soul. Besides, there's plenty of money in his wife's retirement fund to help finance his "vacation."

Can you say *self-absorbed*? Talk about a sluggard, this guy defines one! Check out Proverbs 6:9-11; 20:4; and 26:16. Ring any bells? What do you do with a guy who thinks only of himself? He hasn't shown a shred of consideration for his wife and family. Their existence has been all about his needs. Small wonder they both ended up in my office for counseling. Just who does he think he is? Has he forgotten the four other people in his household who need his leadership and protection?

Thankfully, I remembered something in the nick of time. I'm a lot like this guy. Left to myself, I want everything to be about me. It's so easy for us to lack consideration for our wives and ignore all they do for our families. Still, I couldn't let this guy walk out of my office without giving him a small piece of my mind. I let him know in no uncertain terms what a self-absorbed man he is, and how lucky it is for him that he isn't married to Minnie. His "tiny-hatchet" lifestyle wouldn't last ten seconds in her home.

The rest of our session was anything but dull. I simply explained to the poor little man's wife that his greatest need in life was for a wake-up call. Too tired to take out the trash? Put it in the front seat of his pickup. Still can't remember to take it out? Dump it in the front seat of his pickup. Too tired to help with the laundry? Roll up his dirty socks and underwear and put them right back in the drawer. Too tired to mow the lawn? Wait until it's up to the top step of the back porch and toss his remote into it. Too tired to help train the kids to put away their toys? Maybe it's time he finds them in his shower one morning. (This was just starting to get good when we ran out of time.) Oh well.

What do you think, Mitch? Do you think any woman should put up with that kind of nonsense? That woman needs a man who stands on his feet, not sits on his thumbs. What's the worst that could happen? If he gets angry and storms out of the house, the kids can play with his remote and bounce in his recliner until he comes back. Let him scream. Trust me, he won't like shoveling trash out of his pickup for long. Wearing dirty underwear has a way of getting a man's (and his coworkers') attention. Hauling toys out of the shower will give him an opportunity to interact with the children. If he gets angry and raises his voice, it's time for milk and cookies to celebrate his reentry into reality.

Enough about him. What about you, Mitch? How self-absorbed are you? Take a moment and look at your family. Any comparisons? Any similarities? Are you working with Stacy and the children to make a great family happen, or are you absorbed with yourself? This whole thing is not hard to figure out. Is it time for Stacy to store "Sparky droppings" on the floorboard of your nice "family" car? Or have you already noticed the smell of self-centeredness?

Before I sign off, let me give you something to consider from the Bible. Remember, it's the final authority and "plumb line" for what makes marriage work best. Pay attention to what the apostle Paul says in Philippians 2:3-4: "Do nothing from selfishness or empty conceit, but with humility of mind regard one another as more important than yourselves; do not merely look out for your own personal interests, but also for the interests of others."

So many divorces and broken homes testify to the absence of this teaching. The main problem in marriage isn't communication breakdown, it's being overly absorbed with our tiny little selves. The problem isn't sexual. The problem is that (too often) sex is all about me. *Everything* is all about me if I'm not careful. My rights, my stomach, my image, my relaxation, my bodily functions, and hundreds more. When men become self-absorbed, it creates a "marital disease" that attacks the vital organs of love and unity. It's no longer about *us*; it's about *me*. Isn't that a sad commentary on modern marriages?

Selfishness and conceit will be noticeably absent from a family that is working together and living by principles of selflessness. Humility characterizes such a family. Rather than being absorbed in themselves, the members of this family consider the other members first. This is an all-important distinction. When you see a family on the brink of divorce, you'll usually find family members who are drunk on themselves, focused on their own needs, and dominating their own universe.

Mitch, I know you don't think Stacy loves you anymore, and I can understand why you feel that way. But do you suppose her leaving could simply have been a wake-up call? Many times it's not that a wife doesn't love her husband, it's that she can't bear to spend another second with a man who thinks only about himself. I hope this all makes sense. Get back to me if you have questions.

For my part, I'm off to put a bull back into the pasture. He broke through the fence without one thought of how it would affect me. That self-absorbed critter! I should put him into a bologna tube. (Did you see the attached *Life at the Lazy-U* comic? Maybe I should ask Minnie to repair the fence. Then again, maybe not.)

The Rev

P.S. Just thought of this. Romans 12:10 reminds us, "Be devoted to one another in brotherly love; give preference to one another in honor." Also, Romans 15:1-2 tells us to "bear the weaknesses of those without strength and not just please ourselves. Each of us is to please his neighbor for his good, to his edification." Pretty simple, isn't it? Whose needs come first?

FROM: Carter

TO: Mitch

SUBJECT: The self-willed man

Well, I didn't exactly *forget* that yesterday was Minnie's birthday, I just neglected to wish her a happy birthday within the first fifteen seconds of waking up. Actually, I was tardy by about nine hours. In fact, by the time I did get around to it, most of our friends, both of our mothers, my family, all of the kids, most of our neighbors, and my best friend had already done so.

I tried to explain that I really didn't forget, I was just preoccupied with other things. After all, I was up at first light shipping cattle to market. The brand inspector was coming early in the morning, and I needed to haul them to the sale barn some hundred miles away. I told her I had thought about her throughout the day and even hummed the song, "How Great Thou Art," to the beat of the auctioneer's crooning, which incidentally sounded like a chain saw running low on gas. Well, that explanation went over like a lead Frisbee.

Thinking a bit of humor might help, I told her how much she would bring at the sale barn if I sold her by the pound. I was just kidding, of course, but she about broke the china cabinet with the plate she "accidentally" threw at me. I even raised the price a little thinking a higher price might cool her off some, but that didn't seem to help. Apparently it wasn't the price per pound that bothered her, but the number of pounds I assessed. I explained I was just trying to humor her a little, but mixing weight, cows, and her "price per pound" didn't seem to strike her as humorous. In fact, I could tell by the way she was holding the long-handled fork that she was still pretty uptight!

Finally it occurred to me I could simply say, "Honey, I'm sorry for not being the first to wish you a happy birthday." Then, remembering how helpful it often is to change the subject when things are tense, I asked when dinner would be ready. I guess she must have had other plans for dinner because she threw the fork into the sink (phew!), ran for the car, and shot out of the driveway in a cloud of dust. Funny, we usually eat dinner together on our birthdays. Women are so hard to understand! Maybe it would have been better if I had actually said I was sorry instead of just thinking about it.

OK, I confess to exaggerating a little, but this incident reminded me of an important lesson: We must have the will and determination to say we're sorry when we should be sorry. We men need to put aside our wants and feelings and treat our wives with the respect, care, and concern they deserve. Mitch, there are many bumps and bruises in a marital relationship. We're constantly stepping on each other's toes. How can anyone live every day with the same people without having trials and tribulations? It's impossible. We get our poor feelings hurt over the most trivial things. Do these hurts and pains just go away? Of course not! Someone must exercise his or her will to make matters better. It takes an act of the will to say, "I'm sorry," "I forgive you," "I'll be patient and wait," or "I'll do it for you." If you are ever going to forgive Stacy for her relationship with Mr. X, it will take an act of your will. If you wait until you feel like forgiving her, it will never happen. It will also take an act of your will to be patient with her and wait for her forgiveness for the way you've treated her in recent years.

Here's the trouble. Most of us are so self-willed that we do only what pleases us. Our will is to *not* forgive, to *not* understand, and to *not* be patient because we don't *want* to.

How about a little test to see if you're up on current events? If you get this right, you can have a handful of peanuts sprinkled on some ice-cream. Ready? Who said, "Not My will but Your will be done?"

A. Benjamin Franklin
B. Martin Luther
C. Mother Teresa
D. Paul the apostle
E. Aladdin

If you picked any of the above, you're wrong. Go directly to bed, do not pass the refrigerator, do not collect 1,000 calories. Jesus Christ said it. He was willing to put his will on the back burner and do the will of His Father. In doing so, he set a supreme example for us to follow. What *we* want must take the backseat to doing what *God* wants. The trouble is, we tend to be dominated by our self-centeredness. We want our own way, period! A self-willed man will never have a healthy marriage. His wife will tire of it. Mitch, as Stacy's husband, you must be willing to yield your will to the higher will of God for the good of your family. It's difficult to do, but in order to please God and mature in character you must seek His will over yours. Doing whatever you want is dangerous. Think of how far Adam fell because he placed his will above God's will and the good of his family. You must take charge of your will in order to change your marriage for the better.

I realize this isn't easy. Doing our own thing is part of our culture. "My way or the highway" is as common as tumbleweeds in Wyoming. It's also the root cause of many marital breakdowns. Exterminating self-will is like getting rid of grasshoppers. They're everywhere, they eat everything that's beautiful, and they reproduce like dandelions. Same with self-will. It's in all of us. It destroys everything that is important to a marriage. And the more it takes, the more it wants. Like termites, self-will eats away at unity, intimacy, and companionship. Pretty soon the whole marriage comes crashing down. After all, who wants to hang around with someone who always has to have his own way? (Unless he's the only one with car keys—did you see the attached *Lazy-U*?)

Your self-will has gotten you into a real mess. But you can get out of it by simply following the example of Jesus Christ. Tell Stacy, "It's not my will but yours that I want." Statements such as, "I'm going to help you with the kids," "No, let me take out that trash," or "Let me stay home tonight so you can go visit with your friends" all speak of a will that is working for your marriage, not yourself.

Take some advice from one of the biggest self-willed men of all time. Your marriage is not just about what *you* want. Your wife has hopes and dreams as well. You need to help her realize her expectations and not just be concerned about yours. Our wives want us to share their plans and dreams as well as responsibilities at home. Don't you think it's time for you to engage Stacy at this level? It'll make more difference than you can imagine.

Well, I'm out of here! It's time to start planning for Minnie's next birthday!

The Rev

P.S. The thing about holidays and wives is tricky. Last Valentine's Day I stood in a flower shop for thirty minutes trying to decide which bouquet to buy for Minnie—imitation roses or real roses. I decided the imitation roses are timeless (like our love). After all, they won't wither in two weeks like real ones do. Although the smell was a bit different, they both looked the same and the imitation roses were cheaper. All I'm going to say, Mitch, is *never buy imitation roses* unless you want imitation steak for dinner!

FROM: Stacy

TO: Carter

SUBJECT: Things are actually looking up in Cheyenne!

Dear Carter,

Thank you for sending me copies of the emails you wrote to Mitch. They've been so helpful to me, and they must be doing a number on my husband's heart as well because he did the strangest thing this week. You're not going to believe this!

Before getting to "the strangest thing," I want to report that things are actually going well with our controlled separation. Gerry is meeting with us regularly, and we have even gone on a couple of dates. It's really been different because we've been able to be together without strangling each other. At the beginning, there was so much conflict, defensiveness, and hurt we could hardly say a nice word to each other. Then after my confession and Mitch's rage about Mr. X, neither of us wanted to see the other again. However, this separation (plus your persistence in keeping us talking) has given us both time to gain perspective. Now we discuss our problems openly and reasonably with Gerry and Sue. Gerry has really helped Mitch understand his abusive behavior. The books you sent were also helpful. Before Mitch could change his abusive ways, he needed to understand how he was hurting us and why he was doing it. I'm so thankful Mitch is willing to learn how to overcome his weaknesses. Most men would not even consider such a thing. And Gerry is great. In our joint discussions, he never allows nasty or hateful expressions from either of us. I guess he must have learned that from you.

The books you sent helped me understand what abuse is and how to be a wife who does not tolerate an abusive man. Understanding abuse helped me understand myself, too. Fear, intimidation, and wishful thinking have controlled me for as long as I can remember. Thanks again!

As far as the children go, we're doing pretty well. Mitch picks them up at the proper time and brings them back at the proper time. That really helps me. When you wrote about being self-willed, I was pretty convicted! I wanted my way with the visitation of the children. I wanted to tell Mitch what he could and could not do with them. I think what I really wanted was to hurt him through the children, but you've helped me see how wrong I was. After all, they're Mitch's children as well and they need him. When parents get so self-absorbed, they actually forget the needs of their own flesh and blood. Mitch is sad for the children and so am I. They don't understand why mom and dad fight so much and don't live together anymore. I can see it clearly now, but early on I was so wrapped up in my emotional needs I barely considered them. Here I was sleeping with Mr. X, blaming Mitch for everything, and denying the hurt we were causing our kids. I wish I could somehow go back and protect them from what has happened. However, in the midst of it all, I see God's hand moving us along. He has used my broken marriage to draw attention to my sin. I pray that Mitch will also see God's hand in this and accept Jesus as his personal Savior.

We have about one month left in our controlled separation, and I'm beginning to believe Mitch and I will get back together again. I know my heart has changed about many things. But you know something else? When Mitch did "the strangest thing ever," I could feel that his heart is changing, too.

It all began with an unusual call from a pay phone. When I picked it up, there was this odd voice on the other end. It was like a combination of a man crying and laughing at the same time. I couldn't tell who it was at first. While trying to hold back the tears, he was also attempting to hold back his laughter. The man said, "Hello, Stacy. This is Mr. Y. I would like to meet with you." It took me a moment to sort out my thinking because the strangest thing was happening to me. I figured out it was Mitch and that he was faking a different voice.

Trying to be serious, he was having a hard time with it. Rather than telling him to straighten up and act his age, I got caught up in whatever he was doing and ventured a little role-playing of my own. I said, "You must have the wrong number because this is Sally speaking." "Well Sally," he said without skipping a beat, "I know I have the right number, and I would like to meet with you. Would you be willing?" This little role-playing game was the strangest thing I've ever done, but I whispered back, "I need one minute to think about it. Will you call me back in one minute?" With a simple "Yes," Mr. Y hung up the phone. I had this deep sense of being cared for like never before in our marriage. Mr. Y had stirred up the strangest emotions in my heart. At one level I knew it was Mitch, but it was like we were starting something new and exciting. I even had a new name!

Before I could land on my emotional feet, the phone rang. The caller ID confirmed it was from the same phone number. I answered and said, "Hello, this is Sally speaking." Is this strange or what? Anyway, Mitch asked, "Sally, have you made a decision about meeting me?" In a soft and almost seductive voice, I responded "Yes, I'll meet you, but where?" "How about at the mall near your house?" he answered. Instantly there was a knot in my stomach. The mall? Why the mall? I wondered why Mitch would want to meet me at the mall? What was he up to? I began to cry because the last meeting I had at the mall ended up in an adulterous affair, as you know. But then I remembered I was Sally, a different person than before, and that I wasn't meeting Mr. X, but rather my husband, Mr. Y. Cautiously I said, "I'll meet you at the mall, but is there a place where we can talk privately there?" Mr. Y immediately answered, "There's a bench near the water fountain. I'd like to meet you there." That's the very place I met Mr. X. Was Mitch mocking me? I felt anger building up inside of me like steam in a boiler. I felt so ashamed of what I'd done, and now Mitch was going to rub my face in it again. (I've confessed my sin to the Lord and haven't seen Mr. X since.) But now all of those feelings were coming back again. I was feeling heartsick.

For some reason a Bible passage came to mind at that moment. It was 2 Corinthians 5:17, which says, "Therefore if anyone is in Christ, he is a new creature; the old things passed away; behold, new things have come." With the Lord's confidence in my heart and a true sense of His forgiveness, Sally, the new creation in Christ, said, "Is that the bench near the soda shop?" "Yes, that's the one," said Mr. Y. "Can we meet there tomorrow at 3:00 PM?" I told him I'd be there and hung up.

Now, isn't that the strangest thing you've ever heard? It was kind of like having an "out of the body" experience, only this was an "out of the marriage" experience. I was meeting with Mr. Y who is also my husband. I spent the entire evening thinking through possible scenarios. When the time finally came, I felt pretty strange. I wanted to simply call my husband and say, "What are you up to, anyway?" What I decided to do instead was this—I called Mitch at his office and left a message that went something like, "Hi, Mitch! It's Stacy calling. I just wondered if you would be free to meet me at 3:00 this afternoon? Sue has the kids so I have a window of free time. Let me know." Within the hour, I got a call back from him. He apologized for not being able to see me because he had another commitment. I told him that was OK and that we would connect some other time.

Well, what do you wear to a meeting with a man you've never met before? I knew he would be dressed up for work, so I wanted to look nice myself. "Who knows," I thought, "it might even turn into something special." I arrived right on time and took my seat on the same bench where I'd met Mr. X. As I sat there, I began reflecting on all that had happened. I wanted more than anything to have a happy marriage. It had always been my dream growing up—a great marriage, lovely children, and a beautiful life. "Well," I thought to myself, "you've certainly ruined those dreams, Stacy girl." As I felt the tears running down my cheeks, someone said, "Sally are you all right?" I looked up and there was Mitch, I mean Mr. Y, offering me a napkin.

When I finally got control of my emotions, Mr. Y began to speak. He asked if he could be the new man in my life. He told me my "old man" was so absorbed with himself it was a wonder I hadn't left him years earlier. Mr. Y said he understood about the affair. He understood how Mr. X had won my affections and how my husband had destroyed them. He seemed angered by the abuse I'd suffered at the hands of my old husband. Mr. Y said, "If I had children like yours, I would love them dearly, teach them gladly, and train them to be as loving as their mother." We spoke like this for twenty minutes, then he went to get us each a soda.

When he returned, he was Mitch. He said, "It seemed so easy for me to assume a new name and start all over again. I thought if I were a new man we could date for a while, and I could take you to special places—like hockey games!" We laughed, then he continued. "I figured we could communicate as Sally and Mr. Y without all the baggage from our past. But that would be a coward's way out. After what I've done to our family, it wouldn't be right to pretend it never happened. Stacy, this is reality. I'm Mitch, your husband. I know I've done a horrible job of it and that we face serious problems in our marriage, but I need to tell you something." Then he held my hands and looked me straight in the eyes. "Stacy, I'm sorry for what I have done to you and to our children. I've destroyed everything that was beautiful. Our love was at one time a wonderful thing, but my arrogance and self-centeredness have killed it. While my name isn't Mr. Y, I can promise you that I'm a different man than the Mitch you married. I want to tell you I'm sorry for the way I've treated you. I've been abusive, self-absorbed, and every other "self" thing Carter has been telling us about. Frankly, I'm no longer worthy to be your husband, but I'm asking you to forgive me. I don't even want you to answer me now because you have many things to consider. I've been manipulative and deceitful, and you should consider those things in making your decision to forgive me. I know there's only one month left before our controlled separation is supposed to end, but I want you to be ready when that time comes. If you aren't, I'll wait."

After saying all that he gave me the longest hug and then left. Now the ball is in my court and I need some help!

Stacy

P.S. Isn't forgiveness a new start? Isn't forgiveness like getting a new name or a new chance? What about all the awful things that went on between us? What happens to all that happened if I agree to forgive Mitch? These questions have been running through my head all day. Thanks for letting me run on like this. I know you understand.

FROM: Carter

TO: Stacy

SUBJECT: A crawl in the mall

Dear Stacy,

You were right. That's the strangest get-together I've ever heard of. Mitch must have fried his brain thinking of something that creative. I only wish other men I know would be as creative. I'd say Mitch was standing pretty tall as he was "crawling through the mall." I sensed a real honesty about him, and I'm sure you felt sincerity in his confession. Things might just be looking up!

Now the ball is in your court and you need help. Well, what do you think God would want you to do? I'm wondering if you have considered Ephesians 4:32. Paul tells us to be tenderhearted and forgiving, even as God in Christ has forgiven us. Does this apply to your response to Mitch? Stacy, remember how God (who is perfect and holy) has forgiven your sins because of the work of Jesus Christ. Doesn't it seem reasonable that you (an imperfect, unholy person) should forgive Mitch for his sinful treatment of you? That doesn't mean you should be naïve or careless in the future. Rather, it calls upon you to be Christlike in your forgiveness today.

If you fail to forgive, you might just fall into *self-righteousness*. Come to think of it, I'm sending Mitch an email about that tomorrow. I'll forward you a copy.

The Rev

FROM: Carter

TO: Mitch

SUBJECT: The self-righteous man

Greetings, Sport! Thanks for taking the time to call me. I was touched by your humility and willingness to confess your faults to another person. Actually, Mitch, this is exactly what the Bible teaches in James 5:16. "Therefore, confess your sins to one another, and pray for one another so that you may be healed." Maybe you're not too far from being truly healed by receiving Jesus Christ as your Lord and Savior. Thanks for your honesty and boldness. You are a courageous man for being such a weenie!

Here's a story for you. In the late 1950s and early 1960s, I was one of the best gymnasts in the state of Colorado and surrounding region. I'm not bragging here—I just ran out of good illustrations! I was also one of the best springboard divers in the region. Somewhere in our attic is a box full of medals and trophies to remind me of those defining days. Don't get me wrong—those days are long gone. I could no more stand on my hands today than jump over the recliner. These days I break a sweat just running to the fridge, but at one point I was a real gymnast. Want proof? Check out the medals. When my kids were doing gymnastics and diving in school, lots of parents on the sidelines bellowed advice on the "right" way to do everything, but they were all full of hot air. Most had never done it before, and it was painful to listen to them instructing their children. They didn't know a front flip from a back handspring, yet they were dishing out a sled load of advice.

I'm sure it's the same in your profession. There are those who are highly skilled and those who act like they're highly skilled. How can you tell the difference? Recognition and respect. When a man is truly good at something, he doesn't have to brag about it. Conversely, when a man does a lot of boasting and strutting and proclaiming, we consider him a buffoon. Any man who thinks he's better than he is—or better than the rest of us—is a *self-righteous* man.

A great illustration of a self-righteous man is a male turkey. No, not you, Mitch. I'm referring to a real turkey. Have you ever watched a male "tom" when he does his "I am the greatest turkey in the world" dance? He puffs his chest to the size of a basketball and struts around like he's the most impressive thing in feathers. His head turns blue, the hangie-down thing on his nose gets real long, and he's quite a sight. That's about how silly men look when they get puffed up with self-righteousness. The self-righteous man thinks, "I'm smarter, more important, and better than you." How would you like to live with such a person? How did Stacy feel about living with such a person? (I'm guessing you don't really need to ask her at this point.)

What is it about a self-righteous man that makes him so hard to live with? Self-righteous men live under the delusion that they are the final authority on all things. You can't shut them up. They have rules for everything, and those rules are the right rules. Do this and don't do that—everything from where the dishrag hangs to when the turn signal in the "turkeymobile" should be activated. What self-righteousness really amounts to is being in total control. It's about power. Insecurity demands it!

I recently counseled with a self-righteous husband who wouldn't allow his family to play with cards. Cards were evil and nobody in his family was going to get away with doing evil things. Nobody but him, that is. While his family was downstairs cowering in fear of his wrath, he was upstairs viewing pornography on his personal computer. That's what self-righteousness usually amounts to. The standards I set for you don't apply to me, but you sure as shootin' better not violate them in any way. Ugh. This guy needed a huge wake-up call, like a pine paddle over the old pumpkin.

If there's one thing that bugged Jesus, it was self-righteousness. He called it what it was and didn't disguise the problem in cordial or polite terms. Self-righteousness is an evil and relentless enemy. It ruins marital communication, destroys the sexual relationship, and causes wives to lose respect for their husbands. Self-righteousness is one of the ugliest sons of self-centeredness.

Just to make sure this one hits home, I have a small assignment for you. No, I'm not talking about taking out the trash. I'd like you to sit down with your wife and get her input on this subject. There's not a person in the world who can spot a man's self-righteousness better than his wife. (You might want to take her out to dinner first.) I've included some questions to help you get the discussion started.

1. Are men particularly susceptible to being self-righteous in marriage? How about me? Have I been overly self-righteous? (Or, when you saw today's *Life at the Lazy-U* did it remind you of me? Ouch!)
2. Does their leadership role cause men to be self-righteous? Does it have to?
3. What does self-righteousness do to a marriage?
4. How does self-righteousness express itself within a marriage?
5. Do you feel that I look down on you, or do you feel I validate your opinions and value your counsel?
6. Have I ever encouraged you to express what you really think, or have I made you afraid to disagree with me?
7. Do I always have the right answer and final word on family decisions?

Mitch, you have been making big changes in your life, for which I congratulate you. This is not an attempt to rub your nose in the past, but to make sure we all understand the destructive nature of sin in our lives. To face the worst in ourselves is to make changes for the future. I know you're already on your way.

The Rev

P.S. I think the following passage (taken from Romans 12:3) is worth memorizing: "I say to everyone among you not to think more highly of himself than he ought to think; but to think so as to have sound judgment." Jesus defined "self-righteous" people as those who trust in themselves, consider themselves righteous, and view others with contempt. Check it out in Luke 18:9-14. Isn't the Bible a great resource for getting the "hot air" out of our systems, you old turkey?

FROM: Mitch

TO: Mom

SUBJECT: I need your help even more than your support

Hi Mom,

As you know, Stacy and I have been working hard on our relationship. We're committed to making our marriage work, and it has caused us to change some things. One thing I'd like to change is the way I've misrepresented Stacy to you. I'm sorry about it and would like to set things straight.

Somehow I've allowed you to become biased against Stacy. I know I was the one who called to give you the "heads up" about our marriage problems. I also know my angry phone call was how you found out about her affair. Now I'm sorry for making those calls.

You see, I wanted you to jump on the "Stacy-bashing bandwagon" and sympathize with how she had hurt me. Your anger made me feel better. I understand you're my mom and you love me a lot, but I think I overdid it to gain your sympathy and support. It was only natural for you to immediately side with me against Stacy without really knowing the facts about our marriage. I appreciate your love for me, but I have to confess I wasn't altogether fair in my description of things. To be honest, I've not been a good husband these past several years.

The purpose of this email is to confess to you that I've failed as a husband and to ask you to understand and love Stacy. It says a lot about her that she stayed with me as long as she did. She has been a good wife and mother considering what she has had to put up with. What I really need from you now is not so much your support as your holding me accountable for being a kind and loving husband.

I've never challenged your criticism of Stacy throughout our married life. That has hurt her a lot. She has always sensed that your feelings, traditions, and desires take priority over hers. I have consistently defended you, protected you, and sided with you whenever there was a conflict between her needs and yours. That was wrong of me! I've come to understand how that has hurt Stacy.

We're trying to put our lives back together by getting counseling from a man in Colorado. He just wrote me about being self-righteous. I was so taken aback by it I decided to go back to the beginning of our marriage and fix some things I've done wrong. This has been a big one. Stacy is my wife, and I need to honor her needs above all others, including yours. Not that I plan to abandon you or Dad from now on! I just have to get my priorities straight for the sake of my marriage. I do love you and hope this makes sense. It never seemed like Dad honored you as he should have, and I don't want to make the same mistake he did.

I know I probably haven't done a great job of communicating about this, but my bottom line is that I could really use your help when it comes to honoring and loving Stacy, rather than just supporting me when I don't really deserve support in the first place.

With love,
Mitch

FROM: Carter

TO: Mitch

SUBJECT: The self-pitying man goes hunting

Greetings, my good friend! How have you been these past ten days? Better than me, I hope. I got skunked while elk hunting. At least I'm glad to be back home—my sons don't make fun of me here at the ranch. Why do young people gain so much pleasure from making fun of older people? If it isn't teasing us about the way we dress, it's the way we walk or how badly we snore. Even my grandson said I sounded like a growling bear all night. Kids are so insensitive.

Can I tell you about my trip? Great. I knew you'd want to know how it went. From the time we left there wasn't one ounce of consideration given to my considerable age. In many countries, older people are treated with respect. Not here in the US of A. In our country everything is about young people—from diets to clothing. Who cares about seniors?

Anyway, my boys (who are my favorite hunting partners) wanted to leave at 5:00 in the morning, which means I had to get up at 4:00. Our roosters aren't even awake at that hour. It took me almost twenty minutes to find the floor (where my clothes were piled), the light switch (to make sure I didn't get dressed backwards), and my toothbrush (not that I'd need it on a hunting trip). Then, still half asleep, I tossed all my stuff into our family car instead of the pickup. Oops.

To the untrained eye, my stuff might have seemed pretty disorganized. Real hunters know better. They know if it's organized, it's not true hunting. After all, a real hunter needs lots of stuff. Plenty of bullets are at the top of the list, along with your favorite rifle. (It will minimize frustration if the bullets are the same caliber as the rifle.) Then come all the secondary items like your tent, stove, meat saw, rope (in case you have to tie up one of your smart-alecky kids), dry matches (as if anybody ever packs wet ones), space blanket (in case you need to be airlifted), coat, boots, pants, one shirt, and a grungy old cowboy hat. After going through the list with Minnie the night before, she reminded me that since I'd be gone for more than a week, I might need a change of underwear. She was right, of course, so I threw in another pair of socks.

Finally I fired up the old pickup and pointed it toward the nearest coffee shop. (Can't do anything without caffeine.) Along the way I stopped at my youngest son's house to get him and pick up our food for the week. When I got to his house he was still in bed. (He later informed me that when a real hunter plans to go hunting at 5:00 in the morning, he actually means 7:00. After all, he argued, you can't do anything in the dark.) Young people . . .

After picking up my other son and grandson, we were off to Frasier, Colorado, which is considered the "icebox of the world." My arthritis couldn't wait to get there! Since we were packing into the mountains on horses (borrowed from my son's friend since mine were down with some kind of horse flu), I was feeling upbeat. After arriving at the trailhead, we loaded the packhorses, saddled the riding horses, and took off excitedly. That excitement lasted about five seconds for me. Mitch, let me warn you about something. When the horse you're riding has a name like Stranglehold, Wild Lightning, or Sledgehammer, it means you're about to make a memory. My first clue that something was wrong came when I noticed the tiny pitchfork brand on his rump. I was afraid to ask his name so I just called him Horse. (Thunder & Dynamite is also a bad name for a horse.) Since I've spent a lot of time in the saddle, it didn't bother me that the boys were winking at each other and casting glances my way. I didn't even mind their outright guffawing as Horse began to pitch in the middle of the trail. I'd show them. It's been a long time since any horse unloaded this cowboy. Unfortunately, I failed to check the stirrups before heading out. As you know, the length of the stirrups has a lot to do with the comfort of your ride. This saddle had been fit for a ten-year-old kid. The trouble was, everyone else had already started up the trail, and my horse wasn't about to be left behind. (Nightmare and Black Widow are also bad names for horses.) I was fine for about a hundred yards, but the constant irritation of my knees rubbing against my chin was getting on my nerves. My sons calling me "old jockey" every few minutes didn't help my attitude either.

We eventually came to a small creek. All the other horses waded across, but not mine. He stood on his hind legs and tried to scrape me off with a low-hanging tree branch as he leaped over the water. I was not amused by this, nor by the uproarious laughter coming from my sons and grandson. By the time we arrived at our campsite it took almost two hours before I could straighten my legs and relax my grip. Wouldn't you know the only thing I could do after unsaddling the horses was to sit in a lawn chair holding a cinnamon roll. Lousy horse. Lousy, disrespectful kids.

Well, Tex, there's more to tell about the trip, but it'll have to wait. The memories of what I've just been through are just too painful.

Speaking of which, have you ever been to a pity party? You've now been through at least part of mine. Remember old Mr. and Mrs. Self-Centered? Well, Mitch, one of their favorite children is Self-Pity. He's also the favorite of most men. Let me give you a few tips on how to spot self-pity in men. Listen carefully . . .

1. Everyone takes advantage of me!
2. Nobody appreciates all that I do!
3. Nobody cares how I feel!
4. Nobody understands how hard I work!
5. My wife and kids constantly make fun of me!
6. I work hard every day and I'm tired!
7. I'm not getting the respect I deserve!
8. I never get any time to myself!
9. My wife doesn't pay enough attention to me!

Have you got the picture? Self-pity comes in all different shapes and sizes. I know for a fact that size number three fits me because every time I get the flu nobody cares how I feel. (Not that I ever pull any stunts like our hero in today's *Lazy-U*!) I remember once being up in the bedroom, sick as a buffalo with a blue tongue, and hearing my insensitive wife and her four insensitive children laughing at my groans and prayers for healing. They were even making a series of hilarious comparisons between me and various barnyard animals. Did anyone come to check on how I was doing? Not a chance. They were all too weary from laughing. Poor little me!

When I used to come home from work each day, I'd be shot. Exhausted. Used up. Did anybody understand or care? My wife sure didn't. All she had done the whole day long was mind the kids, fix meals, vacuum the house with our 1957 upright, and do laundry. As if she could relate to hard work. I remind myself how hard it is to get out of bed and tackle each day's challenges, especially when the bagel shop runs out of cream cheese. Frankly, our wives just don't know how difficult it is to go to work. They should have to try driving in traffic while eating a cinnamon roll and drinking a hot cup of coffee, all the while having to shift and steer without dropping the cell phone before the afternoon racquetball game is confirmed. Makes me tired just thinking about it.

The Bible is full of men wallowing in self-pity. Find your Bible and look up 1 Kings chapters eighteen and nineteen. Elijah the hero has just challenged the prophets of Baal (a false god) to a duel. Whichever god would hurl fire from heaven to burn up the sacrifice was the true God. Baal's prophets (hundreds of them) danced around his altar all day long, shrieking and cutting themselves with knives. But no fire came. Imagine how much emotional energy it took for Elijah to make fun of those prophets all day long. Then he had to prepare an ox for sacrifice. That meant killing the animal, skinning it, butchering it, cutting it into pieces, and putting it on top of the altar. No tiny assignment. But first, he had to repair the altar (large boulders), gather firewood (enough to burn an ox), and dig a trench around the altar big enough to hold all the water that would flow down after he completely drenched the ox and the firewood (talk about wet matches).

When all this was arranged, Elijah offered a simple prayer to God. *The* God. The *Almighty* God. Down poured enough fire to burn the ox, wood, stones, and water. Fwooooosh. Gone. While the people fell on their faces in fright, Elijah killed all those prophets of Baal with a sword. Then he climbed back up the mountain, held seven prayer meetings asking God to break the three-year drought, saw the downpour coming, outran King Ahab's horse-drawn chariot for almost twenty miles, got sentenced to death by wicked Queen Jezebel, ran for an entire day to escape her wrath, and crashed under a juniper tree.

Talk about a tough day at the office. No wonder he had a pity party when God's angel woke him up for dinner. "Just take my life," he moaned. "I have been very zealous for the Lord, the God of hosts; for the sons of Israel have forsaken Thy covenant, torn down Thine altars and killed Thy prophets with the sword. And I alone am left; and they seek my life, to take it away." Woe is me.

It's what tired men say best. Even heroes. What's interesting to note is that God showed up at Elijah's party. He ministered to Elijah, first by giving him food to strengthen him, then by giving him loving counsel regarding his emotional and spiritual condition. God enabled him to get up and continue doing his job.

I won't take any more of your time to describe many other men in the Bible who threw pity parties. Some were overcome with self-pity (like Cain who murdered his brother). Others were delivered from it (like Elijah who turned to God). Men who are successfully delivered from self-pity allow God to empower and counsel them through their spiritual and emotional misunderstandings. What I learn from the Elijah story is how God can take a busy, exhausting day and turn it into a time of blessing and healing. Elijah found strength within himself that he didn't know existed. He found God adequate for every tired bone and confused thought. The second part of Isaiah 63:9 reminds us of this: "In His love and in His mercy He redeemed them [Israel], and He lifted them and carried them all the days of old." What God was willing to do for Elijah and Israel, he will do for us.

When you're feeling down about all this, does God care? Yes. He hates for people to sink into self-pity. Feeling sorry for yourself denies the work of God in you. You can live above life's seemingly impossible conditions. God's power is waiting for you in the person of Jesus Christ. His Spirit will come and take up residence in your heart.

Through His strength, you'll not only be able to endure your hard and lonely days, you'll be able to understand God's Word and live a life that is pleasing to Him without feeling sorry for yourself.

OK friend, let's work together and show some pity for the tough struggles our wives face every day. How about thinking of something you can do for Stacy this week? Imagine her getting into the habit of feeling relief when you come around. Wow.

Later, Cowboy.
The Rev

P.S. I heard from Stacy about your "mall crawl." What an amazing idea! You're a creative genius. She was not only shocked but was impressed by your honesty and humility. God is working on your heart, it seems to me.

FROM: Mitch

TO: Carter

SUBJECT: The worst shot in the world

OK, mighty hunter. I'm actually feeling a little better knowing your hunting trip left you "skunked." You wrote at a good time since I too have been having a "pity party." Did you know I was also hunting this past weekend near the Colorado town of Radium? It's so beautiful down there. (Why did I move to Cheyenne?) I had the most beautiful shot at a real nice buck, and missed! Did I say missed? That's putting it too close. That animal didn't have a thing to worry about. I'm so disgusted with myself I could spit nails. The chance of a lifetime, and I blew it. Well, there's always next year.

Thanks for continuing to send me emails about self-centeredness. When I got your last one on self-pity, I was really bumming. You know how hard it was for me to reach out to Stacy by meeting her at the mall. I'm normally not much for being mushy. At the same time, I know I've been pretty much of a failure as a husband and father. I just needed to do something and thought the mall might be the place to start over again. I want her forgiveness so badly. I know I told her to take her time, but can you blame me for expecting her to call me back in ten minutes from her cell phone? She didn't even call me when she got home. Nor did she call before I went to bed that night. I spent the entire night "sleepless in Cheyenne" hoping she'd give me a wakeup call. But there was nothing. Nothing by breakfast, lunch, or supper. In fact, she *still* hasn't called me back. I think she's forgotten about me. Why won't she respond? I need her forgiveness, now! Really, Carter, I've really been trying to change, but I'm getting so little in return. It doesn't seem fair. She's living in my house, I'm living with Stu, and she doesn't seem to give a rip.

Gerry assured me Stacy hasn't forgotten, but that it takes a woman more time to heal. He wants me to be patient and just keep loving her. That's OK for a while, but what if it takes five years? I can't keep this up that long.

I even tried the Elijah trick. I went down the elevator and out to the water fountain by my office building to see if God would meet me there. No such luck. No clouds, no rain, and no ravens. What do you think about that? I tried running alongside a guy on a bike to see if I could outrun him, but I couldn't keep up for even twenty feet. OK, wise one, what was Elijah's secret? Whatever he had, I need it quick!

Want to come to my self-pity party?

Mitch

FROM: Carter

TO: Mitch

SUBJECT: The infamous cousins — Mr. Self-Serving and Mr. Self-Indulgent

Dear Dead-Eye Dick,

I was really excited to get your email. It must have felt pretty good getting that big old Buck in your sights. How long did you track the rascal? You were in some really great country. I've hunted that area many times. In fact, my dad took me hunting there when I was a little boy. We always worked the Sheephorn drainage off Piney Mountain near the town of Radium. Want to know a secret? I have two trophy bucks on my office wall from that country. Bang! Bang! Isn't it a kick to go hunting? I absolutely love it.

The area you hunted used to be one of Colorado's best for big bucks. What changed everything was a bunch of lousy poachers. They came in the winter and killed most of the big bucks for their heads and horns. Chased the poor critters down with snowmobiles and shot them. What a bunch of cowards and lousy sportsmen. However, the Division of Wildlife dealt pretty severely with them, and it was a good thing, too. Who knows what would have happened had they fallen into the hands of poacher-hating hunters. We don't want to think about it.

Please don't feel too down about your hunting experience. I'm sorry that after going through all the trouble of getting him in your sights you flinched and missed him. I've missed my target plenty of times. I have had elk and deer filling my entire scope and still missed. There's always next year. (So, how many times did you shoot at him? Now that's what's embarrassing!)

Well, I'd like to share with you more about my hunting experience, but first we need to establish a glossary of terms. Here are some words and phrases that need defining:

Hunting equipment—anything you never want to see again

Pea shooter or heater—a rifle

Lead—bullets

Hunting vehicle—any vehicle that can't go over fifty mph, heats up frequently, and sleeps six

"Sheepherders tent"—a piece of canvas that lets in enough rain to soak you, but not enough sun to dry your sleeping bags

The stove—a combination cook stove, furnace, exhaust pipe, smoker, and barbecue

Impassable road—anywhere you don't want to drive your hunting vehicle

Passable road—anywhere you don't mind driving someone else's hunting vehicle

Five minutes—anywhere from thirty minutes to three hours

Scouting the other side of the mountain—wandering around lost

Impossible shot—any shot you made

Easy shot—any shot made by another hunter

Head shot—an accident

"OOOOOH NOOOOO!"—there's no more TP by the old log

Pneumonia—a sudden illness you come down with when it's your turn to start the morning fire in "the stove"

"I know where I'm at"—what you say when you haven't the fog- giest idea where you're at (often applies when one wanders out of state)

Heart problems—an excuse for why you can't help pack out some- one else's elk

"Let's leave the lantern on for a while"—I'm afraid of the dark

"Wait here until I get back"—See you at supper

"I'll meet you over that ridge"—I'll see you back at camp

"Dinner is ready"—the meat is burned to a crisp and the taters are stuck to the pan

"You'll never hit it from there"—get out of the way so I can fire
"Don't shoot" or "hold still"—it's time to plug your ears
"We need a little snow"—I'm tired and would rather hunt from
    camp
"It's too hot for good hunting"—seems like a great time for a nap

Well, there you have it, Deadeye. Now you're ready for more hunting stories, which I'll send in my next email.

For now, let's focus on another aspect of self-centered behavior in
husbands. Husbands also have their own way of communicating. It's
no surprise that poor communication is considered to be a major
cause of marital conflict. "Vacuum the living room," for example. It
means different things to Minnie and me. For her it means vacuuming the whole house. For me it means vacuuming around the recliner,
but certainly no farther than the electrical cord stretches. Then there's
the issue of timing. She means sometime in the next five seconds. I'm
usually thinking sometime this week if I can fit it in.

Then there's the issue of getting places "on time." For me, that
means at least ten minutes before the show begins. For Minnie, it
means as soon as she's done blowing her nose, putting on hand lotion,
and moving a wheelbarrow full of stuff from one purse to another. As
long as we arrive before the end of the show, we're "on time."

Terms aren't the only things that confuse communication.
Concepts also complicate matters. Take Minnie's 1957 vacuum. I
think household appliances were built better back then, so why replace
when you can repair? Then again, certain "items" (guns, saddles, cowboy hats, binoculars, etc.) really should be replaced almost every year
because better materials are always becoming available.

Isn't it interesting how we men can twist and turn such concepts
so they fit nicely into our schemes and agendas? Do you suppose this
has anything to do with self-centeredness? Of course it does. Mr. and
Mrs. Self-Centered had a set of twins—Self-Indulgent and Self-
Serving. Let's talk about each of these losers for a moment.

Mr. Self-Serving always uses definitions to serve his best interests.
He likes to color the issues to suit himself. When he says, "I'll be back

in five minutes," he actually means, "I'll be back whenever it fits into my schedule." Being considerate is not an issue for Mr. Self-Serving, unless it serves his interests. When the wife of a self-serving man wants the kitchen painted, he has a litany of excuses for why he won't do it this month. The bottom line? It doesn't serve his interests.

It's easy to be self-serving, isn't it? On the flip side, how easy is it to serve others? Jesus Christ called us to be servants. He taught us to look for ways to serve others. He set the example by not coming into the world to be served "but to serve and to give his life" for others (Matthew 20:28). The thing that set Jesus apart from religious leaders of His time (and many other times) was that He chose to serve others. He was selfless. You want a model to follow? Read about Jesus Christ in the New Testament books of Matthew, Mark, Luke, and John. Why would anyone not want to follow such a man? A self-serving attitude, perhaps? Let me know what you think. (Here are some more verses to look up about this: Luke 9:23-24 and Psalm 100:2.) Troubled marriages are the result of self-serving people who are not that interested in serving each other. Healthy marriages are the result of selflessly serving the Lord with gladness and serving each other in the spirit of love.

Mitch, how have you served Stacy lately? Have you done anything this week because you knew it would be important to her? In Galatians 5:13, we are told, "through love serve one another." The Bible is full of exhortations to serve God and serve others. In fact, there must be at least fifteen hundred verses that teach us the principles of being a servant and doing the work of service. This subject must be extremely important to God because he gave it a lot of space in His book. How about listing three things you could do to serve your wife even though you are temporarily separated:

1.

2.

3.

So, what about Mr. Self-Indulgent? This guy has a thousand reasons why he needs new hunting equipment and a thousand more why his wife doesn't need new household appliances. He enjoys meeting his buddies at restaurants for lunch but can't afford to take his family out for dinner. What's that about? It's about self-indulgence. Men are great at this. A self-indulgent husband can spend hundreds on a new gadget but not allow his wife forty bucks for a new hairstyle or manicure. (Can our wives get a new hairstyle for forty bucks? I don't think so. But that's not the point.) So many wives get by on peanuts while their husbands provide amply for themselves. I feel sorry for these women. Do you know how humiliating it is to have to ask for money all the time? And then to have to give an account for every red cent spent? It's downright ugly.

The first followers of Jesus claimed nothing as their own, but "all things were common property to them" (from Acts 4:32). This same passage also tells us there weren't any needy people among them because they had all things in common and shared all things together (see Acts 2:44-45). The Bible is clear about these matters. I know most men bring home the bacon, but their hard-working wives cook it and are entitled to half the meat.

Well Mitch, my fingers can't type any more today, but let me leave you with two final exhortations. First, how about looking for some way to serve Stacy this week? Second, the next time you feel yourself about to make a self-indulgent move, figure out a Stacy-indulgent move you could make instead. You get those two things in your sights, and you won't miss. Guaranteed.

In the meantime, keep your powder dry, you lousy shot!

The Rev

P.S. Notice anything wrong with this picture?

LIFE at the LAZY-U
Sweetheart, could you come rev up the tractor so I can have more bubbles?

FROM: Carter

TO: Mitch

SUBJECT: The self-sufficient man

You're such a crybaby! I never made fun of you missing the buck. Well, maybe a little. But after screwing up the shot so badly, what did you expect? Keep in mind it takes a real hunter to get that close to a trophy buck. You did good, big guy! Your shot reeked, but tracking him was great stuff. Isn't the hunt what really counts, anyway? Frankly, any idiot can pull a trigger, but sneaking up on an old buck is a real challenge. Oh well, I guess you'll have to eat vegetarian this winter.

I didn't do any better elk hunting. I never even saw a legal bull to shoot at, and I'd probably have missed as well. My sons saw about fifty elk—six of which were legal bulls—but never got close enough for a shot.

We had fun, though. When I woke up the first morning, my oldest boy was already up, the fire was started, and a warm cup of coffee was placed in my hand along with a chocolate donut chaser. I was still in my sleeping bag but didn't feel the usual "pneumonia" attack coming on. (Check glossary from my last email). Five minutes later (check glossary), I was on my feet and ready to hunt. My boys took real good care of me for about ten minutes, then I couldn't even see their orange vests through the timber. They said they'd be back to get me shortly (see glossary), but should something happen they'd meet me over the ridge. Nonetheless, I had a great time hunting all morning by myself.

About noon I spotted my youngest son off in the timber. I thought it would be a hoot to sneak up behind him and fire one off, but by the time I got close enough I could tell he was acting serious. He would sneak ahead slowly, then look through his scope. I could tell he had spotted something, so I aimed my scope where he was looking. One peek and my heart started ricocheting all around my rib cage. All I could see was horns. My son must have heard the increase in my heart rate because he turned just in time to see me preparing to dish out some lead poisoning. I told him, "Don't shoot!" (See glossary.) With fear written all over his face, and with his hand moving rapidly across his throat, I could see he was also mouthing, "Don't shoot!" I quickly told him, "you'll never hit it from there" (check glossary) as I sought a better shot. To delay him even more, I motioned for him to figure out how many points the bull had and whether he was legal for "us" to shoot. None of this worked, however. My son kept moving his hand across his throat and emphatically mouthing, "Don't shoot!" Finally, selfless guy that I am, I submitted to his pleas and moved forward for a better shot. As I came up to where he was standing, however, I was shocked by what I saw. This critter had a nose like a horse, a neck like a water buffalo, and horns like a moose. A *moose!*

Sure enough, lying there all by himself in the middle of a million acres was a big old bull moose. Remembering that a bull moose will often fly into a rage and charge, we moved closer. When this magnificent creature rose to his feet, we were only twenty yards away. Careful to locate a tree in case he decided to come dance, we did what any other wise and experienced hunters would do. We moved closer for an even better look. Fortunately for us Bullwinkle was not interested in making our acquaintance and moved gracefully off into the forest.

That old moose reminded me of another ugly descendant of Mr. and Mrs. Self-Centered. Can you guess which one? A second-generation grandson named Self-Sufficient. That bull was satisfied to be by himself without a cow or calf in sight. He was managing quite well, thank you. When ready for action, he'd go find someone, but until then leave him be. Let the cow moose raise the little calf, do the foraging, protecting, and teaching, and he'd just stay in the high country where everything's to his liking. Know any husbands like that?

That big guy was a picture of one of my greatest temptations as a husband. I might be smack dab in the middle of the living room — or in the car with Minnie — and I won't say a thing until someone else does. And then it annoys me. What a self-sufficient weenie! Minnie often tells me that if something ever happened to her, I'd do just fine. (Marriage tip: If Stacy ever says that to you, don't ask her how you'll do just fine without socks in the drawer and meals on the table. Trust me.)

Mitch, our self-sufficiency is a real problem at home, but it's even worse elsewhere. Self-sufficiency is a spiritual danger. Most men are so self-sufficient they don't even feel a need for God. You're a bit that way, aren't you? When we first started exchanging emails, God was the furthest thing from your mind. Thank goodness you've opened up your heart to spiritual things a little bit since then. Nonetheless, we're all wired that way. I often wonder why prayer is so difficult for men. Maybe it's self-sufficiency. We don't pray because we don't need any help, thank you. Need God? What for? Need the Bible? What for? We couldn't be more mistaken. We desperately need God to guide us through the wilderness of human experience. But we're too self-sufficient for that, aren't we?

Of course, having your wife pack her bags and clear out of there with the children has a way of getting your attention, right?

Our self-sufficiency has a negative effect on our marriages. Our wives feel we don't need them and can do quite well without them. This is wrong, my friend! Marriage was designed to be an interdependent relationship. Each person must draw strength from the other and from God. Self-sufficiency kills the fundamental purpose of marriage. It's time we confessed our sin of self-sufficiency to our wives, don't you think?

Well, Minnie just walked in the door from a wedding shower, and I need to move away from this computer and into her world.

Peace,
The Rev

FROM: Gerry

TO: Carter

SUBJECT: I am so excited about what God is doing in Cheyenne

Well, Carter, I hope you're doing fine. I just had to email you because I know you're praying for us. It's exciting to watch what God is doing in the lives of Mitch and Stacy.

Remember when God put Moses in the cleft of the rock and then walked past him so Moses could see what He looked like? That's just how Sue and I feel lately. God hasn't actually walked past us, but we've been seeing His involvement in the lives of people all around us. We've never been so excited.

I know you've experienced the birth of calves, horses, and pigs at your ranch. You even had us come and watch one time, remember? I'll never forget breaking down and crying over it! I don't know what it is, but a new birth seems like such a miracle. So, guess what? Sue and I got to experience a new birth last night, in our home! And yes, it made me cry this time, too. I think I'll always be a softie for miracles.

Here's what happened. You probably know your emails have had a huge impact on Mitch's life. He has copied me on some of his replies to you. You've seen how much he has changed from how he was just four months ago. We're all pretty amazed at his spiritual openness and willingness to admit his failures as a husband. He even initiates conversations about what the Bible teaches. Last night we were all sitting around studying this passage from 1 John 4:8-10: "The one who does not love does not know God, for God is love. By this the love of God was manifested in us, that God has sent His only begotten Son into the world so that we might live through Him. In this is love, not that we loved God, but that He loved us and sent His Son to be the propitiation for our sins." Isn't this a great section of Scripture? Mitch was asking so many questions about God's love and how Jesus could love a sinner like him that we all started getting excited. You could tell God was doing something. Finally I decided to explain God's plan of salvation as simply as I could. All of a sudden Stu piped up (Mitch brought him along last night) and said, "I've been thinking about this for over a month. I feel really convicted about my sin. I realize that without Christ I will surely go to hell. I've been reading the emails your counselor friend has been sending Mitch—sorry Mitch, you keep leaving them on the coffee table, and there's not much else to read since you pitched all our magazines—and I feel like I need to change from being so self-centered and surrender to God. I wonder if you would help me give my life to Christ?"

I was shocked. We prayed with Stu, and he became a Christian, simple as that. There was no pressure from us, and you could tell God had been speaking to his heart. It was such a wonderful evening! I called Stu this morning, and he wants to start coming to our church and get into a men's discipleship group there. I just had to share this with you. Thanks so much for all you've been investing in us up here. And for your many prayers!

As for Mitch and Stacy, they're doing really well. Stacy called Mitch the other day and told him she was prepared to forgive him like Christ had forgiven her for all her sins. She also asked him to forgive her for being such a difficult wife and for being unfaithful with Mr. X. Naturally, Mitch couldn't wait to forgive her so they could put all this ugly stuff behind them. She asked him to go out with her for a romantic evening to celebrate the rebirth of their relationship, but also told him he'd have to pay since she didn't have a cent to her name. Sue and I kept the kids, and they spent the night at a motel in Loveland, Colorado. I happened to glance south later in the evening, and the sky was aglow. I can hardly believe what God is doing in their relationship.

Apparently the stress of it all is getting to Mitch. He called me last week and said he's having a hard time focusing at work. I assured him it was a temporary condition. Hopefully in a couple of weeks they'll be back together again and going strong. The controlled separation has been helpful for them. Are all men this uptight about getting back together again? Mitch has been trying hard to be a good husband and father, but I worry that without Christ in his life he won't be able to sustain it. What do you think? We really thought he would accept Christ last night. Isn't it odd how that worked? Anyway, I'm still proud of him and his efforts.

Well, my brother, that's the latest from the flatlands of Cheyenne. Keep praying!

Love to you and Minnie,
Gerry

FROM: Carter

TO: Gerry

SUBJECT: When it rains it pours!

Reading your email gave me goose bumps. You kept me guessing, too! I was sure Mitch would be the one who would receive Christ as Savior. It is a shocking reminder of God's sovereignty to hear how He is working out His perfect plan behind the scenes. Who would have thought the prayers of God's people for Mitch and Stacy would somehow carry over to Stu? (It's even more amazing that He would save someone who was reading somebody else's mail.) I'm in awe.

Gerry, this surely makes the Scripture come alive. There are some who plant and others who water, but God makes everything grow. I guess somebody planted some emails, and somebody else dumped a whole tanker full of water on the thing. Now look what we have! Stu is a brother in Christ, and Mitch and Stacy are on their way to reconciliation. When it rains, it pours!

Gerry, living with an unbeliever will be difficult for Stacy. However, living with an unbeliever who understands his self-centeredness is better than living with a self-centered unbeliever (like Mitch used to be). To be honest, I know many wives who would gladly trade in their self-centered Christian husbands for someone who would care about them. It's sad but true. Having a Christian husband doesn't guarantee marital happiness. Many Christian husbands are as self-centered as Mitch was, or worse. What really needs to happen is for Christian husbands to follow the selfless example of Jesus Christ and love their wives accordingly. Right? I believe Mitch and Stacy are on their way to improving their marriage, but let's not sell the power of God short. Who knows whether there might be another "downpour" right around the corner that will water the seed you planted last night in Mitch's heart.

I'm off to tell Minnie about Stu, and I think I'll get us some rain-coats.

The Rev

FROM: Carter

TO: Mitch

SUBJECT: The self-defensive man

I should have known better than to give you excuses about why I didn't score an elk. After all, not seeing any elk is no excuse for not coming home with an elk, right? It just means I did a lousy job of stalking my prey.

Come to think of it, we sportsmen always seem pretty defensive. We have hundreds of excuses for why we missed the ball, the hoop, the hole, the goal, the pass, the puck, the net, the runner, the target, the deer, the elk, the moose, the bear, the caribou, or the prairie dog. I can generally find someone or something on which to blame my failures. It's either the referee, the coach, the goalie, the quarterback, the defense, the offense, the pitcher, the guide, the sun, the rain, my partner, my teammate, my boss, my assistant, my wife, my pastor, the mayor, the governor, the president, the Democrats, the Republicans, or the Division of Wildlife. That's who is responsible for my personal failures.

To be honest, defensiveness is second nature. After all, we have to have some excuse for coming up empty-handed when we've invested all that time and money and had every opportunity in the world to succeed. Our wives weren't born yesterday, you know. They can smell a rat from a thousand miles away. Does it matter that we got close, had him hooked, nicked him, rimmed it, misjudged the wind, or let him get away because we didn't need the meat or don't like fish? If you don't need the meat, why spend the money? Any wife can see the bone-headedness of that. "If you're always going to lose anyway, why not buy a racket at the discount store and pay one third the price?" What are you going to say? "I'm really just a weenie out there on the court?" "I couldn't hit a deer if it was impaled on the barrel of my rifle?" "I couldn't hit a watermelon hanging from a rope in the middle of the strike zone?" No. you're going to say something self-defensive, guaranteed.

Self-defensiveness is not a just a sportsman's illness. It's a human illness typically found in men. The enormity of the male ego makes it seem necessary to win. Or to at least have an airtight reason why winning was not even an option. The trouble is, self-defensiveness in men is like "wasting disease" in elk. It causes us to gradually grow weaker and more out of control. As our excuses multiply, we assume less and less responsibility for our failures.

Where's the manliness in that? Who wants to be thought of as a powerless, impotent victim adrift on the sea of bad breaks and unforeseen complications? We have to be very aware of this, Mitch. It's highly contagious! What starts out as a hunting habit soon spreads into a man's spiritual life, then into his business life, and right on down into his family life. Just look at me, weenie! It spreads everywhere! Excuses! Excuses! Everywhere excuses!

It's kind of funny, really. Picture God coming up to Adam and saying, "What have you done? Why have you destroyed My perfect universe and damned all of your descendants for the next who-knows-how-many thousands of years?" To which Adam replies, "Eve gave it to me." Huh? That's like defending yourself against a mountain lion with a dandelion seed. Whatever happened to manliness? "I failed. I was wrong. I am sorry for my sin."

I like what the prodigal son told his father in Luke 15:21, "Father, I have sinned against heaven and in your sight." Period. No nonsense. No excuses. That was an answer his father could work with. It gave his father something to forgive. If you read the story in Luke 15, you'll notice their relationship was completely restored—even though that young man had done horrible things. This is important, Mitch. The self-defensive man says, "I didn't do anything wrong." Consequently he can't be forgiven. There's "nothing" to be forgiven. Such a man bears his guilt to the grave because he doesn't have the courage to confess it and receive God's (and his wife's) forgiveness. This is a serious problem for many men.

Confessing failure and sin is at the core of everything we believe as Christians. The Bible tells us that "if we confess our sins" (1 John 1:9) God will forgive us. However, God refuses to forgive if we make excuses for our sin. Spiritually speaking, God really doesn't want to hear our excuses. I think He couldn't care less about why we turned our backs on Him. More important, He wants us to quit being spiritual cowards. To stop hiding behind the skirts of self-defensiveness and simply admit we have turned our backs on Him.

The same thing applies to marriage. After counseling countless couples (try saying that five times fast!) I'm convinced that men have a whole sled load of excuses to explain why they're such pathetic husbands and fathers. I hear them every day. When a man's wife begins asking questions, self-defensiveness kicks in and excuses begin spilling out like bees boiling out of a disturbed hive. Allow me to treat you to some of the best I've heard through the years:

> But I've been so busy at work . . .
> I just don't have the time . . .
> Our finances had me distracted . . .
> The children are driving me crazy . . .
> I just can't control my anger . . .
> My medical problems make me this way . . .
> My painful childhood made me this way . . .
> God didn't give me the patience that marriage requires . . .
> But I needed to exercise . . .
> I haven't been feeling very well lately (these past four years) . . .
> I've been so busy at church . . .
> I needed to get ready for our men's Bible study where we're learning to be better husbands and fathers (the study is in its seventh year) . . .
> I needed to fix the car . . .
> I forgot . . .
> I'm tired . . .
> I didn't hear you . . .
> I didn't know it mattered . . .

I picked the wrong line at the bank (gas station, grocery store, toll
  booth, etc.)
I don't know what to say . . .
You know you've done it before a hundred times . . .
I was planning to get to it . . .
Nobody told me about this . . .
I was only gone a little while (six hours) . . .
I got caught in traffic / in a meeting / on the phone . . .

Self-defensiveness destroys marriages every day, but it doesn't have
to happen to us. We need to bring a higher sense of honesty and
responsibility to our relationships. We need to take ownership with
down-to-earth words like, "I have sinned against you," "I am sorry for
what I did," "I have done wrong and been insensitive," "I allowed
other things to come between us," "It's my fault this is happening," or
"Is it possible I could have some dinner now?" (OK, maybe not that
last one just yet.)

Well, my fellow sinner, I confess I got skunked because I was more
occupied with eating and enjoying the scenery than rustling up some
elk steaks. I will also confess to Minnie that I'm sorry I didn't call last
evening when I knew I'd be late. I will tell her I was an irresponsible
slob, it was my fault and not anyone else's, and that I have no excuses.
I am simply sorry. I think I will also tell God I have made my marriage unbearable for my poor wife sometimes because of my stubborn
sinfulness. These kinds of statements will help heal our marriages.

Catch you later, unless I come up with a great excuse not to!

The Rev

P.S. Since your marriage is on the road to recovery, you can appreci-
    ate what I'm saying. Thankfully, you told Stacy you've
    failed—without making excuses. You took total responsibility
    for your broken family (unlike our hero in today's *Lazy-U*). Like
    a true husband, you are living proof of what I have just written.
    However, these excuses can creep back into our lives ever so

stealthily, so we must be vigilant! I know God has honored your honesty. You're something special, Mitch.

FROM: Mitch

TO: Carter

SUBJECT: Didn't you forget something?

I enjoyed your last email on self-defensiveness. Problem is, you forgot a pretty important piece of the puzzle. Can you guess what you forgot, Old Wise One? You went through all the trouble of reminding me how important it is to say, "I'm sorry," but you forgot something. What is it you forgot?

I have a notion to end this email and just leave you in limbo. You're always asking me provocative questions that take me all evening to figure out. Now I think it's your turn, Slacker.

How could you possibly forget such an important part? I'm disappointed in you! It's wonderful when Stacy and I tell each other we're sorry, but *what else needs to happen?*

Think about it. Maybe you should get out your Bible and brush up on the subject before you email me again. You're not going to go self-defensive on me and blame Minnie, are you?

Peace,
Mitch

P.S. Maybe I should enroll in Bible school.

FROM: Carter

TO: Mitch

SUBJECT: What did I forget?

OK, you caught me! I won't defend myself by saying, "I was busy at the time of writing," nor will I justify my forgetfulness by telling you, "I just wanted you to think harder."

I failed to mention that after you say, "I'm sorry," you REPENT AND TRY WITH GOD'S HELP TO NEVER DO IT AGAIN!!!

Thanks for pointing that out, Mitch. I love you, my friend, and appreciate the way you're always alert for my mistakes and oversights.

The Rev

P.S. Speaking of justifying myself, stay tuned for my next email.

FROM: Carter

TO: Mitch

SUBJECT: The self-justifying man

I have to laugh because I just got a call from Gerry. Like any non-hunter, he wanted to know if I had killed "Bambi" during my recent trip. Sadly, I had to confess (without any excuses) that I got skunked. Then he wanted to know how I could kill such lovable, brown-eyed beauties? I simply told him you first have to find a legal "Bambi" to shoot, then turn off the safety on the gun you're using, then raise it to your shoulder, then find "Bambi" in the scope, then carefully position the crosshairs on his soft brown fur (just behind the front leg), and then pull the trigger. BOOM! That's how!

Sometimes I get the feeling people don't understand hunting. They think hunters are merciless "psycho" types with a lust for blood. How can they misunderstand us so badly? Gerry wants to know how I can justify such a cruel act. It's pretty easy, really. If hunters don't keep the herds controlled, they'll starve to death during the winter. I've seen elk and deer starving to death, and it's a terrible sight. Herd management through hunting ensures adequate winter grazing and minimizes starvation. Besides, hunting deer and elk has always been a significant part of my family's history. We enjoy the meat, and it helps provide for our family. In fact, the Bible even says, "Kill and eat." Of course, much of my interest in hunting can be traced to my dad. He loved the big breakfasts we always had in hunting camp. In the winter, he'd visit our rancher friends up in the mountains and come home with suitcases full of meat. I always wondered how he could hunt in the winter when no one else was doing it, and why he didn't bring the dead deer home on the hood of the car like most hunters. Why was it always in a suitcase? He called it, "farmer season." I realized even as a young boy not to ask questions when you were having fresh elk roast for supper. After all, "Father knows best."

Although I hope my explanations made sense to Gerry, it really doesn't matter. After all, I was only trying to justify my love for hunting elk and deer.

Come to think of it, all of us spend lots of time justifying what we like to do. It's the natural result of being self-centered. Once we figure out what we want, it only makes sense to tell everybody why it's the right thing.

Now, I know just what you're thinking, Mitch. You're wondering, "Didn't he write to me about this already?" No, I wrote to you about self-defensiveness last week. It may seem similar, but it's not the same. Here's the difference. Both terms (self-defensive and self-justifying) describe how men get around their bad behavior. On the one hand, self-defensiveness offers "valid reasons" (excuses) for why we act inappropriately. When someone challenges or questions us about something that wasn't how it should be, we throw off an excuse or two. ("I couldn't get home in time for supper because I got roped into a meeting just as I was walking out the door.") On the other hand, self-justification provides "valid reasons" for why it was best to do what I did. ("I have got to see every movie that comes out to keep up with where our culture is headed.") This person, when challenged, simply explains his bad behavior by validating what he has done.

Anyway, these ugly children are the "Siamese twins" of Mr. and Mrs. Self-Centeredness. Although attached, they express themselves differently. Together they explain away unacceptable, sick, abusive, or self-centered behavior. Self-defensiveness deflects blame with excuses. Self-justification does it with logical explanations that attempt to validate the behavior in question.

Let's say the Hill family is driving to the beach on vacation. Dad is trying to listen to a football game on the radio, but the kids are making so much noise he can't hear the game. This makes him angry, so he reaches his rubber arm (standard equipment on dads who drive) into the backseat area and smacks both kids on their New York Yankee caps. Mom is outraged and immediately lights into Dad. . . .

OK, Mitch, can you think of something self-defensive Dad Hill might say? How about something self-justifying? I think you probably can. I sure can.

Now let's get personal. My dear friend, can you give me three reasons why you have raised your voice at your wife in the past? Mr. Self-Defensiveness might say, "I have a headache, my father always raised his voice at Mom, and it's just a habit I have. I didn't mean to hurt her." Mr. Self-Justifying says, "She's a little deaf so I do it to respect her handicap. It's good to keep a woman on her toes, and I find volume communicates authority better than gentle words."

Here's another one for you. Why don't you take your family to church regularly? Self-Defensiveness says, "I'm too tired; I've not been feeling well; I always forget it's Sunday." Self-Justifying says, "I'm actually much healthier when I use Sunday mornings to organize my coming week," or "I think it's better to let kids pick out their own religion," or "I golf on Sunday mornings because hard work deserves rest, not religion."

You probably get the message. The difference is small but significant. Jesus took the time to chew out a group of self-justifying males in Luke 16:15: "You are those who justify yourselves in the sight of men, but God knows your hearts; for that which is highly esteemed among men is detestable in the sight of God." That's why this is significant—because there is One who sees right through it, and He doesn't like it.

I've used this sick trick many times over the years. I have a brand-new rifle in my gun cabinet. I bought it "to get meat for the family to eat." Yeah, right. Like all the meat I didn't bring home this year. I'm sure you can come up with a whole bunch of examples from your life and marriage. We endlessly defend and justify ourselves, but we shouldn't. Rather, we should train ourselves to see our sinful ways of thinking and behaving. You must take responsibility for your failures, not hide behind excuses and explanations. The same is true for me. I must take responsibility for not spending as much time with Minnie as I should. Rather than justifying my bad behavior by saying, "God has called me to this great work of counseling," I should confess that

God has called me to an even greater work of being a loving husband and father. (Please don't breathe a word of this to Minnie. She might pass out and hit her head on something.)

What kind of man would you rather be friends with—one who takes responsibility for what he has done, or one who sidesteps every issue and offers a good reason for any offense? Give me a flawed friend any day who will face his failures head-on. Give me confession, repentance, and forgiveness as the pathway to healing broken relationships, not excuses and justifications. Let's commit to becoming that kind of men.

Until we write again, make sure there's oil in the snow blower. Stacy will need you to do her driveway one of these mornings.

The Rev

P.S. By the way, what's the difference between explaining what happened and excusing what happened? Also, what's the difference between giving the reason you did something and justifying what you did? Please shoot me answers to these two questions in your next email. Thanks.

FROM: Mitch

TO: Carter

SUBJECT: MARITAL TOGETHERNESS!!

Dear Soul Hunter,

Well Rev, we've made it through the first part of our marriage counseling. After three months, Stacy and I are finally back together. I can't believe it. At first, three months sounded like forever, but now that we're together it seemed to flash by like a lightning strike. In fact, I understand now why you recommend controlled separations. This time has given Stacy and me the opportunity to get our emotions under control, get good counseling, learn about our self-centeredness, and implement the changes necessary for our marriage to function properly. When you've got bad habits to break and wounds to heal, it takes time. So thanks for sticking to your guns (elk or no elk).

I know you keep up with Gerry and Stacy, so I won't go into all the details about how everything is going, but I want to say that Stacy and I are doing terrific. Before moving back together, we agreed that Stacy would need to be ready and willing for me to return. So the week before, I invited her to join me for dinner at Stu's apartment. Stu was planning to be out for the evening at his "discipleship group," so I had the place to myself. I wanted to cook an outrageous meal, but I can't even boil water let alone fix prime rib with boiled red potatoes, steamed rice, and a Caesar salad. Thankfully, Sue arranged for a couple from church to help me. He's a great cook, and she used to be a waitress. They were great. He prepared the meal at their house, and she waited on us hand and foot. They even brought another friend along who played the violin at our table. When dinner was over and everyone left, we just sat quietly and looked back over these past three months. Stacy was actually eager for me to return—can you believe it? I was prepared to wait in case she needed more time, but it was so nice to have her want me back.

Now that I'm back, I'm excited to keep learning and applying all the counseling we've received. I'm sure it will still take time to establish our "new family tree" of selflessness, but it's great to know we're both eager to work on it. Our relationship with Gerry and Sue has grown into a wonderful friendship. We all want to continue meeting together, and they told us that their season of working with us has deepened their own marriage. What goes around comes around, right?

I have noticed one major weakness. It has to do with the children. I realize how much Stacy and I need to learn about parenting. Systematic or consistent discipline in our home has been nonexistent. We don't follow through with the kids, and a lot of our discipline is fueled by anger. Stacy and I were wondering if in the future you'd be so kind as to email us some parenting tips. Not right now—we still have things to work on in our marriage—but soon.

Sorry I didn't email you sooner. With everything going on (mainly hunting), I just couldn't get to it. Plus, I kept getting massive headaches. Probably stress, because they've gotten better now that I'm back home. I feel like the events of these past few months really took a toll on my health, but Gerry's got me on some vitamins and I've started exercising again.

I can't believe the difference in Stu. When he became a "Christian" at Gerry's Bible study, his whole life did an about-face. I don't think he has even driven near the strip club. He changed his Internet server and put a filter on his computer to block pornography. I can't believe the difference in him. I wish it were that easy for me to believe.

What you wrote about self-defensiveness and self-justifying behavior hit home. I do a lot of that in the spiritual department. For example, I believe I'm a pretty good person. I try to "do unto others" as I want them to do unto me. I've made a lot of mistakes, but they haven't been all that bad. Tell me, Rev, is that self-justifying or self-defending behavior? I can barely stand to go to church with all those folks, but I do it for Stacy. Actually, I have met some nice friends there (like the couple who did our fancy dinner), but some of the others give me the creeps. I know you pray for me, and I thank you for that. Obviously God is doing something because I still want to learn more about the Bible. Stacy really wants me to become a Christian, but I'm still not sure it applies to me. I don't mean your teachings—they've been great. But it's hard for me to take a "relationship" with God personally. It's easy to say "I believe," but you told me "the devils also believe." So what's my next step? I've got a verse taped to my office wall. It's from John 1:12: "But as many as received Him, to them He gave the right to become children of God, even to those who believe in His name." I guess I'm having a hard time understanding what it means for me to receive Him. Is that self-justifying or self-defensive? Please keep saying prayers for me.

On another subject, I want to thank you for your teaching on defensiveness and justification. I think we were both guilty of this, but especially me. No wonder we couldn't communicate. I never gave a moment's thought to trying to understand Stacy's point of view. I was always too busy justifying and defending my own. Out of all your lessons, this one has been most important to me. I've learned a great deal about how our communication failed. You can't really listen to another person while trying to justify your own behavior. Thanks for taking time to send me those emails.

Well, Rev, I need to sign off. We're all going out to the drive-in tonight for a party. The kids are really excited. I've got the top down on the convertible, it's a beautiful night for this late in the year, the popcorn is popped, and we're ready to split. Say hi to Minnie. I'll write again soon.

Thanks, my friend.
Mitch

FROM: Carter

TO: Mitch

SUBJECT: The self-deceived man

Mitch, I didn't think you had it in you! What a creative night you had with Stacy. Every woman in the world deserves to be treated so special. It's about time we husbands got back to being creative, sensitive, and fun to be with. Great job, my friend!

Yesterday I got some bad news. One of my girlfriends didn't get pregnant. You can't imagine how disappointed I am. Now we'll have to turn her into steaks and burgers. Oh well. That's how it goes in the cattle business. By the way, one of my grandchildren told her pastor, "Grandpa keeps his girlfriends in the barn." You can imagine how quickly that little tidbit spread around the church. Thankfully, it got back to my daughter, who explained it was cattle we were talking about. You just can't be too careful nowadays.

While the vet was doing his testing, he informed me that his wife just shot a six-by-six bull elk. He also told me several more of his friends shot some nice bulls and a couple of cows. All within a couple miles of our ranch. Mitch, I don't know if you know it or not, but we have lots of elk where I live. Frankly, it would be much easier to shoot one right off the front porch than to drive hundreds of miles, pack in on horses, set up tents and equipment, and freeze to death for a week. In fact, it would be too easy. For instance, I was working out back of the corral just before the vet showed up, and a "four-by-five nontypical horned buck" walked by not thirty yards from me. He was a thick-necked rutting buck—a real trophy. I could have blasted him from the tractor seat—but what fun is that? I'd much rather spend hundreds of dollars, work my sorry rear end off, hunt to the point of exhaustion, and come home meatless. (Is something wrong with this picture?)

Even my mechanic filled five licenses with three bulls and two cows within five miles of our place. Of course, the worst part of it is that Minnie found out. You can't imagine the questions that were tossed around our dinner table that evening. "Why don't you . . . How come you don't . . . What's wrong with . . .?" You know what I mean.

The worst part was that it got me asking myself questions. Things like, "Am I as good a hunter as I think I am?" "Would I even be able to track an elephant in two inches of fresh snow?" "What if Minnie is right?" All of this is something to consider while resting in the recliner with a bowl of peanuts.

It's the old story. Are we husbands as good to our wives as we think we are? Are we as loving, nurturing, considerate, strong, and brave as we'd like to believe? Are we leading, teaching, protecting, caring, inspiring, providing for, and celebrating our wives as well as we could be? These are difficult questions to answer, especially when we've been in the habit of self-defensiveness and self-justification. How can we know what's true and right when we've been defending and justifying what's not? Now there's a question for you. It's often better to consider such a question from the reclining position with some nuts handy. (Peanuts, not extended family members.)

Being self-deceived is not good. It's like running around in the forest at night. It's much better to be self-aware. Being self-aware is like turning on the spotlight. All of a sudden you can see where you're going. What a concept! A guy in my office reminded me of this the other day. He was living on cloud nine while his wife was despairing in the dungeon. As she sat there pouring out the misery of her soul, he just sat there with a smug grin. Finally I turned to him and asked if he'd heard anything she'd been saying for the past ten minutes. "I don't know what she's talking about," he drawled. "I'm a great husband!"

That guy had nothing but good reasons for everything he did and airtight excuses for all the things he didn't do. He simply redirected each of her observations by reminding her of how badly other husbands treat their wives. In other words, "Quit your complaining; you're lucky to have me on board." Talk about self-deceived. This unfortunate guy is missing one of life's greatest opportunities—the opportunity to become a better man thanks to the invaluable "reality checks" provided by his wife. Instead, he is engaged in one of marriage's most brutal games. Dodgeball!

Every man needs reality checks. And do you know what? That's just the kind of thing most wives are good at giving. In fact, it's like they went to school for it. "How to give reality checks 101, 201, and 301." Some of our wives even pursue graduate degrees in this area. What they fail to learn in those classes is how fragile men are and how extremely large their egos can be. When a man gets a reality check, it often interferes with his ability to think clearly. Some men appear to stare off into space. Others excuse themselves for a restroom break. And most slip into intense anger, defensiveness, and self-justification. In all honesty, women have a few things to learn in this area. For one thing, they need to learn about timing. Women who continually do reality checks without stopping long enough to take a breath run the risk of coming off as nags. And women who engage in reality checking in front of a live audience (friends, relatives, fellow church members) add shame and humiliation to the obstacles husbands must overcome. Not good.

If I had my way, there'd be more order to the process. Forget this "any time of day or night" stuff. So often, Minnie wants to perform a reality check on me around 11:00 PM, just as my eyes are as heavy as garage doors. She loves telling me what a sorry husband I've been just about the time my sorry carcass hits the sheets. No, if it were up to me, there would be an approved time and place for reality checking. Say, the third Tuesday morning of every other year.

In all seriousness, this is not something I really want to avoid. Rather, I have my mind open to hear what I need to hear and my heart willing to accept Minnie's help. My wife isn't trying to blow me to pieces. She's not my enemy, but my loving helper. She is doing what God wants her to do as my helper. She is trying to give me insight into who I really am. She actually wants me to be successful and be who

God wants me to be. If I'm not careful, I'll continue in my self-deception and miss out on what she's sincerely offering. Fundamentally, my wife does know me better than I know myself. She sees my hypocrisy, indifference, disregard of others, moodiness, anger, impatience, and neglect much more clearly than I do. God has given me this wonderful partner so I won't go through life totally self-deceived. But I must be willing to face reality. There's no room for self-deception in a healthy marriage.

I'm not saying it's enjoyable. It's more like pulling a barbed hook out of your nostril. It hurts everywhere! But, like any corrective surgery, it heals over time (generally by supper). Then I'm on the way to a greater sense of self-awareness, and a greater sensitivity to my wife's needs and desires.

Deceit in the Bible speaks of lying to others. According to Mark 7:22-23, deceitfulness comes directly from our hearts and defiles us. Psalm 5:6 tells us God actually hates deceit. Psalm 101:7 instructs us to avoid deceitful people. So, how does a man avoid himself? He can't. He has to abandon the self-deceit instead. Galatians 6:7 warns us not to be self-deceived. Instead, we are to fill our minds with truth, and we must be humble enough to embrace it.

OK buddy, what did we learn in this email? Hopefully that self-awareness is very important to a healthy marriage. Listening to your wife is extremely important if you want a nice dinner. I mean a nice marriage. If you listen more to your wife, you'll also have a better understanding of yourself. After all, our wives want to respect us as husbands and fathers, so their reality checks are designed to turn us into true heroes rather than imaginary gods.

Time to check on my pregnant girlfriends in the barn. Until next time, keep in touch with the *real* you!

The Rev

P.S. No comment on the attached *Lazy-U*.

FROM: Stacy

TO: Carter

SUBJECT: Are Mitch and I in a state of self-deception?

Dear Carter,

As usual, thanks so much for working with us. You'd be surprised how each email triggers a fresh look at our lives and marriage. It's not easy, but I believe we're stronger for it.

Don't misunderstand my reason for writing this email. Mitch and I are doing fine. After about three weeks, we can really see and feel the difference in our relationship. However, I've been having some doubts. Do you think I made a mistake in letting Mitch move back into our home? Three months doesn't seem like much time to change years of bad habits. Did I deceive myself into thinking Mitch has really changed? I was becoming very insecure about my finances, and now I'm wondering if my financial fears pushed me into thinking we'd be all right. Mitch is really trying to do a great job, by the way. It's just that I can't believe we could possibly be so different in such a short time. Isn't it more likely these are just temporary behavioral changes? I worry about whether Mitch's behavioral changes will last. Will they?

Carter, I'm a Christian, yet I totally deceived myself. How else could I have justified an affair? I want to believe that my repentance is a true change of heart, but is it really? If our relationship changes for the worse, will I turn to another man for comfort and understanding? It seems to me that both of us could be self-deceived. How can we know we're not?

Mitch has never become a Christian. Where does that leave us? How can he make heart changes without Christ? At the same time, I'm a professing Christian. I thought I trusted Christ as my Savior and

Lord, but I still did whatever I wanted. How can a person know what's self-deception and what's reality?

Developing a policy of total honesty between God, Mitch, and me seems to be the only real answer. If I could be sure we were being honest with each other, maybe these questions would go away. But how could I ever know this for sure?

Marriage is a lot of work. It's not easy to keep the lines of communication open. At Gerry's suggestion, we meet twice a week for open and honest discussion of how we're doing. Sometimes I talk and Mitch listens. Other times Mitch talks and I listen. We're learning to let each other be honest about how we feel without overreacting. We discipline ourselves to not raise our voices, interrupt each other, or withdraw into silence. These times of communication have enabled each of us to stay current on how the other is doing. Furthermore, it also "builds a fence" (as Gerry says) around our differences so our disagreements don't get out of control. I suppose I'm answering my own questions now. We're doing our best to be honest with each other, and with Gerry and Sue. It's just that I often am tempted to worry about everything.

Anyway, thank you for your emails. They're certainly making me think.

Love to you and Minnie,
Stacy

FROM: Carter

TO: Mitch; Stacy

SUBJECT: Marital "hide-and-seek"

It's been half a century since I've played "hide-and-seek," but I still remember the game. One time I hid so well the rest of the gang stopped looking for me and went on to something else. Kind of took the fun out of it.

Now, how do you think "hide-and-seek" works in marriage? Is "seeking" for your partner any fun? What about "hiding" from your partner? Is that any fun? How about when your partner loses interest in "seeking" and gets involved in other things? The truth is, marriage works better as a team sport.

Mitch and Stacy, marriage is about openness, honesty, and living totally exposed before God and each other. (Remember "naked and not ashamed"?) A healthy couple talks openly about everything and can "come out of the woods" to discuss anything.

I would say you're doing a great job of moving in this direction, but there's still one thing that will be difficult for you both. Your spiritual lives. They are truly different. Don't be deceived! Mitch, I'm not ragging on you here but just explaining a substantial difference between you and Stacy. If you understand that difference, you will be able to work together—providing you don't try to make the other person just like you. That's God's department, and both of you must leave it in His hands.

If you remain open, honest, and humble toward each other, you'll remain free from self-deception and enjoy this ride.

Keep up the good work.

Carter

FROM: Carter

TO: Mitch

SUBJECT: Mr. Self-Ambition — I sure like doing what I like to do!

Hey Mitch! Have you ever observed the complex nature of "energy" in men? Never have I observed anything so unusual as this matter of energy fluctuation in the male species. I'm taken aback by how tired a man can be at one moment and how thoroughly energized he can be just seconds later. I regret to say that my wife has also observed this unusual phenomenon. Actually, all wives notice it. I hear about it in almost every counseling session I'm privy to.

What do you suppose it all means? Guys have an amazing amount of energy for certain activities, yet seem totally worn-out just at the thought of others. From leaping tall buildings to landing in the recliner in a matter of seconds. What's going on here?

Allow me to shine a little light on this subject. You see, men have what I call self-ambition. They get unbelievably excited about things that serve their interests, and even more lethargic about the things that don't. I have prepared the following list to demonstrate my point. The items on the left generate massive bursts of energy, whereas the items on the right deplete energy faster than your wife can say, "Honey, would you hang a few pictures for me?"

MASSIVE ENERGY	*HUGE ENERGY DRAIN*
1. Sexy lingerie	1. Pajamas with feet
2. Barbecued steaks	2. Tuna casserole
3. Monday Night Football	3. Sad or sentimental movies

4. Channel surfing	4. Wife has remote
5. Loading hunting gear	5. Taking out trash
6. Meeting the guys after work	6. Playing Scrabble after work
7. Slow-pitch softball	7. Slow-pitch house cleaning
8. Riding a horse	8. Getting "ridden" about the finances
9. Polishing the rifle	9. Polishing the furniture
10. Branding calves	10. Wrapping presents
11. Hunting coyotes	11. Hunting bargains at the mall
12. Pulling a truck out of the ditch	12. Pulling weeds out of the garden

There you go! Now you have some understanding as to what gives men enormous energy and what sucks energy right out of them. Let me help you get an even better hold on this with a few illustrations.

ILLUSTRATION #1

You arrive home from work at 5:30 and your lovely wife says, "Let's ride over to my mother's house for the evening." Immediately your body starts hemorrhaging energy like air escaping from a one-inch hole in a car tire. The labored response coming from your fading voice is, "Honey, I would love to do that, but I'm so exhausted." Your loving wife totally understands and brings you your slippers, something to eat, and the remote so you can rest your tired bones. But then an amazing thing happens. A guy from work calls and asks if you can take his place in a game of slow-pitch softball. Suddenly, as if struck by lightning, you're on your feet and dressed for the big game. Confused, your wife stares in disbelief. Then, with a knowing look, she leaves the room. You know the look I mean. It's the one that says, "I'll be asleep when you come home, Romeo." Feeling slightly guilty for at least half a second, you're off to the game!

ILLUSTRATION #2

It's going to be a spectacular Saturday. The hills are calling. The old truck is just begging for a mud bath. Your mind is spinning, and the energy is building in volcanic proportions. You can already taste the magnificent adventures that await you. However, as you begin to sell the idea to your wife, she reminds you that the carpet cleaners are coming and you need to get your rear in gear moving furniture around this very instant. Your energy disappears faster than a hundred dollars at Disney World.

ILLUSTRATION #3

You have two choices about what to do this weekend. Both choices involve a ride in the old truck, followed by walking twelve miles through difficult terrain and carrying a lot of weight. Both involve hunting, and both are demanding. Where's the energy going to be— trekking up into the mountains for some elk? Or trekking down to the mall to buy winter clothes for the kids. Be careful which you pick, or you'll be in deep manure, my friend.

Now you can understand the matter of self-ambition. When a man has enough energy only to do what he wants to do, he is up to his neck in self-ambition. He is striving for only what he wants to achieve and using his resources only for what he desires to do. Like I said at the beginning of this email, I meet with countless women whose husbands cannot control their self-ambition. These guys follow their own agendas, strive toward their own goals, and have enough energy only for their own activities.

As you might have guessed, the Bible is not silent on this topic. In 1 Corinthians, husbands are advised to do things that please their wives. There's no way around it—self-ambition is sacrificed in the life of a loving husband. Before a husband understands this marital principle, his energy is controlled by his own ambitions. After a husband understands this principle, his energy is influenced more by the ambitions of his wife. Are you still with me, Mitch? Hello, Mitch? Don't have a nervous breakdown yet. Never have I heard a wife say she wants her husband to give up all of his life goals, dreams, and passions just to do what she wants. (At least not any wives that are still married.) Rather, most wives simply want their husbands to share some of their goals, dreams, and passions. To participate, not ignore.

I'm excited now. It's time for dinner, and I'm going to ask Minnie to take her seat so I can serve her. My goodness, will she be surprised!

The Rev

P.S. I understand that they bottle all kinds of energy drinks that beef up one's capacity for rigorous activities. We could make a fortune if we bottled a drink that would make husbands energetic about household chores. On the other hand, we wouldn't have any-body to fish with anymore because all our buddies would hate us. Maybe we'd better go fishing and think about this before acting too quickly.

FROM: Mitch

TO: Carter

SUBJECT: I feel like I'm running out of gas

Hey Carter,

Your last email was deeply troubling. I appreciated your corny humor, as always, but it struck me in a serious way and made me sad. Remember, I'm now reading your emails from two perspectives. The first is from where I was at before Stacy and I separated, and the second is from where I'm at now that we're back together. Just so you'll understand me, I'm reading them with painful memories of being a "tiny-hatchet" man even though I now have a "double-bitted axe."

Before we separated, I was the guy you described. I found energy only for what I wanted to do. Plain and simple! Now that we're back together, I'm working hard to be a different man. I'm still finding energy only for what I want to do. Wait, did I write that correctly? Yes I did, and that's what's troubling me about your email. I'm struggling, my friend. There's a battle going on in my soul. I know what I'm supposed to want (energy for Stacy's interests), but I can't get myself to want it. When it comes right down to it, I still want what I want. What am I supposed to do about that?

You recently emailed me about being self-deceived. When I returned home to live with Stacy, I honestly felt committed to becoming all she deserves. I believe my commitment was genuine and that I was not being deceived, but already I find myself being drawn back into old habits. I seem to lack the power to pull this off. I'm slipping back into unhealthy ways of thinking, and though I fight against it, I'm losing more than a few battles. For instance, I'd hate for you to see what I've been viewing on the Internet lately. It's not that I set out to look, I just can't help it.

Am I missing something? Or is this just the way it goes? Stu keeps telling me about all his personal victories and newfound commitment to love others. He told me his relationship with Christ is making all the difference because he's no longer a "slave to sinful attitudes and actions." Is that true? I sure feel like a slave right now, but it's so hard to understand how something I can't see could make such a difference in my life. On the other hand, I don't seem to have it in me to be the kind of husband I want to be for Stacy. Got any ideas?

Mitch

FROM: Carter

TO: Mitch

SUBJECT: The self-satisfied man

Hey, my old buddy, how's it going? How are you guys doing up there in Marital Bliss, Wyoming? I'll bet there's no snow around your house—too warm and sunny!

Let's start off with an easy quiz, OK? (Don't worry, it's a no-brainer.) Picture yourself settling down in the recliner for an evening of Monday Night Football. You've got your refreshments spread out to your left, today's newspaper on your right, and the remote in hand. Suddenly you hear a noise from the kitchen where Stacy is cleaning up every single pot, pan, and dish from supper because you bolted the moment your napkin hit the empty dessert plate. The noise you hear is Stacy asking you to "take out the trash."

We're not talking "yank the bag from under the sink and toss it in the outside bin." We're talking "take out the trash" from a woman's point of view:

1. The trash container must actually be removed from under the sink.
2. All the slimy, gross items that spilled out of the container must be scooped up from under the sink and placed back into the container.
3. All the trash from the whole house must then be collected.
4. Even the pieces of garbage scattered around the various wastebaskets must be picked up and placed in the wastebaskets.
5. It doesn't matter that some wastebaskets contain only four pieces of tissue or a few nail clippings. They must be emptied.

6. Rubber gloves must be employed while collecting trash or else your wife won't let you touch her for the next several days. (This is a problem if you gather the trash every day.)

7. Where each wastebasket was sitting is often dirty, so those areas must be scrubbed or vacuumed.

8. The scrubbing agent is not a dry tissue but a special rag laden with evil-smelling detergent.

9. Every last piece of trash must be dumped into the outside bin. Even the trash that you didn't know was trash because it was still lying on the coffee table or countertop must be gathered and disposed of. You should have known it was trash.

10. All the wastebaskets throughout the entire house must be washed and disinfected.

11. A new plastic trash bag must be inserted into each wastebasket.

12. All wastebaskets must be returned to their proper place. The wastebaskets that are left over because you forgot where they came from must be carried throughout the entire house until you find their happy homes.

13. You must take off the gloves, rinse them, dry them, and hang them under the sink, then wash your hands twice with antibacterial soap. (Don't wipe them on your pants, or you'll have to do it all over again.)

So here's the quiz. What are you going to do next?

> A. Take out the trash.
> B. Forget to take out the trash.

Like I said, it's a no-brainer. I mean, you don't want to miss the game, do you? Now, let's add to this scenario being asked to "make the bed" (a project requiring at least forty-five minutes), "feed the dog" (don't you dare just throw some food in a dish), "vacuum the living room" (there are other outlets scattered around the room, you know, and the furniture isn't exactly bolted to the floor, you weenie), and "mop the floors" (don't forget to put vinegar in the water). Is it any wonder men are so forgetful? After all, things are just fine *the way they are.*

We men like things the way they are. We're happy with them that way. Contented. Satisfied. Why bother with the bed? Just toss the covers up over the pillows and you're ready for reentry. And vacuuming under the furniture? Why wear out the carpet? And what's up with vinegar in the mop water? How about just bringing in the hose?

It's amazing how easily a man can be satisfied—and that's the trouble. When a man is satisfied with the way things are, he'd better watch out. I can't think of a better example of this than King David, *the conquering hero.* (You can read about him in the books of 1 and 2 Samuel). King David was *the man.* Handsome, brave, and blessed by God, he won every fight and was the heartthrob of every woman. He raised the nation to legendary status and amassed an unrivaled fortune. But somewhere in all that success, his pilot light went out. He no longer saw the need to keep trying. Rather, he was satisfied to wander about his palace acting kingly. "Let Joab and the boys fight the battles," he thought. "That's their job. They're the army."

One night he decided to relax, chill out, have a cool drink, and take a kingly stroll around the roof of his kingly palace. Why not? Wasn't this his kingdom? Didn't he have the right to enjoy it? (Besides, it's tough to sleep when you're not doing anything.) So he climbed out of his kingly bed, mounted his kingly stairs, walked to the kingly banister, and gazed across his kingly accomplishments. He was having a kingly time of it, too, until he caught sight of something not so kingly. A woman bathing.

Was it an accident? Who knows? Is it an accident to spend hours "browsing" the Net until you happen to click on a porn site? All we know is that she took his kingly breath away. The text says this woman was very beautiful. Picture a nine out of ten, totally in the buff. No, better yet, don't picture it. Just keep reading. You can bet your bottom dollar the heat was building in David's kingly loins. He was so taken by the beauty of this woman he suddenly didn't feel satisfied with anything anymore. In fact, he could think of only one thing that would give him satisfaction. With that in mind, he sent for the woman and committed the kingly act of adultery. Followed by a kingly attempt at "bait and switch," followed by some kingly cloak-and-dagger shenanigans, followed by a kingly murder, marriage, and cover-up scheme.

Self-satisfaction was very important to King David. He really didn't give a rip that the woman (Bathsheba) was married to Uriah, one of his most loyal and courageous soldiers and friends. What mattered was that Uriah stood between David and his new dream toy, Bathsheba. His new *pregnant* dream toy.

The problem was, what David did "was evil in the sight of the Lord." Yup. Even kings are accountable to the Almighty God! When a man's interests shift from becoming a better man, husband, and father to being a more satisfied man (forget the husband and father part), he's in trouble. When building his character or developing his mind is lower on his list of priorities than taking it easy, eating lots of pizza, and dabbling in voyeurism, he's on dangerous ground.

The natural flip side of self-satisfaction is dissatisfaction. I'm happy with myself (don't force me to improve in any way), but I'm not happy with what I have (don't tell me I can't have more). I need more, and I need it now. When personal satisfaction rules in a man's heart, he ends up with this strange combination of personal laziness and compulsive self-seeking. Go do something fun? Sure! Go do something for someone else, develop a hobby, study another language, write a letter to a discouraged friend, memorize Scripture, or visit the sick? Talk to me after the game. Next week's game.

The self-satisfied man is a lump until some self-serving notion pops into his head—another woman, a new rifle, or a better truck—then he has all the frenzied zeal of a fanatic. Stay out of his way because he will spend whatever resources he has (or doesn't have) to be satisfied.

What do you say, Mitch? Does any of this smell familiar? Probably. It does to me. So why not nail it in the can by looking for creative ways to bring a little satisfaction to your lovely wife? And how about your personal commitments to becoming a man of character and integrity? What about developing your mind and strengthening your physical body? What about reading something deeper than the sports page? How about reading a book on being an interesting father? What about helping out at the local service group one evening a week? Or, are you becoming satisfied with the way things are?

Men can do many things to give our wives joy and satisfaction. In order to get that job done, we must follow the biblical command to love our wives "as Christ loved the church and gave Himself for her" (Ephesians 5:25). In other words, we must sacrifice our personal satisfaction and strive to make our wives more satisfied and fulfilled. This takes discipline and commitment—the very qualities David seemed to be lacking at that stage of his life. Over and over, the Bible warns us to "be on guard" and "beware." Can you understand the peril of being self-satisfied? (See the attached *Lazy-U*.) The devil seeks to destroy our families through our tendency to become self-satisfied or complacent. Don't let him do that to yours. How about this—I'll pray for you, and you can pray for me. Oh yeah, I forgot. You don't have anyone to pray to yet. Hmmmmm. Sounds like some room for self-improvement to me.

The Rev

FROM: Carter

TO: Mitch

SUBJECT: What happens when a man comes to the end of himself

Mitch, forgive me for responding to your email so quickly. I have another "teaching" email almost ready to send on "the self-exalting man" but it will have to wait. Responding to your email is much more important.

Mitch, when a man comes to the end of his abilities and personal resources, what's next? For the person who has never received Christ, there's nothing next! There isn't anything he can do except tread water for the rest of his days. When you run out of personal resources—like the power to do what's right or to avoid what's wrong—where exactly do you go for a "refill"?

It comes from Jesus Christ. I've told you this over and over, so it's nothing new. But what *is* new is that you've come to the end of your-self. You realize you're no longer able to do what is best for your family. Your self-centeredness has made you its *slave*, just like Stu talked about. Why not get your Bible and read Romans 7:18-25? Let me just highlight a couple of verses that should comfort "Mitch the slave." The writer (apostle Paul) experienced the same frustration you're experiencing when he wrote "For I know that nothing good dwells in me . . . for the willing is present in me, but the doing of the good is not. For the good that I want, I do not do, but I practice the very evil that I do not want. . . . I find then the principle that evil is present in me, the one who wants to do good. . . . I see a different law in the members of my body, waging war against the law of my mind and making me a prisoner [did you get that?] of the law of sin which is in my members."

Mitch, it's of great importance to read about the solution to your state of *slavery*. This passage goes on to ask, "Who will set me free from the body of this death?" *Can you guess who?* "Thanks be to God through Jesus Christ our Lord." Mitch, this is the answer you've been looking for!

Now, I want you to be thinking as you read this next sentence. If any man is in Christ, he is a new creation. Old things have passed away, and all things have become *new*. That's the *new* life you're looking for. It's the power to be a different man, the man Stacy deserves to live with. Jesus Christ will set you free from self-centeredness if you'll receive Him as your personal Savior and Lord. In that verse you said you have taped to the wall in your office, John 1:12, God tells us that "as many as received Him [Jesus], to them He gave the right to become children of God, even to those who believe in His name."

Mitch, I think it's time I just came right out and asked you to "believe in the Lord Jesus Christ and be saved." If you believe you're a sinner in need of Christ, simply speak to Him and invite Him into your life. He paid the debt of your sin through His death on the cross, and He'll give you the power to live rightly (abundantly!) through His Holy Spirit once you receive Him. Isn't it time to part company with self-centeredness and become centered on God?

I'll send you another email tomorrow on the self-exalting man. As you read it, remember that the greatest act of self-exaltation is walking away from God's offer to save you.

With love,
Carter

FROM: Carter

TO: Mitch

SUBJECT: The self-exalting man

Hey, big guy! Stacy tells me you're back at work full speed. I'll bet the past months have taken a toll on your performance. It's bound to happen. You're doing the right thing to get yourself back up to speed. Then again, if you were to lose your job you wouldn't have to stay in Wyoming. Just pace yourself and make sure you don't ignore the needs of your family.

Do you know anyone who exaggerates? How about virtually every man who has hoisted a gun to his shoulder or cast a line into the water? These guys have somehow managed to ignore their consciences when it comes to lying. Let me give you a short list of statements typical of an exaggerating man (read: hunter or fisherman). Here we go:

HUNTER

I've been hunting since I was old enough to walk.

My first gun was a .300 H & H Mag.

That first night it snowed six feet.

The timber was so thick you couldn't see daylight.

I shot the elk at a thousand yards.

I shot the elk at four hundred yards.

I shot the elk at two hundred yards.

I got within ten yards of a royal bull, and my gun jammed.

I sat in subzero whiteout conditions for twelve hours.

I always make a clean head shot.

I slept out all night without a fire, and my only blanket was a hand-
   kerchief.

FISHERMAN

The wind was blowing at least a hundred mph.

I made a perfect cast into the hundred mph wind.

That fish was the size of a whale, and it took my fly before it even hit the water.

I've been dry-fly fishing since I was a baby.

My smallest fish of the day was twenty inches long.

I caught more fish last weekend than you can count.

I lost one that would have broken all existing records.

We fished all night.

I caught a fifteen-pounder on a two-pound tippet and released it.

I was standing in white water about four feet deep when this big fish pulled me right into the current, and I almost drowned.

My fishing partners caught some fish, but none as big as the one I released.

Who's the best person you know at cutting right through all that bull in a nanosecond? You know who it is, you bozo. It's Stacy. Wives may not act like it, but they know exactly what's going on. Guaranteed. The old saying, "it takes a man to know a man" isn't true at all. It takes a woman to *really* know a man. More specifically, it takes a wife. Wives can see through all our exaggerated stories, but they're usually too compassionate to let on. They know it would devastate our teensy egos to be flushed out.

Where am I going with this? Husbands use exaggeration as a means to an end. The end is that a man likes to feel good about himself. He likes to feel important—more important than the next guy, if possible. He likes to appear to know a lot more than anybody else knows. Even though we can't eat missed meat, losing a really big trophy fish is always more satisfying to the frail male ego than only catching a tiny one. It just sounds more important. Making a tiny deal sound bigger through exaggeration always makes the businessman feel more impotent. I mean important! Self-exaltation through exaggeration is a great way to prop up one's self—except it isn't worth squat with our wives. They can all see right through us.

Why do we continually exalt ourselves? Why do we keep reminding our wives that we're so smart, so skilled, so intuitive, so brave, so helpful, so resourceful, so trustworthy, so macho, so strong, and so right when in fact the only thing that's true about us is that we're so hungry? It's about time for us to come back to earth and realize we're just like everyone else. It's about time we acknowledge the futility of self-exaltation and admit our limitations to our wives. They would pass out if we humbly asked them for ideas on how to be better husbands or fathers. We should be thankful they're willing to give us guidance about family life. When we exalt ourselves and think we know it all, it's difficult for our wives to respect our leadership.

The Bible tells us a man "not to think more highly of himself than he ought to think; but to think so as to have sound judgment" (Romans 12:3). The Bible also reminds us we shouldn't deceive ourselves by thinking we're something when we're nothing (Galatians 6:3). Rather than exalting ourselves, we need to see ourselves from a proper perspective. We do fail! We don't have all the right answers! We're not as smart as we think we are! We could benefit from our wives' insights on parenting, marriage, and life! The Bible warns against boasting and pretending to be something we're not. This is good advice. Self-exaltation is a form of mental blindness. It's skating on thin ice. (It's also a good way to enjoy a horse ride all by yourself— see the attached *Lazy-U* and grow wise!) Jesus said in Luke 14:11 that "everyone who exalts himself will be humbled."

What do you think Mitch? I know you're doing a great job of trying to be a terrific husband and father, but make sure you don't put too much stock in how things look. Don't be afraid of being honest about the situation. Stacy knows the truth, anyway, and she'll respect you far more for being valiant and genuine than for being self-exalting. I know this from experience.

We continue to pray for you guys and can't wait to see you again.

The Rev

LIFE at the LAZY-U
LAZY U
Will ya hurry! I could shut the gate in half the time!

The trouble with reality is that it doesn't always turn out like you expect. To be honest, as this tale came to an end it left me feeling angry and depressed for weeks.

I ended up angry with Mitch for putting us through it all. I was also angry with God for allowing the whole thing to seem so pointless. For more than six months, Sue and I worked our tails off, and this was the thanks we got? I couldn't believe it. I'd always been taught that God is loving and merciful, but I suddenly found myself wondering. How could He allow all this to happen? Is He really sovereign? Does He really love us? I know He has ultimate authority over human events, but He also promised to answer our prayers. Bringing those two truths together was difficult for me following the events that took place after Carter's last email.

I realize this sounds selfish, but I couldn't help it. Sue and I spent countless hours with Mitch and Stacy. They were in our home every week, and some weeks every day. Stacy was growing like a thirsty plant, and I continually stayed in touch with Mitch, praying always for his salvation. Why did God allow us to waste all our time and energy? Do you know how many times I went through the gospel with Mitch? I explained over and over how Christ died to pay the penalty for his sins and rose from the dead to give him a new and better life. I answered many of his questions of unbelief. He seemed so close to accepting Christ as his Savior and Lord. Was I the only one who noticed his spiritual interest? I didn't feel that God was paying attention. We're told in Psalm 139 that He knows everything about us, right? "O LORD, You have searched me and known me. You know when I sit down and when I rise up; you understand my thought from afar. You scrutinize my path and my lying down, and are intimately acquainted with all my ways. Even before there is a word on my tongue, behold, O LORD, You know it all." At least that's what it says in my Bible.

When Stu became a Christian, Mitch seemed truly amazed at God's power. As you surely picked up from these emails, Stu's lifestyle left a lot to be desired. His drinking, womanizing, going to strip bars, and other outrageous behaviors seemed unforgivable to Mitch. He once told me, "If God can save Stu then God can save anyone— me included." From that moment forward, I was convinced God would save Mitch. Soon. So what happened?

Here's what happened. One night, shortly after that last email from Carter, Mitch took Stacy and the kids out to dinner and a movie. Even though it all went well, Stacy could tell something was on his mind because he wasn't talking much. "He seemed a little distant," she said afterward. The movie was about an angel helping a preacher get his church and family back on track. The movie sparked an interest in Mitch because he observed how spiritual renewal had redirected the future of the preacher's family. According to Stacy, Mitch commented how Carter's emails had altered the future of their family as well. He also called attention to something Carter had written in his last email about "when a man comes to the end of himself."

After putting the children down for the night they continued talking about what a spiritual home is supposed to look like. Mitch got pretty emotional. He kept saying he wanted to believe in Christ but had a lot of unanswered questions. Stacy tried to fill in the blanks but Mitch simply couldn't bring himself to decide.

Here's the kicker. Stacy felt something wasn't quite right about the way Mitch was acting. It wasn't like him to be so undecided, uncommitted, and unsure about things. *I wonder if he's hiding something*, she thought while getting ready for bed. Then Mitch came into the bathroom and said he was going out with Stu for a while. "I know it's late, but I need to talk to somebody."

That was the last time she saw him. She lay awake for a couple of hours and then tried calling him on his cell phone. He didn't answer. Then she called Stu's apartment to see if Mitch was still there. When Stu finally answered the phone he was so groggy he could hardly speak. Mitch had apparently tried to reach him earlier that evening (there were voicemails), but Stu had been out and missed the calls.

As you can imagine, Stacy became frantic. She called us around 2:00 AM to see if Mitch was here. As we were discussing what to do next, Stacy's "call waiting" signal began to click, so she put us on hold and took the call. So many questions were rushing through my mind. "What is Mitch doing out at 2:00 AM? Where is he? Is he with another woman?" It seemed an eternity before Stacy came back on the line. She told us Mitch was OK, and that he'd simply been driving around for several hours trying to put the pieces together (he always thought more clearly behind the wheel). His driving landed him in Loveland, Colorado. By the time he reached Loveland he didn't feel the best, so he checked into the hotel he and Stacy had visited during their separation.

Naturally, Stacy was furious that he'd driven her half crazy with anxiety, but also relieved to know he was safe. Like any woman, she wondered what was really going on. Was he alone? Was he being truthful with her? Did he mean it when he closed their conversation with, "Stacy, I want you to know I love you with all the love that is in me"? He said he'd be back in the morning and hung up.

By 11:30 the next morning she was half crazy with anxiety all over again. She hadn't heard anything from him, and her repeated calls to his cell phone brought no response. She was just getting ready to drive down to Loveland herself when an unmarked police car pulled up in front of the house. A man and a woman got out of the car and the man introduced himself as Detective Adams. Before the woman could introduce herself, Stacy felt her emotions beginning to take over (she'd been awake all night), and she clumsily sat down on the front step. Detective Adams asked if she was Stacy, and if she had a husband named Mitch. She whispered, "I am," and the strangers went on to say they were from the Cheyenne Police Department and had received a call from the police in Loveland, Colorado, regarding her husband. All she could think of was what Mitch had said about loving her "with all that is in me" just before hanging up. As the woman sat down next to Stacy, Detective Adams said, "I'm very sorry to be the one to tell you this, but your husband passed away last night. He was discovered this morning in a hotel room. The cleaning woman found him slumped over in a chair by the window. He must have died sometime during the night. There was no sign of struggle, and the cause of his death has not yet been determined. There isn't a whole lot more information available at this time, but the authorities will continue to investigate. While we're here, we'd like to call someone who might be able to come stay with you. Is there someone close by you'd like us to call?" Stacy gave them our number and there you have it.

As it turned out, Mitch died from a brain aneurysm. After all the desperate scenarios Stacy had imagined during her sleepless night, the truth came as a relief of sorts, but it was no less devastating.

Suddenly it was all over. Our friend was gone and I had countless questions. *Did he know this was going to happen? Did he have a premonition that caused him to leave the house that night? Why didn't he go to the doc like I told him to? Why didn't God wait for Mitch to come to faith in Jesus? Or did He? Should I have pushed harder for Mitch to accept Christ?* There were times when I know if I had asked Mitch to pray with me, he probably would have agreed. Maybe I should have tried harder. What do you think? Do you suppose God introduced Himself to Mitch during that car ride? Do you think Mitch became a Christian in his hotel room?

We drove to the hotel right away and saw photographs of the room as it had been discovered that morning. The Gideon Bible was on the floor by his chair. Did he meet Christ? If only we could know what happened during those last few hours of his life. It's possible that Mitch resisted right to the end but I, for one, thought God had Mitch in His sights and would eventually bring him in. One day we'll know.

My questions persisted for a time, but gradually they served to strengthen my understanding of God. His ways may not make sense to us, but because He is completely wise, loving, powerful, and good, we can trust Him even in the darkness and experience inner peace. Besides, it wasn't long before we began to experience the fruit produced by those difficult months. For example, let me share with you one final email from Stacy . . .

FROM: Stacy

TO: Carter

SUBJECT: Texas or bust!

Well, Carter, what a day we have had! I'm sitting here at Gerry and Sue's one last time. It's 2:30 AM, and we've had a *very* long day of packing, cleaning, and talking about the things that happened this year. What an emotional roller coaster!

The moving people will be here by 8:00 AM, and then we're off to Houston! My family is thankful to have us coming back home. Carter, I feel this is a good move because I need family support right now. It'll be great for the children to be close to their grandparents. My father can fill in some of the holes left by their dad. Believe me, the kids really miss Mitch. Looking back, if we had gotten divorced it would've been so hard on them. No wonder children of divorced parents are angry and discouraged. God never meant for people to divorce, did He?

We went to the cemetery yesterday to say good-bye one last time. It was painful. As I looked back over the past months, I couldn't believe where I was standing. Life is filled with uncertainty, and now I'm facing even more of it. What will I do for a career? How will I handle the children by myself? God will have to carry us for a while. My Christian friends here in Cheyenne have been a wonderful support. I hope I'll be able to find a fellowship near our new home.

I wanted to say again that Mitch became a different man as a result of your counseling and emails—an even better man than the one I fell in love with! For the first time in his life, he had a spiritual awareness that influenced his attitudes and actions. Rather than flying by the seat of his pants, he was thinking, reasoning, and planning on the basis of what would be best for the children and me. If only every wife could enjoy such treatment! I was so proud of him.

Standing there in the cemetery, I sobbed because we never shared Christ together, never prayed together, never read the Bible together, and never worshiped together as a family. Carter, do you think Mitch became a Christian? The headstone marking his grave hints at that question. Do you remember what it says?

> Where you stand I used to be
> Where I am you soon shall be
> Prepare yourself to follow me!

Many years ago, his father saw that "statement" on a tombstone in an old Colorado ghost town, and Mitch always joked that he wanted the same thing on his gravestone. Little did he know how quickly the time would come. Back when he joked about it, he was skeptical about religious beliefs. He made fun of people who believed in life after death. Carter, I don't believe Mitch was still a skeptic when he died. He knew there was life after death—hell for those who reject God's love and heaven for those who accept Christ's payment for their sin. The problem is, Mitch seemed to run out of time before making that decision.

Before I sign off on this part of my life, I want to share some of what Gerry, Sue, and I discussed this evening. Once the kids went to bed, we ended up talking past midnight, and it probably won't surprise you to know Gerry wrote some of it down so we wouldn't forget—just like that day he took notes on Tanya's questions after we left Mitch. We came up with some interesting things, and I wanted to send them to you as a sort of "thank you" gift. Your friendship has meant more to us than you'll ever know.

First, we listed some of the reasons our marriage got into trouble in the first place. I can tell you one thing. If there's ever a "next time" for me to consider marriage, I'll be looking through different eyes! I won't be as blind as I was the first time around. I guarantee it!

1. We didn't keep our premarital physical relationship in check.
2. We didn't pay attention to our premarital counseling (sorry!).

3. We didn't bother with any of the first-year checkup counseling you advised us to pursue.
4. Mitch failed to establish a male accountability partner.
5. I failed to hold Mitch responsible for his abusive behavior.
6. I withdrew into my own miserable world for too long before seeking help.
7. Having an affair didn't help . . .
8. We wouldn't (or couldn't) give up our self-centeredness.
9. We allowed petty disagreements to escalate into full-scale battles!

We also came up with some things we did right in the process:

1. We finally acknowledged we had marital problems.
2. We confessed what we'd been doing to each other.
3. We were willing to meet with Gerry and Sue for counseling.
4. We accepted your "controlled separation" as the initial step toward our reconciliation.
5. We were willing to start learning about solutions instead of just feeling sorry for ourselves.
6. We eventually shut the door on divorce as a solution.
7. We began thinking about our kids instead of our differences.
8. We began trying to live selflessly and even made sacrifices for each other.
9. We separated our problems from our commitment to each other and actually started enjoying each other again.
10. We understood that love is first a discipline, not a feeling.

Finally, at Gerry's recommendation, we listed some of the things God did for us:

1. He allowed this to happen for our mutual good.
2. He opened our hearts toward Him.
3. He convicted us of our sin.
4. He caused Mitch to become interested in spiritual matters.

5. He made us aware of how self-centered we were.
6. He made me aware that since I was His child, I should be living like one.
7. He helped us see the potential for growth and maturity that could come from working at solving our problems.
8. He enabled us to forgive each other and start over.

When it comes down to it, God is the real reason Mitch and I got a second chance. He's the answer to marital conflicts and disagreements. Without Him, we would never have gotten over loving ourselves more than each other. I used to think I loved Mitch, but I realized through this experience that I loved myself far more. Honestly, as I look around at the many couples I know, I think almost everyone is guilty of the same thing. It's too bad. What Mitch and I had our last couple of months was far better! So, thanks for helping us develop a healthy marriage and for making us see what the Bible says about love. I hope many couples will benefit from your counseling.

Well, my nervous energy is finally fading, so I'd better try for a least a couple hours of sleep! I'll be out of the loop until things settle down in Houston. However, I'll keep this same email address so feel free to write us anytime!

With much love and affection, and more thanks than I can possibly express,

Stacy

So, my friend, there you have it. Not the kind of ending I'd ever attach to a story, but God has His own ways. While we'll never know the conclusion of Mitch's spiritual journey it is a sobering reminder that "today is the day of salvation" (from 2 Corinthians 6:2). So don't harden your heart and put off your decision to receive Christ until another time, for that time might never come.

On the other hand, the Bible tells us that God's mercies are new every morning and that His compassion never fails. Just when you think everything's over and done, along comes tomorrow! How true that turned out to be in Stacy's life. She left with her hands full when she packed off to Texas. Between supporting her family as a single mom and trying to raise two "energetic" children, we hoped and prayed for God to make her paths straight. But God wasn't finished showing kindness to them. The "detours" He led them through down in Texas still make us smile to this day. But that's another story—a "parenting" story—and it'll have to wait. (I haven't finished sorting through all the emails yet!) Until then, may God richly bless your marriage as He has blessed ours!

Gerry

From the beginning, Doyle Roth's marriage was destined for disaster. Between his entrepreneurial interests, oversized ego, and the demands he inflicted on his young bride, he nearly joined the ranks of those "unnecessarily divorced" in record time.

Then, as a last-ditch effort to save his dying marriage, Doyle agreed to see a counselor. What he heard in that office opened his eyes to the real meaning of being a husband. "Husbands, love your wives, just as Christ also loved the church and gave Himself up for her" (Ephesians 5:25). Suddenly, it all made sense:

1. Loving your wife isn't something you feel, it's something you do for her.
2. Christ set the example for husbands to follow.
3. Christ's example was one of sacrifice and serving, not self-centeredness.

That simple verse (and the man-to-man confrontation that accompanied it) changed his marriage. It also convinced him that the Bible speaks with authority to every facet of a man's life. If God's Word could transform his marriage, it could do the same for others.

As a successful businessman and long-term elder in his church, Doyle has worked with hundreds of couples from every walk of life. He's seen the power of God's Word heal hurting marriages and he's watched man-to-man confrontation revive hardened hearts.

In addition to his counseling work, Doyle has now enjoyed over forty years of "happily ever after" marriage with his wife, Nancy. They have four grown children, twelve grandchildren (at last count), and make their home on the family ranch in Colorado.